Why
We Still
Need
Public
Schools

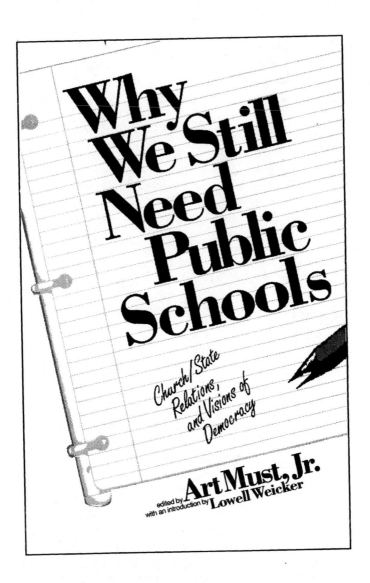

Why We Still Need Public Schools

Church/State Relations, and Visions of Democracy

edited by **Art Must, Jr.**
with an introduction by **Lowell Weicker**

PB Prometheus Books

59 John Glenn Drive
Amherst, New York 14228-2197

May America continue to be a pathfinder on the frontier of democracy.

Published 1992 by Prometheus Books

Inquiries should be addressed to
Prometheus Books
59 John Glenn Drive
Amherst, New York 14228–2197
VOICE: 716–691–0133, ext. 207
FAX: 716–564–2711
WWW.PROMETHEUSBOOKS.COM

08 07 06 05 04   6 5 4 3 2

Library of Congress Cataloging-in-Publication Data

Why we still need public schools : church/state relations and visions of
democracy / [edited by] Art Must, Jr.
    p. cm.
Includes bibliographical references.
ISBN 0–87975–758–2 (alk. paper)
    1. Education and State—United States. 2. Church and State—United States.
I. Must, Art.

LC89.W48 1992
379.73—dc20

92–4404

Printed in the United States of America on acid-free paper

Contents

PART TWO: THE NEED FOR PUBLIC SCHOOLS

Preface

Art Must, Jr.

Today, many people, including the president, are promoting the idea that we can reform public education by patterning it after our economy. We are told we need to throw our public schools into competition with private schools by providing tax money to pay for the tuition of children in private schools. This is the concept of "private school choice." There is little evidence, however, that such choice would improve public education; on the contrary, the probability of damage to public education—and to the country—is high. The only certainty is that private schools and parents currently sending their children there would benefit. And since the great majority of private schools are parochial, they would be the biggest winners of all. This is no coincidence. Even though the movement for private school choice has acquired the veneer of education reform, it is essentially only the most recent and most sophisticated incarnation of the periodic campaigns by parochial interests to appropriate public money for religious education.

It used to be that the Supreme Court could be counted upon to prohibit the public subsidization of parochial school tuition but that is no longer so. Today the only real obstacles that the proponents of private school choice must overcome are state constitutions and public opinion. While private school choice is exalted, therefore, those who desire a closer partnership of government and religion wage a subtle campaign to deemphasize

Art Must, Jr., is Executive Director of the National Coalition for Public Education and Religious Liberty (National PEARL).

separation of church and state by emphasizing governmental "accommo-dation" of religion.

This anthology, which represents National PEARL's* way of commem-orating the recent bicentennial of America's Bill of Rights, contains articles that help to remind us why separation of church and state and public education are bedrock American institutions to be fought for and preserved. At issue here is not whether public schools need to be improved. It is assumed that improvement is a necessity.

The book falls loosely into two parts. Part One contains articles that testify to the need for separation of church and state, explore the intent of our country's founders on the subject, and deal with issues of separation within education. Part Two includes discussions of the dangers of heeding the current call for private school choice and addresses the question of why we need public schools.

Part One begins with Sam Rabinove and Charles Bergstrom explaining why separation of church and state is essential. John Swomley then refutes the argument frequently used by those hostile to separation: that those who wrote the Constitution and Bill of Rights felt that it is appropriate for gov-ernment to aid all religions equally as long as it does not create a national religion or coerce anyone into participating in religious activities. Robert Alley reinforces Swomley's rejection of the idea that the original intent of those who crafted the First Amendment was to allow nonpreferential aid to re-ligions, and takes the argument one step further: even if orginal intent coun-

---

*The National Coalition for Public Education and Religious Liberty, a coalition of organizations and individuals dedicated both to a strong public school system that is free from sectarian control and to the guarantee of religious liberty for all by ensuring strict separation of church and state in the financing of education.

PEARL's members are: the American Association of School Administrators; the American Association of University Women; the American Civil Liberties Union; the American Ethical Union; the American Federation of Teachers; the American Humanist Association; the American Jewish Congress; Americans for Religious Liberty; Ameri-cans United for Separation of Church and State; the Anti-Defamation League of B'nai B'rith; the Baptist Joint Committee; the Central Conference of American Rabbis; the Committee for Public Education and Religious Liberty; the Council for Democratic and Secular Humanism; the General Board of Church and Society of the United Methodist Church; the General Conference of Seventh-Day Adventists; the Michigan Council about Parochiaid; the Minnesota Civil Liberties Union; Monroe County, NY, PEARL; the National Capital Area Civil Liberties Union; the National Center for Science Education; the National Congress of Parents and Teachers (PTA); the National Council of Jewish Women; the National Education Association; the National Service Conference of the American Ethical Union; Ohio PEARL; Public Funds for Public Schools of New Jersey; the Union of American Hebrew Congregations; and the Unitarian Universalist Church.

tenanced aid to religion in general, one of the strengths of our democracy is that we are not tied to policies from the past that are bad for us. T. Jeremy Gunn then refutes the argument employed in November 1991 by the U.S. Justice Department, when it urged the Supreme Court to make presence or absence of coercion the fundamental question for determining violation of the establishment clause of the Constitution.

We then change pace with a little-known example of failure to adhere to the principle of church-state separation. Most of us know about the more egregious church-state incidents, such as the banishment of Anne Hutchinson; the murder of Joseph Smith; and the persecution at one time or another of nonreligious people as well as Baptists, Catholics, Jews, Mormons, and numerous other religious groups. We know that at one time one could not hold elected office in many of the colonies and states unless one was a member of an officially approved religion. We know that even patriots and heroes like Thomas Paine were vilified for espousing unpopular religious beliefs. Michael Oleksa recounts a little-known piece of Alaska history as yet another example of the arrogance of those who force their religious beliefs on others.

William Schulz's article "Prayer in School: Why It Does Religion No Favor" leads us more specifically into discussion of the need to honor the principle of separation of church and state within education. He explains why most of the major denominations do not want government to compose, lead, or endorse prayer within the public schools. In a similar vein, August Steinhilber relates the problems associated with interpreting the Equal Access Act in such a way that students are authorized to proselytize others with religious literature on public school grounds.

The effect on the public schools of continuous attempts by the Religious Right not only to dictate curriculum but to attack public schools themselves as immoral institutions, is discussed by James Wood. Both he and William Schulz note that because of fear of running afoul of the First Amendment's establishment clause, there is virtually no mention of religion in public school curricula. Both promote teaching *about* religion; that is, the role of religion in history.

Eugenie Scott follows James Wood's brief introduction to the creationism movement with an entire article devoted to the problems creationists pose for science education. She contends that although the Supreme Court—at least until now—has thwarted creationists' plans for the public schools, the battle to keep science education free of sectarian bias may still be lost at the grassroots level unless many more Americans join the fight.

Oliver Thomas asserts that the main church-state battles of the 1990s will remain the same but be fought on a different battleground. He notes that the Chief Justice of the United States Supreme Court has stated that separation of church and state is "a metaphor based on bad history," and that the Supreme Court is likely to refer more and more church-state issues to state legislatures. He joins Eugenie Scott in alerting us to the need for much greater grassroots involvement in the battle for separation.

Part One ends with an excellent illustration by Florence Flast of the type of state battle Oliver Thomas warns us we must be increasingly prepared to fight in the 1990s.

Part Two of this volume begins by focusing on the campaign to authorize tax money for tuition in private schools, the great majority of which are parochial. The campaign for public subsidies of private school tuition, whether it be via vouchers, tuition tax credits, or tuition tax deductions, is led, for the most part, by the same religious groups that give mere lip service to or actively attack separation of church and state. This drive to pay parochial tuition would create not only a dangerous entanglement of government with religion but could lead to the eventual demise of our public schools. In fact, for the advocates of tax-supported private school tuition to succeed in getting the necessary legislation, it is in their interest actively to promote as much discontent with the public schools as possible. Private school choice is then conveniently pressed into service as not only the way to improve student performance but as the means of deliverance from a sorry and immoral mess.

Ironically, many of those most enthusiastically touting the efficacy and democratic qualities of choice in the debate on school reform, will deny to others the use of the same argument in the debate on abortion even though—in contrast with choice in the church-state context—the Constitution presents no obstacle to choice in abortion.

Donald Frey provides an analysis of the economic implications of subsidies for private school tuition and gives a short history of the campaign for such subsidies. He asserts that subsidies would have very little impact on overall academic performance of American students; stimulate less than expected growth in private school enrollment; cost the public more than what has been estimated; and give most aid to parents who already have children in private schools.

Edd Doerr and Al Menendez demonstrate that there is less support for choice than a simple reading of opinion polls and newspapers would lead us to believe. They point out that among all the hoopla for choice, we tend to overlook the fact that only one of eighteen parochiaid referenda held in this country since 1966 has endorsed using public money for paying private school tuition.

In his article "Private School Vouchers: Separate and Unequal," Arnie Fege provides a summary of the most frequently heard claims made by voucher proponents and gives responses to each.

Bill Honig addresses the popular argument first espoused by John Chubb and Terry Moe in the Brookings Institute's *Politics, Markets, and America's*

Schools, namely that public schools are poor because they are incurably bureaucratic. He asserts that Chubb and Moe came to faulty conclusions and demonstrates that school reform efforts in California achieved in only three years what Chubb and Moe claim would be the best their proposed system of private school choice could offer. Honig cites private trade schools to refute the idea that a less regulated, market-type approach to education will deliver us from poor schools. He adds that the system envisioned by Chubb and Moe would most likely require a whole new bureaucracy of its own to have any chance of being successful.

In "The Milwaukee Parental Choice Program," Herbert Grover and Julie Underwood discuss problems of accountability inherent in Milwaukee's experiment with private school choice.

J. William Rioux directs our attention to the fact that most Americans have no children in school and that we must convince them that public schools are in their interest nevertheless. He and Shirley McBay remind us that simply setting higher standards for academic performance will not produce the results we want unless we devote more energy and resources to ensuring that those students who are currently failing do not continue to fail.

In "Why Public Schools?" Michael Casserly tells why he, a Catholic, has his child in a public school.

Colin Greer then gives an overview of how the role played by public education has changed since public schools were first established. He adds that "we still need to evolve the public schools we believe we once had," and that choice will not help us make the necessary transition. Greer contends that the problems of public schools cannot be solved without removing the socioeconomic inequities in America, and that to accept the current dissatisfaction with public schools as the final verdict on their usefulness makes as little sense as saying the electoral process should be discarded because of terribly low voter participation rates.

Everyone knows about Jefferson's wall of separation between church and state. Anne Bastian observes in her article that Jefferson also felt very strongly that the government should have a plan for educating citizens. She maintains that the choice plan being pushed by President Bush and Education Secretary Alexander is really not a plan at all and ignores issues of funding and social stratification which must be addressed before public schools can improve. Bastian suggests that "offering people the chance to choose is not the same as offering people good choices," and points out that after dwelling upon the evils of bureacracy, Chubb and Moe actually come to the disturbing conclusion that the fundamental cause of poor public schools is "direct democratic control."

This volume ends with Robert Bullough's article "Democratic Schooling and the Revitalization of the Public World." He asserts that the problems of our schools are due precisely to *lack* of truly democratic control, resulting from our degeneration into a consumer-oriented society that lacks a coherent sense of community essential for the success of democratic institutions. Bullough observes that "high test scores and a work force able to beat the Japanese do not a social vision make" and insists that before we ask how we are going to improve the schools, we must first ask what purpose we want them to serve. He urges us to transcend thinking of schools as factories meant simply for improving our productivity and to ensure first that schools serve the larger purpose of teaching the knowledge and skills necessary for democratic living.

This volume emphasizes that in order to solve our public school problems we must address other more basic social problems that lead to poor schools. It's not bureaucracy that produces poor education. Japan, for all its rigid bureaucracy, has excellent schools. Nor will enhanced achievement in math and science and high productivity alone sustain us. Nazi Germany excelled at math and science and was phenomenally productive.

The quality of our schools is a direct reflection of the quality of our democratic system, of how truly we are maintaining a democratic course. It is not enough simply to be charitable toward those who lanquish outside the warm circle of the American Dream. Many slaveholders were charitable to their slaves as long as the slaves stayed in their place. At this time, when many lament the lack of a sense of national unity, we need to ensure that all Americans have a real probability—not just a theoretical possibility—of leading personally rewarding and productive lives. Rather than throwing essential democratic institutions like public schools and separation of church and state overboard because we are encountering rough seas, we must check our democratic bearings and get all hands on deck.

Part One

The Need for Separation
of Church and State

Introduction

Lowell P. Weicker, Jr.
Governor of Connecticut

History makes the point time and time again: No greater mischief can be created than to merge the power of religion with the power of government. To find religious liberty is what drove many of our ancestors to these shores.

The Founding Fathers knew precisely what they were doing in writing the First Amendment to the Constitution guaranteeing the separation of church and state. They did not want government meddling in religion in any fashion; they wanted the constitutional barrier between the two to remain absolute.

Thomas Jefferson wrote in 1802 to the Danbury, Connecticut, Baptist Association: "Believing with you that religion is a matter which lies solely between Man and his God . . . I contemplate with sovereign reverence that act of the whole American people which declared that their legislature should 'make no law respecting an establishment of religion, or prohibiting the free exercise thereof,' thus building a wall of separation between Church and State."

Why, only eleven years after the adoption of the Bill of Rights, did Jefferson feel compelled to address the establishment issue? It is because, in many parts of the country, people were not taking the First Amendment seriously.

Recent developments indicate that the Moral Majority and the lucrative liars of televangelism, as well as some U.S. senators, are still not taking it seriously.

I find nothing moral in those who pray and then become chief apologists for apartheid. I find nothing moral about those who pray and then sanctimoniously speak of divine justice in response to the cries for help from those suffering with AIDS. I find nothing moral in those who pray but then deny resources to the retarded and disabled. And there are those who, in the name of good old-fashioned morality, would radically amend the First Amendment. It is the task of all committed clergy, laity, and public office holders to fight against them.

Our nation was built upon the premises of freedom, competition and individuality. The secular and the ecclesiastical spheres need to compete, not merge, in the continuing process of creating a better nation and world. I have come to believe with Mark Twain that mandated religion "means death to human liberty and paralysis to human thought."

I stand with Jefferson. I stand with Twain. I stand at Plymouth, Massachusetts, with those 102 English Calvanists who were persecuted because they denied the ecclesiastical authority of the King and who, in the lonely cause of civil and religious liberty, stood on the shore of America.

1

Religious Liberty and Church-State Separation: Why Should We Care?

Samuel Rabinove

Jews know in their bones how important it is to be able to live in a society where true religious liberty for all prevails. So do Baptists. Yet, regrettably, some Jews, both in the United States and in Israel, sometimes forget this vital truth. And so do some Baptists, and other religious people, too. Many of us need to be reminded, from bitter historical experience, how easily religious freedom may be restricted or chipped away.

Of all the religious sects in the early days of America, there is no question that the Baptists were the most impassioned in the fight for religious freedom and separation of church and state. John Leland, a prominent Baptist minister, wrote in 1820, "The liberty I contend for is more than toleration. The very idea of toleration is despicable; it supposes that some have a pre-eminence above the rest to grant indulgence; whereas all should be equally free—Jews, Turks [Moslems], pagans, and Christians. Test oaths and established creeds should be avoided as the worst of evils."

The fight for religious freedom, as we know, was neither an easy nor

Samuel Rabinove is Legal Director of the American Jewish Committee and a member of the Religious Liberty Committee of the National Council of Churches. This essay is adapted from a speech delivered at a symposium on church-state relations at the Southern Baptist Theological Seminary, Louisville, Kentucky, on April 10, 1986.

a short one. In 1843 in New York City, for example, a group of Jewish parents whose children attended public schools, where religion was part of the normal curriculum, protested the content of a textbook called *American Popular Lessons*. The Board of Education appointed a committee to look into the matter. The report of this committee, which rejected the Jewish protest, read in part as follows: "Our committee has examined the several passages and lessons alluded to, and they are unable to discover any possible ground of objection, even by the Jews, except what may arise from the fact that they are chiefly derived from the New Testament and inculcate the general principles of Christianity." Well, what can one say? That kind of insensitivity has its present-day counterpart in the attitude of many sincere, well-intentioned Christians who cannot understand why Jewish parents object to devotional Christmas observances in public schools.

There is no question whatever that religious and spiritual values have contributed immeasurably to human progress from barbarism to civilization. The United States, certainly, has been profoundly influenced for the better by Jewish and Christian moral and ethical values. Unlike countries with established churches, however, many religions have thrived in pluralistic America, hand in hand with our longstanding tradition of separation of church and state, which has served as a bulwark of religious liberty for all. (In Sweden, for example, with its established Lutheran Church, attendance at religious worship is far less than in the United States. In Norway, also with an established Lutheran Church, Jesuits were actually barred by the constitution from entering the country until the constitution was amended in 1956.)

In 1986, John Buchanan, a Southern Baptist minister and former eight-term congressman from Alabama, was the official spokesman for church-state separation at the National Religious Broadcasters annual convention in Washington, D.C. He was pitted in a debate against the Reverend Jimmy Swaggart, the fiery television preacher from Louisiana. Although the audience of 3,500 was heavily predisposed to the Swaggart position, Buchanan pulled no punches. "If you're a Christian or anything else in this society," he said, "if you're a person of faith, you ought to thank God for religious liberty and for the First Amendment's protection of everyone's freedom of conscience, guaranteed by the absolute separation of church and state."

The former congressman, who had been defeated by a Moral Majority campaign in 1980, cited several historical precedents for the abuses that can take place in the name of religion—the Crusades, the Inquisition, the burning of the heretics, the hanging of the witches, and the many religious wars and persecutions. Buchanan declared: "Preachers like Pat Robertson and Jerry Falwell should not forget that in the colony of Virginia, Baptists ministers were beaten and imprisoned and run out of town for preaching their dissenting faith, while Anglican ministers were paid with tax funds from the state treasury."

It is precisely the constitutionally mandated principle of separation of church and state that has guaranteed all Americans in our pluralistic society the freedom to join or not join any denomination. Despite certain shameful episodes involving dissident sects (the Mormons, for example, who were driven as far west as Utah by mob violence), people in America have practiced their religions without hindrance. The separation principle has also allowed nonbelievers, so many of whom are no less moral or decent or patriotic than people of faith, to live as equal citizens without penalty or stigma.

Alexis de Tocqueville, writing of his travels in America in 1830, said this:

> The religious atmosphere of the country was the first thing that struck me on arrival in the United States. . . . My longing to understand the reason for this phenomenon increased daily. To find this out, I questioned the faithful of all communions; I particularly sought the society of clergymen who are the depositories of the various creeds, and have a personal interest in their survival . . . all thought the main reason for the quiet sway of religion over their country was the complete separation of church and state. I have no hesitation in stating that throughout my stay in America I met nobody, lay or cleric, who did not agree about that.

Those who are inclined today to rebuke the "separationist" justices on the U.S. Supreme Court as being outside the American tradition (as the religious "right" has been fond of doing) would do well to note the predominant views enunciated by American courts during the last century. In *Melvin* v. *Easley* (1860), the North Carolina Supreme Court declared: "Christianity is not established by law, and the genius of our institutions requires that the church and the state should be kept separate. . . . The state confesses its incompetency to judge spiritual matters between men or between man and his maker . . . spiritual matters are exclusively in the hands of the teachers of religion." And, in *Davis* v. *Beason* (1890), the U.S. Supreme Court affirmed that "the First Amendment of the Constitution . . . was intended to allow everyone under the jurisdiction of the United States to entertain such notions respecting his relation to his maker, and the duties they impose, as may be approved by his conscience, and to exhibit his sentiments in such form of worship as he may think proper, not injurious to the rights of others, *and to prohibit legislation for the support of any religious tenets*, or the modes of worship of any sect" (emphasis added).

Marginal religions have contributed significantly to our understanding of religious pluralism, as well as to judicial interpretations of religious liberty, far out of proportion to their numerical membership. Consider, for example, Jehovah's Witnesses, who probably have been responsible for more cases dealing with religious liberty than any other single sect. In the Jehovah's Witness compulsory "flag salute" case of *West Virginia Board of Education* v. *Barnette* (1943), the Court squarely addressed the constitutional guarantee of religious pluralism: "If there is any fixed star in our constitutional constellation, it is that no official, high or petty, can prescribe what shall be orthodox in politics, nationalism, religion, or other matters of opinion or force citizens to confess by word or act their faith therein. If there are any circumstances which permit any exception, they do not occur to us."

Many of us recall Jefferson's words in his famous letter in 1802 to the Danbury, Connecticut, Baptist Association: "Believing with you that religion is a matter which lies solely between Man and his God . . . I contemplate with sovereign reverence that act of the whole American people which declared that their legislature should 'make no law respecting an establishment of religion, or prohibiting the free exercise thereof,' thus building a wall of separation between church and state." Yet, the Supreme Court and the First Amendment notwithstanding, there has never been in this country total separation of church and state. Actually, there have been quite a few accommodations between the two in America—including government aid to religion such as military chaplaincies, tax exemption for religious property used for religious purposes, and tax deductibility of contributions to churches and synagogues—which are widely accepted as reasonable and proper. There are other issues of church-state separation, however, which have been in sharp dispute and where the question often is: Where shall an intelligent line be drawn?

The question of school-sponsored organized prayer and Bible readings has been a dramatic illustration of the church-state separation controversy, with major Jewish organizations having supported the challenge to these practices, which were traditional in many states (though not in others). In 1962 and 1963, the U.S. Supreme Court, as we know, in the *Engel* and *Schempp* cases, held that they violated the First Amendment, and that it is not the business of government to compose or sponsor prayers for American children to recite. Although these decisions caused a furor at the time and were widely denounced as being anti-religious, anti-Christian and un-American, they have since gained at least a measure of public acceptance. Thus far, repeated efforts in Congress to amend the First Amendment to permit organized school prayer have not been successful; its advocates have not been able to muster the necessary two-thirds majority in both houses of Congress. Still, public opinion polls indicate that a substantial majority of Americans continues to support school-sponsored prayer on a "voluntary" basis. Let's not forget, however, that the First Amendment is *anti*-majoritarian: "Congress shall make no law. . . ." Congress, by its very nature, represents majorities. The First Amendment was intended to guard against a possible majority tyranny.

Despite the court's rulings, prayer and Bible reading continue today in a good many school districts, particularly in rural areas of the South and Midwest. But their prevalence in the country as a whole is certainly far less than when the Supreme Court's decisions were rendered. Mainstream Protestant leaders today are heavily opposed to a prayer amendment—many of them have so testified repeatedly and effectively before congressional committees.

It must be stressed that there is nothing in any U.S. Supreme Court ruling to stop a pupil from saying a prayer, either spoken or silent, any time the spirit moves him or her to do so, provided only that normal school activity is not disrupted thereby. Why, then, this virtual obsession by some people with organized prayer during the school day? Few adults, after all, expect to be able to engage in organized prayer at their places of work during the work day. Parents for whom it is important that their children pray while in school are free to instruct them accordingly. What is really sought here by the school-prayer zealots is induced prayer by *other* people's children, whether or not this is desired by *other* parents.

Unable to pass a prayer amendment to the Constitution, the Reagan administration threw its support behind an alternative legislative measure. This law provides that public secondary schools which allow non-curriculum-related student activity groups to meet voluntarily on school grounds, before or after classroom instruction, cannot deny "equal access" to student religious, political, or philosophical groups that wish to meet on the same basis for prayer or any other kind of discussion. Advocates of such "equal access," including many in Congress who opposed the president's prayer amendment, argued that the free speech and free exercise of religion clauses of the First Amendment should not be suspended just because students enter a public high school building. Since nobody seriously contests the right of an individual student to pray voluntarily, as long as the school itself plays no part, why should a group of students be forbidden to come together in their "free" time for the same purpose?

Opponents of "equal access" maintained that the law would allow churches, using student surrogates, to set up shop in tax-supported high schools and junior high schools. They noted also that the law does not bar adult outsiders (such as clergy) from attending student meetings, provided they do not attend "regularly" or control the meetings. "Equal access," of course, cannot be restricted to students from "respectable" religious groups (like ours); it necessarily opens the schoolhouse door to all, including aggressive missionary groups such as Rev. Sun Myung Moon's Unification Church. In the view of the opponents, parents who enroll their children in public schools, for the secular education mandated by the state, have every right to expect that their children will not be proselytized away from their own faith and into a sect which may be abhorrent to them. This could happen without their knowledge, let alone their permission.

In June 1990, in the case of *Board of Education* v. *Mergens*, the U.S. Supreme Court upheld, by an eight-to-one majority, the Equal Access Act on free speech grounds. In an opinion by Justice Sandra Day O'Connor, the Court ruled that the Act does not violate the establishment clause because there is no government endorsement of religion. A school need not permit any student activity groups unrelated to the curriculum, said the Court, but if it does, the school is required by the Act not to discriminate against any student group on the basis of its religious, political, or philosophical views.

Although the Court rejected arguments that the Act violated the constitutional principle of separation of church and state, the justices in the majority were themselves divided. There were three separate opinions, none commanding a majority, in support of the result. The lone dissenter, Justice John Paul Stevens, said that the Court had interpreted the Act in a way that left too little discretion to local school districts. In essence, this decision is an extension of a 1981 Supreme Court ruling, *Widmar* v. *Vincent*, in which the Court held on free speech grounds that public universities had to permit student religious groups to meet on the same terms afforded other student organizations.

It is important for all of us to understand the rationale for the drive to inject religion, in one form or another, into the public schools. The reality is that our country has been experiencing a powerful religio-cultural backlash against what are perceived to be the excesses of liberalism and "secular humanism." Traditional and cherished American and Judeo-Christian values seem to be mocked and threatened by developments in our society that many people find acutely unsettling. The list of irritants is long and painful: the epidemic of violent crime, growth of the drug culture, emergence of a militant feminist movement, rising tide of divorce, soaring rate of teenage out-of-wedlock pregnancy, demand for abortion at will, breakdown of discipline in many public schools, growth of "gay liberation," and X-rated films almost everywhere, among others.

Many of our citizens, people devoted to God, country, and family, have been deeply disturbed by many of the contemporary trends in our society. There is a widespread conviction that things have gone too far, that liberty has become license, and that individual rights and freedoms have been exalted at the expense of other equally important values, such as order, security, responsibility, civility, courtesy, and consideration for the rights and freedoms of others. Faced with serious social problems, many people yearn for the "good old days" (which frequently seem far better in memory than they were in reality), and want to believe that restoring organized school prayer and Bible reading, and prohibiting abortion, will somehow enable our society to cope with its complex ills. They seek scapegoats, blaming the Supreme Court, in their view, for expelling God from the public schools. Hence the broad appeal of the religious "right" and its simplistic rhetoric and remedies. In the ringing words of TV preacher James Robison, "We want our country back!"

But those of us who reject the ethos of the religious "right" have a responsibility to go beyond being nay-sayers. We must advance positive, constructive alternatives to their nostrums. For example, the teaching of common core values that are broadly shared by people of all faiths or none, on a nonsectarian basis, in public schools—honesty, decency, sportsmanship, compassion, patriotism, respect, and concern for the feelings of others—can reassure those parents and clergy who are striving to teach the very same values from a God-centered perspective, at home and in religious school, and also provide *some* moral guidance for those children who, sadly, are not receiving any because they don't get it at home and don't attend religious school. Teaching traditional values would be far more useful than having children parrot a prayer each morning.

This right-wing religiocultural backlash was, in my opinion, one key factor in the Republican victory in the 1980 presidential election, and in each election since then. Not surprisingly, therefore, both Mr. Reagan and Mr. Bush have not only reached out to this segment of the electorate but also have given aid and comfort, in various ways, to those who believe that only one brand of politics (their own) meets with the Lord's approval. Sad to relate, there has been a serious erosion of commitment by the executive branch to the separation principle. A U.S. ambassador has been appointed to the Vatican, which is essentially an ecclesiastical entity, its role as a state notwithstanding. And former Secretary of Education William J. Bennett argued that two U.S. Supreme Court rulings in 1985 (*Grand Rapids School District* v. *Ball; Aguilar* v. *Felton*), which barred public school systems from sending their teachers, at public expense, into parochial schools to teach remedial and enrichment classes, were a "ridiculous" expression of the Court's "fastidious disdain for religion that is hard to fathom." The Justice Department had filed briefs on the side of government aid to religious schools in both cases. The American Jewish Committee joined with the Baptist Joint Committee on Public Affairs and the National Council of Churches in the Grand Rapids case, on the opposite side. We maintained that it is not the business of government to subsidize schools whose chief reason for being is to propagate a religious faith—any faith, including our own. President Bush, as did Mr. Reagan before him, has expressed strong support for efforts to enact legislation providing for tuition tax credits or vouchers for parents of pupils in religious schools.

In 1983 in *Mueller* v. *Allen*, the Supreme Court upheld (by a 5–4 vote) a Minnesota statute allowing taxpayers to deduct from their state income tax expenses incurred for their children's tuition, transportation, and textbooks in elementary and secondary schools, both public and private. Since few public school parents incur any such expenses, the real objective of the law was to aid private school parents, 96 percent of whom have their children enrolled in parochial schools. "This statute," said the dissenting Justice Marshall, "is little more than a subsidy of private school tuition, masquerading as a subsidy of general educational expenses." The majority of the Court, however, were unable to see through this obvious fiction.

When, in response to a question from Supreme Court Justice John Paul Stevens during the oral argument in the 1984 Pawtucket, Rhode Island, crèche case (*Lynch* v. *Donnely*), the Solicitor General of the United States could reply that, in his opinion, it would not be unconstitutional for a city to use public funds to celebrate Mass in observance of Christmas (provided nobody is forced to attend), it indicated that something had gone gravely amiss. This is not "conservative." Rather, it represents a radical departure from American tradition. If the principle of separation of church and state is to have substance in America, it should mean at least this: the state must not behave as if it were a church or a synagogue. Nor may it serve as an agent for any religion. The state must not do for citizens things which, in their rightful free exercise of religion, they are perfectly capable of doing for themselves. For government to intrude into religious practices (such as school prayer), or to seek to impose particular religious beliefs or values on citizens who do not share them (such as the prohibition of abortion), constitutes a clear and present danger to Americans of all faiths. In sum, the state must be neutral, not partisan, in matters religious, even when neutrality may be painful to some.

In a major speech in New York City in 1984, Senator Edward Kennedy of Massachusetts eloquently said what needed to be said:

> There is a long and unhappy history of intolerance which still flourishes at the extreme fringe of American politics. . . . But today that extremist tradition also infects the very center of our national authority. We have a president who has announced that those who disagree with him on officially prescribed school prayer or nationally proscribed abortion are "intolerant of religion"—that they are somehow or other anti-God or anti-truth. What is the proper relationship between church and state, between religious values and national decisions?. . . . Religious leaders may say anything they feel bound in conscience to say, but they may not ask government to do something which it cannot do under the Constitution or the social contract of a pluralistic society. . . . In cases like abortion or prayer or sexual identity—the proper role of religion is to appeal to the free conscience of each person, not the coercive rule of secular law.

The observance of the bicentennial of the ratification of the Bill of Rights is a perfect time to spotlight the vital importance of the principle of church-state separation in the perspective of American religious history.

2

The Need for Separation: A Lutheran's View

Charles V. Bergstrom

Preparing this essay was a great privilege and I hope to make it representative of mainline Christian and Jewish perspectives on separation of church and state. Of course, there are differences both of approach and of position on specific issues, but I am made bold to write this as a Lutheran because I present no isolated view. During the eleven years I served as director of the Lutheran Office for Governmental Affairs in Washington, D.C., I reveled in the working relations with forty Jewish, Protestant, and Catholic offices. Most of our testimony and coalition-building was to serve the needs of others, with an occasional opposition to the encroachment of government regulations.

The difficulty is that not all those claiming to be religious will support separation as defined by these national Christian and Jewish organizations. Thomas Jefferson and James Madison warned that religion can make dangerous efforts to manipulate political structures. In our time we have witnessed the veritable onslaught of the Religious Right, who have rallied to make the nation's capitol "Washington for Jesus"; claimed to be the "Moral Majority"—God's voice; and even designed a vicious "biblical scorecard" to rate as "immoral" members of Congress who vote against prayer in school or support freedom of choice for abortion. Interfering as well in the sphere of public

Charles V. Bergstrom is a co-founder of People for the American Way and was a director, from 1977–1988, of the Lutheran Office for Governmental Affairs in Washington, D.C.

education, Pat Robertson, Jerry Falwell, Jimmy Swaggart, and others have regularly attacked the public schools as the enemy of religion!

In 1980, I was privileged to help write "A Statement on Religion and Politics," my church's response to this unbiblical approach to government. We said:

> We support pluralism and freedom of all people in the political process in the United States and maintain that pushing for total agreement on moral issues is not the same as advocation for legislation which will enhance the common good. . . . Thus it is unnecessary and unbiblical for any church group or individual to seek to "Christianize" the government or to label political views of members of Congress as "Christian" or "religious." It is arrogant to assert that one's position on a political issue is "Christian" and that all other are "un-Christian," "immoral," or "sinful." Government under God employs reason and power for social justice, peace, and freedom. To describe one group's political position as "The Christian Voice" and one movement's political agenda as a movement "for Jesus" is wrongly judgmental. It is also an affront to Jewish and other religious advocates whose religions hold social justice as a social form of "love thy neighbor."

Let us make clear that religion and politics are closely related. Your faith should be related to your political beliefs and actions. When talking about separation of church and state, however, we are talking about the institutions of religion and government and are using the word "church" to include not only Christian but Jewish and other religious bodies. These two institutions are to remain structurally separated so that government does not define the Church's ministry and the Church does not seek to write its doctrines of faith into law. Personally, I believe that God is at work in the secular world as well as in the Church. We do not have to drag the deity into our classrooms or the halls of Congress. Nor can God be "kicked out of school," as Ronald Reagan foolishly claimed.

The issue of church and state relations is about justice and civil rights for all—atheists, doubters, and people of faith. There can be what Lutherans call "functional interaction" of church and state. Thomas Jefferson wrote about the wall of separation; former Chief Justice Warren Burger described the division as more like a hedge, occasionally trampled upon from either side; others speak of a river of separation. I like best the description of Lutheran historian and theologian Martin Marty, who envisions church-state relations as a zone in which both can interact with one another. In all cases, it is a grand tension for freedom. To quote again from "A Statement on Religion and Politics":

In affirming the principle of separation of church and state, Lutherans in the U.S. respectfully acknowledge and support the tradition that the churches and government are to be separate in structure. As the Constitution provides, government neither establishes nor favors any religion. It also safeguards the rights of all persons and groups in society to the free exercise of their religious beliefs, worship, practices, and organizational arrangements within the laws of morality, human rights, and property. The government is to make no decisions regarding the validity or orthodoxy of any doctrine, recognizing that it is the province of religious groups to state their doctrines, determine their politics, train their leaders, conduct worship, and carry on their missions and ministries without undue interference from or entanglement with government.

The very best experience of freedom and diversity, and now the most threatened, is public education. Growing up in a small town in Illinois gave me a happy experience. My home town was a community of churches and families, part of the "Bible Belt," but we never had classroom prayers during those twelve years of learning. Public education was supported by parents and others of various religious inclinations. Thus, I took it for granted as a boy, as a college and seminary student, and as a parish pastor for twenty-nine years in New England.

Even though the Lutheran Church has many parochial schools, it has supported public education by action of conventions and by opposing attacks on public schools. The Church has consistently opposed efforts to add prayers in classrooms and to use the schools for sectarian indoctrination. I know hundreds of people in other denominations and faith groups who support similar actions. The Church needs to recognize the civil rights of a first-grade student to be free from any religious pressure. That right applies to the children of atheists, agnostics, and fervent evangelicals.

The Lutheran churches are aware of the serious theological and public policy difficulties that arise when government mandates religious exercises in public schools. Since the landmark decisions of the Supreme Court in 1962 and 1963 (the *Engel* and *Schempp* cases), these churches have consistently resisted legislative attempts to circumvent the court's actions or to enact a prayer amendment to the U.S. Constitution. This activity has been undertaken carefully and deliberately: within these church bodies, consideration has been given to the school prayer issue by lay persons and members of the clergy, by individuals within our congregations, and staff of regional and national church conventions at which congregational representatives gather. Resolutions opposing government-sponsored prayer in the public schools have been implemented in accordance with the churches' constitution and bylaws, and represent the end result of an organized and democratic process that is acknowledged as legitimate by members of these church bodies.

Our position on school prayer reflects our theological and biblical conviction that not only are prayers in public schools not essential to the cultivation of religion in our youth, but that such religious practice can be harmful, especially if offered by an atheist or imposed on a person of different faith. The families—not the school boards—have the overriding responsibility for the children's religious education. We object to "nondenominational" prayers that may uncritically mix nationalism and religion. The more we attempt to insist on common denominator religious exercises or instruction in public schools, the greater the risk we run of diluting our faith and ending up with a vague national folk religion that confuses religious practice with patriotism.

We believe that the purpose of prayer is to praise and petition God, not to serve the secular purpose of creating a moral or ethical atmosphere for public school children. We resist any attempt by legislators or by school authorities to inject religion into the public classroom in an effort to create a "wholesome milieu" for public school learning or to overcome "immorality." Lutherans are offended by untheological calls to "put God back in school," or claims that such efforts are "evangelical." They are political, since they ask Congress to act on a religious matter that divides people. Prayer can be manipulative and used as a tool for trying to convert unbelievers or to make America into this or that group's idea of a "Christian nation."

We are concerned about the quality of public school education and understand it to be inadequate when it is premised either on indifference or antagonism to the religious elements in history, community life, or the lives of individuals. While the Supreme Court has ruled state-mandated prayer unconstitutional, it has not ruled out studying about religion in public schools. In this area Lutherans and others see a positive challenge to interact with public school educators in order to develop programs that acknowledge the religious and moral dimensions of life while also respecting the larger religious neutrality mandated by the Constitution. I have supported teaching about religion as a parish pastor and as a church official. In 1987, Rabbi David Saperstein of the Union of American Hebrew Congregations and I co-authored an article that appeared in the *New York Times* and other daily papers. In it we said:

> In the face of the fundamentalist campaign to require the teaching of "creationism" as a scientific truth and to censor textbooks containing "unacceptable" descriptions of religion, many publishers have found it easier to remove any reference to religion from their textbooks, avoiding the topic of religion altogether rather than seeking to accommodate conflicting viewpoints. . . . The distinction between teaching the "truth" of religion and teaching *about* religion is vital. The first introduces denominational differences and theological strife into the classroom. Teaching *about* religion allows students to study the influences that religion has had on history, culture, and values. Indeed, it is impossible to understand

the development of civilization without recognizing the impact of religious beliefs and institutions. Failing to cover religion in public schools, however, implies that it is not an important element of life. . . . Teaching religion undermines our freedoms and divides our children along religious lines. Teaching *about* religion nourishes these freedoms and offers a genuine opportunity to endow American values with the knowledge of our nation's diverse and rich religious traditions.

The influx of immigrants with varying traditions and creeds and a range of other historical circumstances has contributed to a society that is thoroughly pluralistic. The Lutheran churches view this situation as a challenge and not a threat—an opportunity to articulate clearly the tenets of our faith in this pluralistic culture. The Founding Fathers made clear the difference between reference to God and establishing Christianity as the one religion. Promoters of homogenized prayers exaggerate the practice of prayer in the schools. Macalester College made a survey showing that in the far West, 91 percent of the schools had no prayers. In the Midwest, 74 percent had no prayers. The Supreme Court decisions did not unleash immorality as some claim. We were always as we are now. Many individuals belonging to religious minorities can describe the unfair pressure on children to "pray like everyone else."

Lutherans cherish the blessings of the Bill of Rights. We affirm the fact that government safeguards the rights of all persons and groups in our society to the free exercise of their religious beliefs, and makes no decisions regarding the validity or orthodoxy of any doctrine. The Bill of Rights protects the individual child who is different from the majority; it does not give the religious majority power to bring its practices into the realm of education. It should be noted that when the state deeply involves itself in a religious practice in the public schools, it is thereby not only appropriating a function properly served by the church and the family, but subjecting the freedom of believers and unbelievers alike to the restraint that accompanies the use of government power and public facilities in the promotion of religious ends.

The Lutheran churches, like the courts, do not believe that any school-organized prayer sessions can be completely voluntary. Children attending public schools are there under compulsion of public law. Public school facilities are used, and the teachers—symbols of authority—may supervise the exercise. These factors combine to operate with coercive force on young and impressionable children, inducing them to take part despite freedom to be excused. That cannot be compared with adults praying in Congress or a reference to God on our coins.

During the 1980s a number of bills were introduced in Congress supporting "equal access." This means that any high school permitting clubs to meet on school property during instructional time must also permit religious groups to meet. Much of the legislation was poorly written and would have opened the doors for fundamentalist evangelists. The legislation finally adopted was supported by several religious organizations, but the Lutheran Church still has concerns regarding high school freshmen being pressured to join such clubs. Jay Alan Sekulow of Christian Advocates Serving Evangelism calls our high schools the new mission field to help crumble the wall of separation. It will be important for mainline church groups to support public educators in order to make sure that equal access is not misused in our public schools.

Now and then someone suggests that we might establish community standards to determine the practice of prayer in school. That suggestion, however, ignores the reality and the depth of religious differences, especially regarding religious minority groups. Religious differences, even among advocates of school prayer, will surely find expression in practices offensive to some and will lead to harmful and bitter contention. The most positive contribution that religion can make to the public schools is to support the effort to train and adequately pay the very finest teachers possible and to select the finest leadership in our communities for our school boards and committees.

This lengthy review of prayer and Bible reading illustrates church and state tensions between public education and religion. Early in this essay I spoke of the Religious Right's efforts to use the public schools to evangelize and even to aggressively attack public education as godless. This activity is now most evident at the grassroots level. Here fundamentalists seek to censor books and attack reading programs such as the *Impressions* series, a kindergarten through sixth grade literature-based reading series published by Holt, Rinehart & Winston. A cluster of national far-right groups are involved, including the American Family Association, Christian Educators Association International, Citizens for Excellence in Education, and the Traditional Values Coalition. Phyllis Schlafly, James Kennedy, and Pat Robertson continue to be voices of criticism of our public schools. Parents and others have a clear right to question textbooks and educational programs, but one religious view cannot govern this process. Among others, Lutheran bishops in Texas and California have worked with public school leaders for open discussion of such censorship efforts. People for the American Way, a First Amendment rights organization, has also been active on behalf of education and local school committees. Each year it produces an edition of *Protecting the Freedom to Learn,* which catalogs the censorship efforts in each state.

There has been an increasing concern about the lack of participation in the election process in the United States. Even in a presidential election year, barely one in two registered voters goes to the polls. Cynicism, bitterness, and alienation abound as public officials seem more concerned with getting elected than with governing. Certainly there is a need to reform campaign financing, but we must also look ahead to the future generations of voters. Polls reveal that a majority of youth feel that they can trust government in Washington to do what's right only some of the time at best. Less than a majority feel optimistic about the country's future. What a challenge! Here is an opportunity where clergy and laity, teachers and school administrators, parents and students can begin to develop a positive and concentrated effort to strengthen the positive theme of the First Amendment and the entire Bill of Rights instead of promoting religion over secular education.

And so it is as we begin our third century under the Bill of Rights. Continued vigilance and excellence are important for citizenship and education. Hopefully this book will be a catalyst and a spark. We need to strengthen our often weak knees and bring together more adequate support for the proper separation of church and state.

3

Toleration Is Not Good Enough*

John M. Swomley, Jr.

The original intent of those who framed and adopted the Constitution of the United States was to establish a clearly secular government and thereby separate church from state. The evidence for this is found in each of the following historical facts:

1) Although the Declaration of Independence, proclaimed eleven years earlier, contains various religious terms such as "Divine Providence" and "Nature's God," the Constitution has no such reference. It does not even imply a divine right or purpose. This absence of religious terminology does not reflect any hostility to religion, or imply its unimportance. Rather, it is a recognition that religion would thrive better if left uninfluenced, unaided, and unimpeded by government.

The political philosopher John Locke, who had been a strong influence on many leading Americans, including Thomas Jefferson and James Madison, wrote in his first *Letter Concerning Toleration* that "the care of souls can-

John M. Swomley, Jr., a Methodist theologian, holds a Ph.D. in political science from the University of Colorado. He is Professor Emeritus of Christian Ethics at the St. Paul School of Theology in Kansas City, Missouri, and Chair of the Church-State Committee of the National ACLU.

*This essay originally appeared, under the title "Separation of Church and State: The Original Intent," in John M. Swomley, *Religious Liberty and the Secular State: The Constitutional Context* (Buffalo, N.Y.: Prometheus Books, 1987), pp. 17–24.

not belong to the civil magistrate because his power consists only in outward force; but true and saving religion consists in the inward persuasion of the mind." This means essentially that true religion is a matter of faith and that if a church cannot persuade its members to accept its doctrine or contribute to its work, it is not the business of government to enforce the faith or pay its expenses.

2) Locke's political philosophy also provided the framers of the Constitution with the idea that the Constitution is a social contract between the people and the states on the one hand, and the new federal government on the other. The Tenth Amendment spells out the meaning of the social contract in these words: "The powers not delegated to the United States by the Constitution, nor prohibited by it to the states, are reserved to the states respectively or to the people."

The Constitution, wrote the historian Charles A. Beard, "does not confer upon the federal government any power whatever to deal with religion in any form or manner."[1] James Madison called it "a bill of powers"; he said that "the powers are enumerated and it follows that all that are not granted by the Constitution are retained" by the people.[2] Richard Dobbs Spaight, a delegate from North Carolina to the Constitutional Convention, said about religion: "No power is given to the general government to interfere with it at all. Any act of Congress on this subject would be a usurpation."[3]

3) Before it was amended, the Constitution contained only one reference to religion. That reference, in Article VI, Section 3, says:

> The Senators and Representatives before mentioned, and the members of the several State Legislatures, and all executive and judicial officers both of the United States and of the several states, shall be bound by oath or affirmation to support this Constitution, but no religious test shall ever be required as a qualification to any office or public trust under the United States.

This is the first specific statement of separation of church and state, because it permitted any person, without regard to religious affiliation, to hold public office; and it provided for the use of "affirmation" as an alternative to an oath which is not even described as a religious oath. Oliver Ellsworth, the third Chief Justice of the U.S. Supreme Court and a delegate to the Constitutional Convention, said in one of his writings that in Europe, by contrast, the nations with established churches always had religious tests for holding office.[4]

James Iredell, a Supreme Court justice from 1790 to 1799 who had served in the North Carolina Convention that ratified the U.S. Constitution, referred to the exclusion of a religious test for public office as one way to establish religious liberty. He argued that Congress had no power to create "the establishment of any religion whatsoever; and I am astonished that any gentleman should conceive that they have. . . . If any future Congress should pass an act concerning the religion of the country, it would be an act which they are not authorized to pass, by the Constitution. . . ."[5]

4) Although members of the Constitutional Convention and many others believed that the new federal government had no power or right to legislate with respect to religion, there was a widespread desire for a bill of rights that would guarantee no action with respect to religion.

Thomas Tredwell of New York opposed ratification of the Constitution. He said that he wished that "sufficient caution had been used to secure to us our religious liberties, and to have prevented the general government from tyrannizing over our consciences by a religious establishment—a tyranny of all others most dreadful and which will assuredly be exercised whenever it shall be thought necessary for the promotion and support of their political measures."[6]

Rhode Island and North Carolina refused to ratify the Constitution until a Bill of Rights was adopted. In Virginia, James Madison could not get the state convention to ratify the Constitution until after he gave his personal pledge to secure an amendment against an establishment of religion.[7]

5) Frequently people who know little about the history of religious establishments in American colonial history believe that the early American opposition to an established church was a reaction to the Anglican Church of England or the Roman Catholic Church of Spain or Italy. Chief Justice William Rehnquist made such a mistake in a 1985 statement wherein he tried to justify aid to religion on the basis of the establishment clause in the First Amendment, asserting that it was intended "to prohibit the designation of any church as a 'national one.' "

Those who drafted the First Amendment were not recent immigrants from Europe but the products of American religious pluralism. The Constitutional historian C. Herman Pritchett summarized the American experience as follows:

The phrase "establishment of religion" must be given the meaning it had in the United States in 1791, rather than its European connotation. In America there was no establishment of a single church, as in England. Four states had never adopted any establishment practices. Three had abolished their establishments during the Revolution. The remaining six states—Maryland, Massachusetts, New Hampshire, Connecticut, South Carolina, and Georgia—changed to comprehensive or "multiple" establishments. That is, aid was provided to all churches in each state on a nonpreferential basis, except that the establishment was limited to churches of the Protestant religion in three states. Since there were almost no Catholics in the first group of states, and very few Jews in any state, this meant that the multiple establishment practices included every religious group with enough members to form a church. It was this nonpreferential assistance to organized churches that constituted "establishment or religion" in 1791 and it was this practice that the Amendment forbade Congress to adopt.[8]

The phrase "establishment of religion was defined in the period when the Constitution was drafted, not as the official state religion, but as "a religion which the civil authority engages not only to protect but to support."[9]

6) At the time the First Amendment was proposed, many in Congress thought the Constitution had already made it clear that the federal government had no power to deal with religion. Their concern was one of defining a prohibition so that no future government could assume an authority that had not been granted to Congress in or under the Constitution.

An early proposal by James Madison included the phrase, "nor shall any national religion be established." This was rejected and a House committee reported to the House that "no religion shall be established by law nor shall the equal right of conscience be in any manner or on any pretext infringed."[10]

On another occasion Madison tried to insert the word "national" before "religion," but there ensued so much opposition that he withdrew it. A motion presented by Samuel Livermore was adopted "that Congress shall make no law touching religion or infringing the rights of conscience."[11] This motion was changed before it went to the Senate to read, "Congress shall make no law establishing religion, or to prevent the free exercise thereof, or to infringe the rights of conscience."[12]

In the Senate two attempts were made to change the wording so that it referred to the establishment of "one religious sect or society in preference to another" or to "establishing any religious sect or society." These were rejected, as was the phrase, "Nor shall the rights of conscience be infringed."[13]

Finally, after a weakened Senate version was rejected by the House, a compromise was reached by a conference committee. The establishment clause adopted by both Houses of Congress is that found in the First Amendment today:

> Congress shall make no law respecting an establishment of religion or prohibiting the free exercise thereof. . . .

The word "respecting" meant then, as it does now, "concerning, touching upon, or in relation to, or with regard to." The word "establishment" had two meanings then as it does now. The first refers to the situation that existed in some of the colonies and states, wherein the state provided financial or tax support to churches. The second meaning is that an establishment of religion is an institution of religion. Both Madison and Jefferson in their capacity as government officials were referring to establishment in the second sense. Madison, in a veto of a bill granting a parcel of land to a Baptist church, said, "Congress shall make no law respecting a religious establishment."[14] Jefferson, in drafting a Virginia law about colleges and universities, provided that students "will be free and expected to attend religious worship at the establishment of their respective sects."[15]

Whichever of the above definitions is used, it is clear that the First Amendment does not say, "Congress shall make no law establishing religion," but does say, "no law respecting an establishment of religion." It therefore cannot be construed as authorizing Congress to support religious institutions. It is not, as some partisans of aid to churches indicate, an act of empowerment, but rather an act denying Congress any power to vote laws respecting an establishment of religion.

The question of original intent *does not,* in the final analysis, depend on historical references to a single established church, as in England; or to multiple establishments that received tax support; or to preferential treatment of a particular church; or to the abandonment of such treatment. Original intent *does* depend on the following four things: the secular nature of the Constitution, which gives no power to the federal government to deal with religion; the actual text of Article VI, Section 3, which forbids any religious test for public office or a position of public trust; the actual text of the First Amendment, which forbids any law "respecting an establishment of religion"; and the continuing revolution against government support of religion, to which we now turn.

The discussion of original intent cannot be ended with the adoption of the First Amendment because that might imply that the religion clauses applied only to the federal government. It is an historical fact that political leaders, then as now, usually react to public demand rather than enact legislation that then creates public support. The demand for the religion clauses arose from the people and was manifest in a continuing revolution in each state against government meddling in religious affairs, especially at the point of taxation.

Although it was assumed, when the Constitution was framed and adopted, that matters pertaining to religion and education were the province of the respective states, those states were moving steadily against any state-supported religion and against any religious test for public office. Those states that had such tests gradually dropped them, although they were not required to do so. Delaware in 1792, Vermont in 1793, Tennessee in 1796, and eventually every state in the Union either abandoned religious tests for voting and for holding public office or, as in the case of Rhode Island, never had such tests to begin with.

The states also abandoned the use of public funds or taxation for religious purposes. The New Jersey constitution of 1776, well before the federal constitution was framed, said: ". . . nor shall any person within this colony, ever be obliged to pay tithes, taxes or any other rates, for the purpose of building or repairing any other church or churches, place or places of worship, or for the maintenance of any minister or ministry contrary to what he believes to be right or has deliberately or voluntarily engaged himself to perform."[16]

The Pennsylvania constitution of 1776 had a similar provision, as did the Vermont constitutions of 1777, 1779, and 1782. Rhode Island never had any religious taxes; Virginia eliminated such taxes in 1785, South Carolina in 1790, and Delaware and Kentucky in 1791. The last state to end tax support of its various churches was Massachusetts in 1833, after the state senate, which had favored distribution of tax money to churches on a nonpreferential basis, finally permitted the people to vote on it. The vote was ten to one, an overwhelming rejection of multiple establishments of religion.[17]

In other words, the concept of separation of church and state, including the rejection of government funds to support religious institutions, was not simply the idea of a few individuals like Roger Williams, Thomas Jefferson, and James Madison. It was the general will of the people. The churches as well as the unchurched were a part of that general will.

Not surprisingly, therefore, after the Fourteenth Amendment was adopted in 1868 following the war between the North and South, the legislative history shows that it was intended to make the first eight amendments of the Bill of Rights applicable to the states. The Fourteenth Amendment declares: "No state shall make or enforce any law which shall abridge the privileges and immunities of citizens of the United States. . . ." The floor manager, Senator J. M. Howard, stated that "to these privileges and immunities . . . should be added the personal rights guaranteed and secured by the first eight amendments to the Constitution." He also said that the "great object of the first section of the amendment is therefore to restrain the power of the states and compel them at all times to respect these fundamental guarantees."[18] The House of Representatives took a similar position with respect to the Fourteenth Amendment.[19]

Sometimes it is argued by modern opponents of separation of church and state that various government officials violated constitutional prohibitions against supporting religion, thus proving they did not intend to keep government from aiding church institutions. The answer to this is that the people concentrated their opposition to government interference with religion on such major offenses as taxing the people to support religious institutions or establishments. Neither the people nor their representatives in Congress drew up a list of everything they meant by the word "establishment" or specified whether, for example, prayer at public events or Thanksgiving proclamations would be included. In practice, many of these public manifestations of piety have been perfunctory or have lost their religious meaning. Thanksgiving, for example, is no longer—if it ever was—a day observed by a people at prayer, but is celebrated as a civil observance. Almost no one attends the opening prayer of the chaplain in the houses of Congress or uses the chaplain to perform weddings, funerals, or personal counseling. Each member of Congress relies on his or her pastor, if any, for such services.

Congress and the executive branch, however, have always been subject to pressures from some church leaders to engage in public piety or to appropriate money to aid church projects or to support some other religious expression; but the people, when given an opportunity to vote in state referenda, have continued over the years to support separation of church and state. They have wanted their government to be neutral with respect to religion and to leave the raising of money, the winning of adherents, and the determining of doctrine, church programs, church property and all other religious matters to the respective religious bodies.

Nevertheless, there are some religious leaders and even Supreme Court justices responsive to religious pressures, who have opposed separation of church and state. In spite of the constitutional history, certain myths have arisen to suggest that federal or state governments may or should aid religion or establishments of religion.

The first myth is that religious liberty is a by-product of the First Amendment. Actually that amendment was intended as an additional protection, since the federal government under the Constitution had no power to invade the field of religion. Still, some Supreme Court justices, notably Warren E. Burger, a former chief justice, have argued that aid to religion is permitted if it doesn't lead to the establishment of a state religion.[20] In other words, the clause, "Congress shall make no law respecting an establishment of religion" has been interpreted by some, contrary to its precise wording, as giving the government the power to aid religion so long as it doesn't lead to a state establishment.

The second myth is that the establishment clause does not preclude aid to religion but merely prohibits preferential aid to one or some religions. This is the position of Chief Justice William H. Rehnquist. In his dissent in *Wallace* v. *Jaffree,* he said the establishment clause was "designed to stop the federal government from asserting a preference for one religious denomination or sect over others."[21] This is rebutted by the fact that the first Senate in separate votes on the proposed religion clauses of the First Amendment rejected the following amendment: "Congress shall make no law establishing one religious sect or society in preference to others," and also, "Congress shall make no law establishing any particular denomination or religion in preference to another. . . ." It is also rebutted by the fact that Congress was given no power in the Constitution or the First Amendment to aid religion. The attempt by any judge to use the First Amendment prohibition as a justification for aid is a perversion of its meaning.

The third myth is that the Supreme Court, in those cases where it upheld a strict separation of church and state, gave undue weight to Virginia's experience, which was that of complete rejection of aid to churches. This position, enunciated in an *amicus* brief of the U.S. Catholic Conference in *Mueller* v. *Allen,* holds essentially to the Rehnquist position that aid to churches is lawful provided it is nonpreferential. This is also false. When the First Congress adopted the establishment clause, it was not merely following Virginia's lead, but reacting to the fact that six states had provisions for multiple establishments or for taxing people to support any churches that had the required minimum number of members. In other words, the practice in a number of states at the time the Constitution was adopted and when the First Amendment was debated was that of nonpreferential aid to churches. The opposition to establishment was not just to the establishment of one church in preference to others, but to any governmental support of religion.

Nor did Virginia take the lead in opposing aid to establishments of religion. Rhode Island, New Jersey, Pennsylvania, and Vermont all opposed the use of public funds to aid established churches before Virginia did so. Virginia generated more written arguments on the subject than most states because in that state the controversy had been so prolonged.

It was the conviction of those who framed the Constitution and of those in the First Congress who adopted the First Amendment, that the federal government should stay out of the business of regulating, endorsing, or supporting churches and should maintain the free exercise of religion.

The fourth myth is that the Bill of Rights, including the ban on federal support of religion and presumably the free exercise clause, does not extend to the states. The Fourteenth Amendment, however, specifically says: "No state shall make or enforce any law which shall abridge the privileges or immunities of citizens of the United States. . . ." The Congressional debates indicate that Congress intended, by adopting the amendment, to make the Bill of Rights as well as the rest of the Constitution applicable to the states. The Supreme Court since the 1940s has interpreted the First Amendment's religion clauses as applicable to the states as Congress intended.

The fifth myth is that separation of church and state is not written into the Constitution, but was simply a part of Thomas Jefferson's metaphor referring to the First Amendment as "building a wall of separation between church and state." It is true that the metaphor does not appear in the Constitution, but neither does the phrase "separation of powers," which refers to the distinct powers of the legislative, executive, and judicial branches. Yet both are accurate descriptions of constitutional provisions.

The secular nature of the Constitution provides for separation. The meaning of "separation" at the time the Constitution and Bill of Rights were adopted, was clearly derived from the context of that day when there were religious tests for public office, established churches, taxation for churches and church schools and state laws protecting conscience. There should be no doubt about the original intent to separate church and state at these points and to uphold the free exercise of religion.

Some religious leaders in America do not like the idea of a secular constitution and a secular state. They advocate a Christian republic in which presumably Jews and other non-Christians would be tolerated.

These religious leaders are responsible for a sixth myth: that early America was a Christian society led by committed pastors and religious leaders. The historical fact is that colonial America was composed largely of people who were not church members, although church members in some colonies were influential enough to persuade colonial governments to provide tax support for their churches. William Warren Sweet in his authoritative book, *The Story of Religions in America,* wrote:

> Up until the third decade of the eighteenth century the lower classes in the American colonies were little influenced by organized religion and only a small percentage of the population were members of the colonial churches. . . . Even in the Puritan colonies only a comparatively small proportion of the total population were members of the church, while in Virginia at the opening of the eighteenth century not more than one in twenty were church members, and the proportion was undoubtedly smaller in the other southern colonies.[22]

While those who advocate a return to established churches in the form of a Christian republic claim they would tolerate non-Christians, that is not certain. Even if it were, tolerance would not be the same thing as religious liberty. When any nation-state has a religious bias or preference, it cannot be impartial with respect to all faiths and denominations and to nonbelievers. The secular state can guarantee the religious liberty of all precisely because it has no theocratic pretensions, no religious loyalties, no religious preferences, and no religious prejudices.

Under our constitutional separation of church and state, churches, Quaker meetings, synagogues, other religious institutions, and humanists and atheist societies have been granted religious liberty. In contrast to the state churches in Europe, where membership was a matter of course, there were "more unchurched people in America in proportion to the population than was to be found in any country in Christendom."[23] Under the Constitution's guarantee of religious liberty, that ratio has been reversed, and there are now more members of organized religious groups and a greater vitality of religious life in the United States than in those countries where there exists no constitutional restriction on state aid to religion and no free exercise clause.

In other words, the constitutional text as well as the tradition established by the American people over a period of two hundred years is that of separation of church and state wherein government is neither to aid nor hinder religion. Religion and its support, practices, and beliefs are to be left to the people. This is in harmony with the Ninth Amendment, which also guarantees the right of privacy: "The enumeration in the Constitution of certain rights shall not be construed to deny or disparage others retained by the people."

NOTES

1. Charles A. Beard, *The Republic* (New York: Viking Press, 1944), p. 166.

2. *Annals of the Congress of the United States* (Washington, D.C.: Gales and Seaton, 1934), 1:438.

3. Jonathan Elliot, ed., *The Debates in the Several State Conventions on the Adoption of the Federal Constitution* (Philadelphia: J. B. Lippincott and Company, 1941), 4:208.

4. Paul L. Ford, ed., *Essays on the Constitution of the United States* (Brooklyn, N.Y.: The Historical Printing Club, 1892), p. 168.

5. Elliot, *Debates,* 4:194.

6. Ibid., 2:399.

7. Sanford H. Cobb, *The Rise of Religious Liberty in America* (New York: Macmillan Co., 1902), p. 508.

8. C. Herman Pritchett, *The American Constitution* 3rd ed. (New York: McGraw Hill, 1977), p. 401.

9. Anson Phelps Stokes, *Church and State in the United States* (New York: Harper and Brothers, 1950), 1:510.

10. *Annals of the Congress of the United States,* 1:434.

11. Ibid., p.731.

12. Ibid., p. 766.

13. *Journal of the First Session of the Senate* (Washington, D.C.: Gales and Seaton, 1820), p. 70.

14. Leo Pfeffer, *Church, State and Freedom* (Boston: Beacon Press, 1953), p. 140.

15. Ibid.

16. Stokes, *Church and State in the United States,* p. 435.

17. For a detailed discussion of state actions to end establishments of religion see John M. Swomley, *Religious Liberty and the Secular State* (Buffalo, N.Y.: Prometheus Books, 1987), pp. 27–37, 57–60.

18. *Congressional Globe,* 39th Congress, 1st Session, p. 2765.

19. Ibid., pp. 1088-90. See also *Congressional Globe,* 42nd Congress, 1st Session, Appendix, p. 150, where Bingham restated his intention in drafting the Fourteenth Amendment.

20. See *Wallace* v. *Jaffree,* 104 S. Ct. 1704 and *Grand Rapids School District* v. *Ball,* 104 S. Ct. 1412.

21. Ibid.

22. William Warren Sweet, *The Story of Religions in America* (New York: Charles Scribner's Sons, 1953), p. 7.

23. Ibid.

4

Nonpreferentialists: Modern Advocates of Court-Mandated Second-Class Consciences

Robert S. Alley

In August of 1990, at Touro Synagogue, I was privileged to participate in the 200th anniversary celebration commemorating a letter from George Washington to that congregation in which the president affirmed the nation's commitment to religious freedom. My mind drifted back to the seventeenth century and the circumstances that had brought that small Jewish community to Newport, Rhode Island, in 1658. The crazed urge by Christians to convert or destroy Jews, an attitude still present in many quarters of Christianity even today, drove the Sephardim to seek refuge from persecution. Roger Williams's grand experiment drew them to that unique colony where they enjoyed religious freedom unknown elsewhere.

In every era there are moments when, to borrow words from Harry Emerson Fosdick, we are challenged to seek wisdom and courage "for the living of these days." Williams accepted that challenge. There do appear to be those special moments when choices made determine the direction of history. The problem is that the actors who play out their parts in the drama can never be certain which moments are the special ones. Walter Rauschenbusch was acutely aware of this when, in 1907, he wrote his introduction to *Christianity and the Social Crisis*:

Robert S. Alley is a professor of Humanities at the University of Richmond and author of *The Supreme Court on Church and State*.

45

> In a few years all our restless and angry hearts will be quiet in death, but those who come after us will live in the world which our sins have blighted or which our love of right has redeemed. Let us do our thinking on these great questions, . . . with a wise outlook on the fields of the future and with the consciousness that the spirit of the Eternal is seeking to distil from our lives some essence of righteousness before they pass away. (p. 3)

While the founders of this nation would likely not have phrased it that way, when they spoke of the "natural rights of mankind" or mused on "the trust committed to them," they did sense the inestimable value of those moments. Speaking at a symposium on religious freedom in 1982, Henry Steele Commager remarked on the character of those nation builders of the eighteenth century. America, he says,

> . . . relied on reason as well as on faith, embraced mankind rather than the individual, and was ever conscious of the claims of posterity—a word that has all but disappeared from our vocabulary today. . . . Its testaments, moral, philosophical, or political, celebrated virtue, happiness, equality in the sight of God and the law, justice, and life here rather than hereafter. It believed in one form of immortality—the immortality of fame—which was the spur: "Take care of me when I am dead," Jefferson wrote Madison; it was in a sense the *cri de coeur* of their generation.[1]

One of the legacies from that era is the Bill of Rights. And it is not, I think, overly dramatic to insist that the third century of that great document is fraught with considerable peril for our posterity. Tortured arguments about original intent of the founders threaten the spirit to which Commager referred. Sadly, one of the reasons for the looming risks to our freedoms is a massive historical ignorance that grips our citizenry. That ignorance is all the more distressing because, to some large degree, it stems from ever more frequent academic disdain for American culture in historical perspective. Our college students are left to vague generalities about the founders, establishing heroes without substance. We haven not taken care of those women and men after their death.

Creators of the Constitution provided a dynamic document that transcended them. It loses its character and genius when attempts are made to incarcerate that document in the dead forms of heroic figures, no matter how profound their leadership in their lifetimes. Neither Jefferson nor Madison ever appear to have contemplated the extension of political freedom to women, nor were they and their peers prepared to extend the natural rights they espoused to slaves. Their gift to us is no less significant because of their own blindness, but their original intent was radically flawed. It is only the ideas released in those crucial years that may, two centuries later, free us from a mindless commitment to original intent, an intent, Leonard Levy observes, "most likely to be determined by the conclusion that the Court wishes to reach."

Strained efforts to recover the "intent" of the founders is a conservative effort to restrict the very genius that gave wings to democracy. Levy rightly notes,

> Ours is so secure a system, precisely because it is free and dedicated to principles of justice, that it can afford to prefer the individual over the state. To interpose original intent against an individual's claim defeats the purpose of having systematic and regularized restraints on power; limitations exist for the minority against the majority, as Madison said. Original intent analysis becomes a treacherous pursuit when it turns the Constitution and the Court away from assisting the development of a still freer and more just society.[2]

Fifty years ago, it was in this direction of thought, rather than in his sometimes flawed historical analysis, that Justice Hugo Black captured the dynamic character of the Bill of Rights.

> Under our constitutional system, courts stand against any winds that blow, as havens of refuge for those who might otherwise suffer because they are helpless, weak, outnumbered, or because they are nonconforming victims of prejudice and public excitement.[3]

However, citizens ignorant of 200 years of American history will not easily grasp the import of Levy's and Black's words. Arguments focused on a presumed knowledge of intent, hallowed by passage of time, trade on this ignorance. There arises a dogma based upon mythologized dead heroes, ignoring the framers as sentient political activists. Such thinking denies the efficacy of education for the future. Advocates of public education, including Jefferson, believed that only an educated electorate could sustain democracy. In any valid education there must be a tension between an understanding of the past and a robust claim to the future by those who are living their own days. Public education is the best hope for this nation to claim its legacy.

Trapped by a recalcitrant public mood that refuses to heed the spirit of *Brown* v. *Board of Education,* a religious fundamentalism that rejects the very principles of diversity, an educational hierarchy that often forces teachers to become little more than crafters of elaborate lesson plans, and irresponsible attacks by civic leaders on public school teachers, our children face an uneasy future, a future suggesting a reghettoization of education. Rather than search for constructive alternatives to build a stronger, more vibrant public educational system, political leaders and all too many self-styled educators see the current situation as hopeless; they turn to plans of privatization that require redistribution of public funds to private schools. Sadly, religious schools stand ready for the dole, while their parent bodies spend large sums plotting strategies they hope will result in massive aid to parochial schools. As will be noted later, an original intent argument that turns the First Amendment on its head, rejecting fifty years of precedent concerning establishment of religion, looms as a primary means to finance parochial schools.

I take it as a given that the spirit of our Constitution and Bill of Rights is an expansive spirit. It is one that asks not what limits did Madison imagine existed on the First Amendment in 1790, but how would the imaginative mind that conceived those words construe them for a multi-cultured, giant democracy in the 1990s. In the final analysis, we do not honor Madison because he wrote words or performed acts beneficial to another time, but because his spirit and vision have credibility for today; in short, they speak to those living today.

Standing on the front lawn of Madison's Montpelier a few months ago, I experienced the living quality of the Madison legacy as I listened to the president of Hungary speak about his nation and the significance of the Bill of Rights. He was so moved by the moment that, although he speaks fluent English, he announced that the emotions he felt could only be expressed in his native Hungarian. In comments later that day, political historian James MacGregor Burns argued that while Madison may have to share credit for the writing of the Constitution, he most assuredly was the Father of the Bill of Rights. That being the case and recalling Jefferson's plea to his dear friend, we might inquire how our generation may best take care of Madison in a world he could not have imagined. On June 28, 1836, Madison's niece, Nelly Willis, visited her uncle while he ate. Noting his difficulty in swallowing, she asked what was the trouble. He replied, "Nothing more than a change of mind, my dear." Appropriately, his final words seem to ridicule the whole notion of original intent.

THE FORMATION OF RELIGIOUS FREEDOM: 1784–1790

Ralph Ketcham, in an excellent biography of James Madison, comments,

> . . . when Madison went to the middle colonies and to the Presbyterian strong-hold at Princeton [The College of New Jersey], he placed himself at the center of the English dissenting tradition in North America. He found there that enlightened men took for granted the pattern of thought which from Cromwell's day had opposed religious establishment [and] ecclesiastical hierarchy. . . .[4]

But Madison did not gain from that exposure any explicit rejection of all forms of establishment. It was his genius—coupled with harsh experiences—that moved him from those early influences supporting a liberal form of toleration to a grander concept—religious liberty.

When, in 1772, Madison returned home to Montpelier, he entered into correspondence with his close friend, William Bradford of Philadelphia. Perusal of this material reveals some interesting facts. In November of 1772, Madison appeared despondent, anticipating an early death. In September of the following year, he was less introspective and offered serious advice to Bradford about choosing a profession. On December 1, 1773, Madison learned that Bradford had chosen the law. At this point we come upon Madison's first reference to a serious political interest. He asked Bradford for a draft of the Pennsylvania constitution, "particularly the extent of your religious Toleration." One can feel Madison come alive as he asks, "Is an Ecclesiastical Establishment absolutely necessary to support civil society in a supreme Government? And how far is it hurtful to a dependent State?" Something was clearly at work on the young man.

On January 24, 1774, Madison wrote, "Ecclesiastical Establishments tend to great ignorance and Corruption all of which facilitate the Execution of mischievous Projects." He spoke of poverty and political corruption before making the following moving observation:

> This is bad enough but it is not the worst I have to tell you. That diabolical Hell-conceived principle of persecution rages among some and to their eternal Infamy the Clergy can furnish their quota of Imps for such business. This vexes me the most of any thing whatever. There are at this time in the adjacent County not less than five or six well-meaning men in close Gaol for publishing their religious Sentiments which in the main are very orthodox. I have neither patience to hear talk or think any thing relative to this matter, for I have squabbled and scolded, abused and ridiculed so long about it, to so little purpose that I am without common patience. So I leave you to pity me and pray for Liberty of Conscience [to revive among us].[5]

By April of 1774, Madison was writing about the "rights of conscience."

Madison's vexation appears to have raised him from his lethargy and eliminated his predictions of an early death. He had a cause that ignited him. And in two consecutive letters we find him recognizing the fundamental difference between toleration and liberty of conscience. There is little doubt that in the few months since his previous letter, Madison had answered his own question about establishment and moved to a new level beyond toleration.

The word toleration has a sweet ring in modern America. It denotes a sense of justice and respect for differing views. We urge our children to retain that natural spirit of tolerance in mind and action which characterizes five-year-old girls and boys. But for a state to be tolerant is quite another matter. Here the implication is that the state has the right to tyranny and exercises tolerance out of its largesse. Tom Paine would later characterize the term as despotism. It was this point that quickly affected Madison; in 1785, he cast his concerns in the following classic mold:

> Who does not see that the same authority which can establish Christianity, in exclusion of all other Religions, may establish with the same ease any particular sect of Christians, in exclusion of all other Sects?[6]

As he expressed it in his *Autobiographical Note* of 1832, Madison contended for freedom of conscience as a "natural and absolute right." Toleration presumed a state right that, for Madison, did not exist, for the right to tolerate religion presumes the already existing right to persecute it.

It may be fair to surmise that the young Madison first felt his intense, life-long commitment to freedom focusing on political action as he observed the persecution by his own government of those ministers in close jail. Whatever sent him to the Virginia Convention two years later, the emotional reactions to the abuse of the dissenters in 1774 cannot be dismissed as an insignificant factor.

In May of 1776, Madison was elected to the Revolutionary Convention in Virginia. He was selected to serve on a committee to compose a declaration of rights for the new government. George Mason, a Virginia elder statesman, proposed an article about religion that read, "All men should enjoy the fullest toleration in the exercise of religion." Madison proposed to supplant the word toleration. He already appeared to view the term as an "invidious concept," and proposed to substitute, "All men are equally entitled to the free exercise of religion." Historian George Bancroft would describe that phrase as "the first achievement of the wisest civilian in Virginia."

A little-noted suggestion by Madison respecting the Declaration of Rights, included with his move to insert free exercise, was a concluding phrase of justification. It read, "unless under colour of religion, the preservation of equal liberty and the existence of the State be manifestly endangered."[7] This may be the clearest statement by Madison of his dual fear of establishment. He was concerned over not only the loss of religious freedom but the threat to a democratic state posed by religious establishment. The all-consuming character of the continuing war with Britain, however, left little time to make further changes in the laws of Virginia. Jefferson was unable to have his Bill to Establish Religious Freedom in Virginia passed during his time in the legislature.

In 1784, the year following the conclusion of the war, Madison took his place in the governing body of Virginia. Almost immediately he was confronted with two threats to the freedom he so clearly articulated in 1776. First, there was the renewed effort to establish the Episcopal Church in the state as the natural successor to the Anglican establishment. Second, there was a General Assessment Bill that would assign tax monies to support religious education by Protestant churches, a project justified by its supporters as a means of curtailing the sin and immorality of the youthful population. In the fall of 1784, Madison knew that he could not deflect both these pieces of legislation. Politicians were not likely to cast two votes "against God" in the same session. Madison had already indicated his opposition to the established Church of England in his letters to William Bradford in 1773; in 1784, he quickly resolved his dilemma. He voted for Episcopalian establishment, and the measure passed. But Madison convinced his colleagues to postpone a vote on assessment until the next session in 1785. He believed that the Assessment Bill was an even more insidious form of establishment, and was convinced that it would result in an established Protestantism in Virginia. Combining, as it would, the interests of all religious factions, the consequence could well be a permanent condition. Writing to his father on January 6, 1785, Madison explained his decision:

> The inclosed Act for incorporating the Episcopal Church is the result of much altercation on the subject. In its original form it was wholly inadmissable. In its present form into which it has been trimmed, I assented to it with reluctance at the time, and with dissatisfaction on review of it. . . . I consider the passage of this Act however as having been so far useful as to have parried for the present the Genl. Assesst. which would otherwise have certainly been saddled upon us: & If it be unpopular among the laity it will be soon repealed, and will be a standing lesson to them of the danger of referring religious matters to the legislature.[8]

The reason for Madison's choice in the fall of 1784 is clear enough, confirming as it did his consistent view that the state had most to fear from the "tyranny of the majority." He was certain that Presbyterians, Methodists, and Baptists would not long tolerate the preeminent position of the Episcopal Church. Indeed, this turned out to be the case. Within a decade, the Episcopal Church had been stripped not only of its established status but also of its land holdings obtained in pre-revolutionary times. For Madison the great danger was an establishment of a coalition of Protestant groups that would be impervious to arguments against it. He foresaw a classic case of majority tyranny relegating minority religious views to a "tolerated" status.

Madison now faced two tasks: he had both to enlist public opposition to the Assessment Bill and to deal with the oratory of his chief adversary in the Assembly, Patrick Henry. Commenting upon Henry, Jefferson wrote his friend Madison in December 1784: "What we have to do I think is *devoutly* to *pray* for his *death*, in the meantime to keep alive the idea that the present is but an ordinance and to prepare the minds of the *young* men. I am glad the Episcopalians have again shewn their teeth & fangs. The dissenters had almost forgotten them." Rather than take Jefferson's religious option concerning Henry, Madison used, as Ralph Ketcham wryly notes, the secular humanist alternative and helped elect Henry as governor, thereby silencing his silver tongue.

After the Assembly adjourned, having authorized distribution of the Assessment Bill to the voters for their thoughts, Madison was convinced by his friends that he must write a document attacking the Assessment Bill which had been laid over to the fall of 1785. This he did in his brilliant *Memorial and Remonstrance*.

Newly elected delegates, and a massive petition activity by dissenters in the state, as well as his *Memorial,* gave Madison his victory over the Assessment Bill without ever having to argue in the Assembly against it. He chose the moment to introduce Jefferson's Bill to Establish Religious Freedom in Virginia; with some minor alterations, that Bill became law in January of 1786. As predicted by Madison, Episcopal establishment was repealed shortly thereafter. Meanwhile, Madison was off to Philadelphia to help fashion the new Constitution.

Little information is forthcoming from examination of Madison's notes on the Constitutional Convention concerning the two occasions in 1787, when religion became an issue before that assemblage. On June 28, Dr. Franklin addressed his colleagues:

> The small progress we have made after four or five weeks . . . is methinks a melancholy proof of the imperfection of the Human Understanding. . . . How has it happened, Sir, that we have not hitherto once thought of humbly applying to the Father of lights to illuminate our understandings?[9]

Franklin went on to credit God for victory over Great Britain and asked whether "we imagine we no longer need his assistance?" He concluded,

> I have lived, Sir, a long time, and the longer I live, the more convincing proofs I see of this truth—*that God governs in the affairs of men.* . . . I therefore beg leave to move—that henceforth prayers imploring the assistance of Heaven, and its blessings on our deliberations, be held in this Assembly every morning before we proceed to business, and that one or more of the Clergy of this City be requested to officiate in that Service.[10]

Madison makes no indication that he himself entered the debate, noting only that "Mr. Hamilton and several others expressed their apprehensions that however proper such a resolution might have been at the beginning," it might now lead "the public to believe that the embarrassments and dissensions within the Convention, had suggested this measure." And of course it had done precisely that by Franklin's words. Mr. Hugh Williamson of North Carolina suggested the omission was due to a lack of funds. Madison concludes, "After several unsuccessful attempts for silently postponing the matter by adjourning, the adjournment was at length carried, without any vote on the motion." Seemingly an embarrassing interlude followed when the delegates, anxious not to offend the elder statesman, fumbled about until they simply dispersed. The idea for prayer never resurfaced.

This is a revealing episode. Franklin clearly believed the prayer would secure success in their deliberations. His point was never addressed, as those who spoke all dealt with public opinion, suggesting that for most of the men prayer was a form without substantial benefit other than good feelings and appearances. And the remarkable observation that they could not afford to pay for prayer tells us that at least one delegate considered prayer as a cultural prop. Hamilton and others construed the Franklin suggestion as having good public relations value to the extent that it might convey a positive message to the electorate. But the efficacy of prayer was not at issue for the leaders in Philadelphia. These were men satisfied that their creator had endowed them with minds with which to think. Their religious sentiments were consistently expressed in an enlightened humanism that respected the image of the deity which, many felt, resided in the human mind. At most, prayer was a habit of affirmation of that humanism, little more. So much for Franklin's views on the God of history.

Respecting Article VI, Madison's notes provide no clue as to the reasoning behind the religious test provision. Charles Pinckney of South Carolina submitted a set of propositions on August 20. Among them was, "No religious test or qualification shall ever be annexed to any oath of office under the authority of the U. S." This was referred to the Committee of detail without debate or consideration. On August 30, Pinckney moved to add to what was to become Article VI: "but no religious test shall ever be required as a qualification to any office or public trust under the authority of the U. States." Roger Sherman of Connecticut "thought it unnecessary, the prevailing liberality being a sufficient security against such tests." Gouverneur Morris of Pennsylvania joined in support of the amendment. The motion was then agreed to. In a letter to Jefferson in 1788, Madison noted reservations among some about this provision. "One of the objections in New England was that the Constitution, by prohibiting religious tests, opened the door for Jews, Turks, and infidels."

When he left Philadelphia, Madison was satisfied with the decision to omit a Bill of Rights from the new document. He felt such provisions were unnecessary and, further, "because there is great reason to fear that a positive declaration of some of the most essential rights could not be obtained in the requisite latitude." Knowing that Jefferson felt strongly the need for a Bill of Rights, Madison therefore explored the matter thoroughly in a letter to his friend in October 17, 1788. Among other things, Madison affirmed his support for such an enumeration if "it is anxiously desired by others." In point of fact, he and many other leaders assured delegates to Constitution ratification conventions that, when Congress convened, a Bill of Rights would be a first order of business. Enough support was generated by these promises that it provided for the Constitution a margin of victory, sometimes slim, in the conventions of the more populous states.

As James Madison made his way to New York for the opening of Congress in April, he carried with him promises made to seek a Bill of Rights. He wrote to George Eve that the first Congress "ought to prepare . . . the most satisfactory provisions for all essential rights, particularly the rights of Conscience in the fullest latitude." In a campaign letter to voters in Spotsylvania County he wrote, "It is my wish . . . to see specific provision made on the subject of the Rights of Conscience. . . ." James Burns has recently commented that the most important ingredient in those early days of democracy was "trust." When political leaders agreed to pursue passage of a Bill of Rights, they were trusted by those who questioned the Constitution without such enumeration. In Madison they were not to be disappointed. The same, however, could not have been said of most of his colleagues. The House had more pressing business than a Bill of Rights and Madison found himself confronted with serious resistance when he said on June 8, "this house is bound by every motive of prudence, not to let the first session pass over without proposing to the state legislatures" a Bill of Rights. Only on July 21 did the House refer Madison's proposal to committee. A report was made on June 28 and finally began discussion on August 13. On August 24, the House sent seventeen amendments to the Senate. The third read, "Congress shall make no law establishing religion, or prohibiting the free exercise thereof; nor shall the rights of conscience be infringed." In an eighteenth-century version of nonpreferentialism, a motion was made to strike "religion, or prohibiting the free exercise thereof" and substituting "one religious sect or society in preference to others." The motion was defeated. As finally reported, the Senate did strike the final phrase. Another article written by Madison read, "No State shall infringe the equal rights of conscience, nor the freedom of speech, or of the press, nor of the right to trial by jury in criminal cases." Addressing his peers in the House on August 17, Madison said he considered "this to be the most valuable amendment on the whole list." The

Senate, however, demurred. Twelve amendments emerged from committee, not including the restrictions on the states. Victory on that front would have to wait until 1868 and the Fourteenth Amendment. On September 25, Congress sent the amendments to the states. The states in turn rejected the first two—regulation of number of representatives in Congress and regulation of congressional pay. Appropriately, it was Virginia that, on December 15, 1791, became the final state required to bring about ratification of the remaining ten amendments.

In its 1833 ruling, *Barron* v. *Baltimore*, the Supreme Court affirmed the obvious: the Bill of Rights imposed limitations only upon federal power. It is perhaps an irony that in the same year, Massachusetts, the last state to retain an establishment of religion, abolished it. It was the Civil War, finally, that ushered in a new approach that would ultimately be consistent with the spirit of Madison. In 1866, the Congress entered into extended debate over amendments in an effort to establish a satisfactory basis for reunion. Representative John Bingham set forth the following views on the Fourteenth Amendment, "I have advocated here an amendment which would arm Congress with the power to compel obedience to the oath, and punish all violations by State officers of the Bill of Rights. . . ."[11] Thaddeus Stevens concurred: ". . . the Constitution limits only the action of Congress, and is not a limitation on the States. This amendment supplies that defect, and allows Congress to correct the unjust legislation of the States, so far that the law which operates upon one man shall operate equally upon all."[12] Finally Senator Jacob Howard affirmed, "The great object of the first section of this amendment is, therefore, to restrain the power of the States and compel them at all times to respect these great fundamental guarantees."[13] Constitutional scholars Charles Fairman, Raoul Berger, and Leonard Levy all reject an original intent conclusion from these statements, noting contrary evidence from other legislators not quoted by Black. It is likely an irrelevant argument. Levy writes, "The imprecision of the text of the Constitution's litigated provisions makes 'strict construction' a faintly ridiculous concept."[14]

One thing is clear to me: our proclivities, whatever our vocation, are invested with our conclusions. We know that in 1619 basic human rights were denied to slaves. We know that the Bill of Rights did not apply to slaves, and not in any genuine way to women. A war and constitutional amendments corrected, partially, that diabolical defect. But the conscience of a nation was still in slumber. The 1896 Supreme Court decision, *Plessy* v. *Ferguson,* which enunciated the "separate but equal" doctrine of racial segregation, is testimony to that. If the historical record offers no undisputed direction in reference to the applicability of the Fourteenth to the First Amendment, the precedents of Supreme Court decisions over decades have led us to ever more inclusive interpretations. Respecting the religion clauses, the precedent of the

Fourteenth driving the First Amendment in terms of jurisdiction has been established since 1940 and the *Cantwell* decision. Delivering the opinion of the Court, Justice Roberts wrote:

> The First Amendment declares that Congress shall make no law respecting an establishment of religion or prohibiting the free exercise thereof. The Fourteenth Amendment has rendered the legislatures of the states as incompetent as Congress to enact such laws.

And in that incorporation of the Fourteenth Amendment, now well established by the Court, the role of judicial review respecting state laws properly took on an expansive flavor. Leonard Levy goes to the heart of the matter:

> The historic mission of judicial review is supposed to be the vindication of individual freedoms. To acknowledge that, yet to understand and protect only the most obvious and conventional freedoms, cancels two centuries of democratic growth by returning us to the world of the Framers. But even in that lost world of two centuries ago, rights were still in evolution, people understood that new rights emerge, and the Ninth Amendment put the Framers' thumbs down on the "rights" side of the scales that weigh rights against power.[15]

NONPREFERENTIALISM

In stark contrast to the Court tradition begun in *Cantwell* (1940) and *Everson* (1947), is a long-standing, articulate opposition that argues from the premise of original intent to assert that the First Amendment is the bedrock of some type of plural establishment. In more recent years this position has assumed the label nonpreferentialism. In 1986, Levy defined nonpreferentialism as,

> . . . a plausible but fundamentally defective interpretation of the establishment clause to prove that its framers had no intention of prohibiting government aid to all denominations or to religion on a nonpreferential basis. The nonpreferentialists are innocent of history but quick to rely on a few historical facts which, when yanked out of context, seem to provide a patristic lineage to their views.[16]

Michael Malbin, a scholar sympathetic to nonpreferentialist thought, phrased it succinctly in his 1978 volume, *Religion and Politics: The Intentions of the Authors of the First Amendment*, setting forth what would become nonpreferentialism: "The legislative history of the establishment clause shows that the framers accepted nondiscriminatory aid to religion."[17]

Since 1985, persons who would eviscerate fifty years of Supreme Court precedent have found a vital and critically important ally in Chief Justice

William Rehnquist. In his vigorous dissent in *Wallace* v. *Jaffree*, Rehnquist dismissed the Jeffersonian phrase "a wall of separation between church and state" as inapplicable to the First Amendment. As the reader may recall, President Jefferson used the wall analogy in a letter to a group of Danbury Baptists. Rehnquist asserted that,

> the greatest injury of the "wall" notion is its mischievous diversion of judges from the actual intentions of the drafters of the Bill of Rights. . . . The "wall" of separation between church and state" is a metaphor based on bad history, a metaphor which has proved useless as a guide to judging. It should be frankly and explicitly abandoned.[18]

Justice Rehnquist appears to ignore the fact that Jefferson may be a far more reliable source for the "actual intentions" than a Supreme Court justice some 180 years later. Jefferson was in constant discussion with Madison, via voluminous correspondence, during the entire period from 1784 through 1789. One may differ with Jefferson's insights, but it is the height of arrogance to assert that his observations, based upon intimate knowledge of the subject and the events, has provided modern judges with a "mischievous diversion." Rehnquist's easy dismissal of Jefferson's thoughts is an instant clue to the justice's own lack of historical judgment. For Rehnquist, the "wall" idea is an impediment to a goal he espouses, therefore in need of expurgation.

Unfortunately the decision of Jefferson to use nonconstitutional language to define the religion clauses has become a nonpreferentialist means to divert the argument. Jefferson's central role in the struggle provides him credibility, but his absence from the debates in Virginia, Pennsylvania, and New York allows critics to use that against him. The Court, however, from 1879 to the present, has found a reasonable correlation between the wall idea and the First Amendment. Justice Waite wrote for the Court in *Reynolds* v. *United States*, in 1879, that the Danbury letter, "coming as it does from an acknowledged leader of the advocates of the measure, . . . may be accepted almost as an authoritative declaration of the scope and effect of the amendment thus secured." But Justice Waite does use the word "almost." It is important because none of the cases from that time on have been based upon the Jefferson metaphor alone. The decisions stem from the clear and precise language of James Madison and other participants spanning a period from 1774 to 1833.

In 1833, Madison received a pamphlet from Jasper Adams of Charleston, South Carolina. Adams wanted Madison to endorse the idea of Christianity as a national religion. Adams asserted that "the people of the United States have retained the Christian religion as the foundation of their civil, legal, and political institutions." Justice Story had already commented, "My own private judgment has long been that government cannot long exist without an alliance with religion." He concluded that Christianity "is indispensable to the true interests and solid foundations of free government." He had expressed similar sentiments in his 1815 decision in *Terrett* v. *Taylor*:

> . . . the free exercise of religion cannot be justly deemed to be restrained by aiding with equal attention the votaries of every sect to perform their own religious duties, or by establishing funds for the support of ministers, for public charities, for the endowment of churches, or for the sepulture of the dead.[19]

Though plagued with infirmities that made it difficult to write, Madison took up the challenge. He stated the proposition thus:

> . . . the simple question to be decided is whether a support of the best & purest religion, the [Christian] religion, itself ought not, so far at least as pecuniary means are involved, to be provided for by the Govt. rather than be left to the voluntary provisions of those who profess it. And on this question experience will be an admitted Umpire, the more adequate as the connection between Govts. & Religion have existed in such various degrees & forms, and now can be compared with examples where connection has been entirely dissolved.[20]

Madison then listed several examples of church-state connections such as the papal system, "most of the Govts. of the old world," and Holland with its combining of a "liberal toleration with the establishment of a particular creed." He rejected them all with the observation, "the prevailing opinion in Europe, England not excepted, has been that Religion could not be preserved without the support of Govt." Finally Madison set forth his own view on a national religion:

> It remained for North America to bring the great & interesting subject to a fair, and finally to a decisive test. In the Colonial State of the Country, there were four examples, R.I., N.J., Penna. and Delaware, & a greater part of N.Y. where there were no religious Establishments, the support of Religion being left to the voluntary associations & contributions of individuals; and certainly the religious conditions of those Colonies will well bear a comparison with that where establishment existed. As it may be suggested that experiments made in Colonies more or less under the Controul of a foreign Government, had not the full scope necessary to display their tendency, it is fortunate that the appeal can now be made to their effects under a compleat exemption from any such controul.[21]

Madison's last words on this subject came in 1833, the same year that Massachusetts finally abolished its establishment. The point here is not to insist that Madison must be the only voice considered respecting First Amendment matters. Clearly, Justice Story had a contrary opinion. Rather, it is to suggest that historical integrity demands fairness to the admitted author of our constitutional right to free exercise and of its prohibition of establishment. I would rest on his arguments, not his stature as a founder. It is not original intent at issue here, but experience with principles of freedom.

Nonpreferentialism is certainly not new as an alternative reading of tradition. Story makes that clear. Indeed, his version would provide funds to support ministers and endow churches. These seem reasonable extensions once the barrier—or the wall, as Jefferson put it—is abandoned. But the wall metaphor has not been necessary to support the Court's findings since 1940. It has become a straw man by which nonpreferentialism seeks to discredit the Court precedents, thereby rendering a disservice to Jefferson and Madison alike.

Nonpreferentialism and its correlative thesis that "the Establishment Clause did not require government neutrality between religion and irreligion nor did it prohibit the federal government from providing nondiscriminatory aid to religion" (*Wallace* v. *Jaffree*, Rehnquist dissent) are unapologetically, if not admittedly, tolerationist to the core. Rehnquist's failure to understand that conscience may lead one to irreligion is a fundamental flaw in his argument.

Undoubtedly Justice Rehnquist would insist upon a much more inclusive net than did Justice Story. However, given the population of Virginia in 1784 and its religious proclivities, the net was broad in the Assessment Bill. Few non-Protestants populated Virginia in 1784. It is not clear how large a net the Chief Justice would employ, but any net is restrictive of freedom. And, to extend the analogy, nets not only exclude, they ultimately imprison the included. Free exercise resulted in a rejection of any notion that the government possessed the right to tolerate in matters of conscience. The conscience is inviolate, beyond the power of the state to control. Jefferson phrased it well in his Bill for Establishing Religious Freedom:

> . . . the rights hereby asserted are of the natural rights of mankind, and that if any act shall be hereafter passed to repeal the present, or to narrow its operation, such act will be an infringement of natural right.

Working from the principle of natural right, the establishment clause should not be interpreted as creating for the state a resident power to select among creeds, endorsing some, tolerating others. Unfortunately nonpreferentialism rejects this principle.

A serious problem with nonpreferentialism lies in the necessity for the federal government to "define" religion. One can hardly go about the task of plural establishment without definitions about inclusion and exclusion. This problem is solved in the First Amendment by assigning to each citizen the responsibility of defining religion according to individual conscience. Hence, the government should accept, without debate, all conscience claims by citizens as of equal worth. To be sure, practical implementation of some beliefs (snake handling or polygamy) have been restricted in the name of "compelling state interest." But the Court, at the same time, has been prepared to affirm that the beliefs that inspired such actions were unquestionably protected by the First Amendment.

Parenthetically, concerning "compelling state interest," the 1990 *Employment Division* v. *Smith* case (popularly known as the "peyote" case) has delivered a blow to that approach. In turn, a coalition of right- and left-wing groups, ranging from the Rutherford Institute to the ACLU, have endorsed "The Religious Freedom Restoration Act" to counter the effect of the Smith ruling.

Any effort to provide a "generalized endorsement of prayer," as Rehnquist says the establishment clause allows, necessitates a definition of prayer. But prayer, as many prominent religious leaders (Bailey Smith, Jerry Falwell, and Billy Graham) have recently noted, is not generalizable. Falwell and Smith deny that prayer, other than in the name of Jesus, is prayer at all. What is the state's position to be on this matter? Did the Regent's Prayer of New York qualify as prayer? It did not for millions of Christians in this nation. Is the State of New York, then, to tell them otherwise by endorsing a particular religious perspective, no matter how innocuous?

Some years ago, I testified on behalf of a young man who had been ordained by a mail-order religious group in California. He had become a chaplain in the state penitentiary and was, on occasion, performing marriages. The city attorney in Richmond became alarmed that such a person was acting in that capacity and took the matter to court. The judge in the case, a devout Episcopalian, questioned me about the particulars. I told him that when the state authorizes ordained clergy to verify marriages by signing the licenses, it is a blanket acceptance of ordination without definition. He was offended by this, noting that such an interpretation would allow atheists (read here the irreligious) to perform marriages. Precisely so! The other choice is for the state to "establish" criteria for ordination. One does not need the *Lemon* test to understand the morass into which the state would plunge itself if it chose that avenue. The state taking sides with religion against irreligion poses a fundamental dilemma: Who will define either? The Rehnquist ploy is merely a means of establishing "traditional" religions or it is a meaningless concept. If no definition of religion is forthcoming, then the argument is moot. In any definition, no matter how broad, some will be excluded.

In a scholarly treatment of similar subjects, Daniel Dreisbach, a nonpreferentialist, has written that, the modern Court should not limit its interpretation of the First Amendment to the presumed ambitions of Madison. Rather, judicial interpretations of the First Amendment should reflect the views of the majority of the First Congress, which apparently diluted Madison's "sweeping" intentions.[22]

Two comments are in order. First, Dreisbach appears to differ with Rehnquist and others when he asserts that Madison had sweeping intentions as reflected in Court opinion since 1940. Second, why should the Court "limit its interpretation of the first amendment" to the "views of the majority" in the 1789 Congress? Let's examine that proposition. Many of the states had establishments at the time. Were we to be guided by their proclivities we would have little of content left. Indeed, senators defeated Madison's proposal that the First Amendment apply to the states because they were protecting their home environment. The miracle of religious freedom as incorporated in the Bill of Rights is that it came in spite of a narrow, unenlightened sentiment that pervaded the new states. Most members of Congress in 1789 probably had about as much sympathy for thoroughgoing separation as they did for women's suffrage and emancipation.

The advocates of nonpreferentialism have an emotional edge with the average Christian congregation. The intention of mainstream Christianity is to mobilize believers to live Christian lives. Accepting this challenge and unencumbered by competing claims, people in the pew may well wonder why a faith that lays absolute claim to their lives should not equally lay such claim on the nation's domestic and foreign policies. The tragedy is that Christian leadership has been so remiss in teaching about the voluntary principle of church affiliation, which is the American model. Many in the Christian mainstream often become partners in betraying the constitutional principles establishing a secular state. "Secular" takes on a negative meaning for many as it is so frequently equated with "atheist." Thus, an unholy alliance takes shape. Many intelligent ministers know better than to accept the notion of a Christian nation, but seldom say so.

As we focus on nonpreferentialism, it is helpful to consider one of its most vigorous advocates, Richard John Neuhaus. He insists that "the entire purpose of the religion clause of the First Amendment" is religious freedom. "Any use of 'no establishment' that restricts 'free exercise' is a misuse of 'no establishment.' "[23]

Neuhaus hopes by this ploy to cure what he abhors: the "secular state in a secular society," "the naked public square," "secular humanism," and "suppression of religion in the classroom." Justice Scalia's de sent, iopposing the taxing of religious booksellers, in *Texas Monthly* v. *Bullock* (1989) is a natural extension of the Rehnquist dissent in *Jaffree*, but it is also remarkably close to the language of Neuhaus:

It is not always easy to determine when accommodation slides over into pro- motion and neutrality into favoritism, but withholding of a tax upon the dissemi- nation of religious materials is not even a close case. . . . If there is any close question it is not whether the exemption is permitted, but whether it is con- stitutionally compelled in order to avoid "interference with the dissemination of religious ideas."

Justice Brennan, voting with the majority, noted,

Justice Scalia's opinion, conversely, would subordinate the establishment clause's value. This position, it seems to me, runs afoul of the previously settled notion that government may not favor religious belief over disbelief.

The argument being advanced by Justice Scalia is that free exercise man- dates a tax exemption, no matter how such practice might violate establish- ment. He believes, with Neuhaus, that "no establishment" is intended only to support free exercise. Both argue that the founders had no intention of protecting the state from the church, a badly reasoned point clearly disputed by Madison's notes on the Virginia Declaration of Rights and the *Memorial and Remonstrance*. Only by accepting the superiority of religion over irreli- gion can the Scalia position be seriously considered. But even given that as- sumption, the fact is that single *or* plural establishment, as proposed in the Assessment Bill in 1784, impinges necessarily upon other citizens whose reli- gious views differ from those receiving government approval. It would tilt the state toward one or more confessions and against others.

In arguing in the *Texas* case that the state may be mandated to extend tax exemption "to avoid 'interference with the dissemination of religious ideas,' " Scalia is establishing the role of government to define religion. Justice White recognized this problem in a 1989 Illinois case where he insisted that neither Court nor Congress can place itself in the position of defining religion. The result, he noted, would be a clear violation of establishment. Justice Stevens addressed the problem directly in 1982:

There exists an overriding interest in keeping the government—whether it be the legislature or the courts—out of the business of evaluating the relative merits of differing religious claims. The risk that governmental approval of some and disapproval of others will be perceived as favoring one religion over another is an important risk the establishment clause was designed to preclude.[24]

The motive for this nonpreferentialist mischief appears to be the estab- lishment of a moral tone for the nation and a "return" of the country to a specific set of values. Those values are clearly identified as Christian in origin. Free exercise then would become a special largesse administered by the congressionally established religions. The inevitable result would be the creation of second-class believers outside the realm of revealed truth who would be, at best, tolerated.

The genius of ideas cannot be captured in their historical context. The ideas concerning democracy and freedom espoused by Jefferson in the Declaration of Independence and Madison in his framing of the Constitution were larger than the minds that gave them voice. The Constitution has made it possible to expand rights while guarding against retrenchment and restriction of them.

Much has been made of Madison's early objection to a Bill of Rights. One of the primary reasons for his reticence was his fear that enumeration of such rights might leave out some that later generations would regret. After listening to the 1987 Bork hearings as they focused on a right of privacy, we are struck by Mr. Madison's prescience.

Those who are committed to Madisonian principles of religious liberty and church-state separation have a series of rational arguments that we hoist on command. Believing in reason as the ultimate arbiter, convinced with Jefferson that "truth is great and will prevail if left to herself, that she is the proper and sufficient antagonist to error . . . ," we fail to educate, much less to inspire, our fellow citizens respecting the "truths" of religious freedom. We often seem convinced that free argument and debate should occur without passion or emotion. We do well to remember the words of John Milton in the opening paragraph of the *Areopagitica*, ". . . The very attempt of this address . . . hath got the power within me to a passion. . . ." One can sense the same passion in Madison in his letters of 1774.

As the Court approaches new challenges in the nineties, its composition has been radically altered: the former lone voices of Justices Rehnquist and White have been joined by Scalia, Souter, Kennedy, and now Clarence Thomas. Justice O'Connor—a swing vote for a brief time—can probably no longer fill that role now that Justices Souter and Thomas have joined the Court. In the next several years, assuming a continuation of the current political climate, the Court could swing more and more toward strict constructionism as defined by the political Right.

Supreme Court precedents are critical for an orderly democracy. As new precedents have emerged in our history, the Court has traditionally expanded on the rights of citizens. In the *Brown* v. *Board of Education* decision of 1954, an 1896 precedent was overturned. Today *Plessy* is an antique, a reminder of a nation's blind past. *Griswold* and *Row* have provided access to the Ninth Amendment. However, the current Court seems poised to move in a quite different direction respecting precedents related to the religion clauses of the First Amendment. The nineties of this century could provide the Court occasion to overturn *Everson* and its successors so completely that fifty years of church-state precedent might become irrelevant overnight.

The Bush administration, through the Justice Department, has seemingly joined forces with the coalition on the Court. In the fall of 1991, the Supreme Court heard arguments in *Lee* v. *Weisman*. On its surface it seems a rather simple case pitting the rights of a middle school student, Deborah Weisman, who was subjected to officially sanctioned prayer, against the long-standing rituals of public school graduations across the nation. The unique factor in this case appeared to be the fact that Ms. Weisman, who is Jewish, objected to a prayer subsequently given by Rabbi Leslie Gutterman. Upon closer scrutiny it becomes clear that the introduction of a rabbi into the situation was an effort to placate the Weismans after they objected to any prayer at all at the ceremony. The Weisman response to the "bribe" is the part of the story that is most compelling and offers a profound argument against the Rehnquist/ Scalia approach.

When Daniel Weisman, Deborah's father, objected to a prayer at her 1989 graduation, he had no specific clergy in mind. Indeed, his objection stemmed from an earlier ceremony involving his older daughter in 1986, an event in which a minister asked the audience to thank Jesus for the children's accomplishments. When informed by school officials, "You don't have anything to worry about; we've gotten a rabbi this year," Weisman responded, "That's going to make someone else uncomfortable. Why do anything? Separation of church and state applies."

If Justice Black or Douglas or Brennan had been looking for an illustration that would solidify his strong anti-establishment position over the past half century he could have done no better than use the *Weisman* case. It is all the more stunning that the Justice Department has chosen to challenge the classic precedents of the Court on church and state, seeking to dismantle them, with the popular eighteenth-century doctrine ". . . that all Men shou'd enjoy the fullest Toleration in the Exercise of Religion." It was this halfway doctrine that led James Madison to alter those very words by substituting, ". . . all men are equally entitled to the free exercise of religion, according to the dictates of conscience," in the Virginia Declaration of Rights of 1776.

French Jews addressing the French National Assembly in 1790 phrased it best:

> America, to which politics will owe so many useful lessons, has rejected the word toleration from its code, as a term tending to compromise individual liberty and to sacrifice certain classes of men to other classes. To tolerate is, in fact, to suffer that which you could, if you wish, prevent and prohibit.[25]

As has been discussed earlier, Rehnquist sets forth the view that the state is not called upon to exercise neutrality between religion and irreligion. That misreading of the historical evidence and of the spirit of the First Amendment is predicated on the dangerous notion that the state can and should define religion. Beyond these objections lies another fundamental flaw in the Rehnquist/Scalia position. Preference by the state for any religion is inevitably a problem not only for the irreligious, but equally for those of other variant traditions. This may be so either because one religious tradition may offend another or because a devoutly religious citizen concurs in the Roger Williams dictum that righteousness gives no one the right to impose upon others his or her own definitions.

Returning to the *Weisman* case, in posing the question, "whether government accommodation of religion in civic life violates the establishment clause, absent some form of government coercion," the Bush lawyers urged the Court, on the one hand, to abandon restrictions on school prayers and the like. On the other hand, they entered a caveat—"absent some form of government coercion"[26]—which they either do not understand or do not believe. If Ms. Weisman wished to attend her own graduation, clearly a citizen's right in a public school, then to be subjected unwillingly to a prayer was to be coerced in conscience. Conversely, to avoid offense to conscience, she would have been coerced to absent herself. How the lawyers for the Justice Department can, with any seriousness, enter the argument that prayer at graduation is a "noncoercive religious practice in civic life" is incomprehensible.

The Justice Department would undoubtedly reply with the guidelines for prayers at nonsecterian occasions issued by the National Conference of Christians and Jews (NCCJ) and quoted in their original *amicus* brief. The NCCJ urges that such prayers be composed with "inclusiveness and sensitivity." It is one thing for a private group to urge citizens to be responsive to a plurality of sentiments, but quite another for the government to compose or instruct to be administered "inclusive" prayer. An inclusive prayer (read here the omission of the Jesus formula) is an immediate offense to millions of Christians who worship an exclusivistic God who demands, they believe, commitment to Jesus as God. And on what grounds does the state invite a minister to pray and then tell her or him *not* to pray according to conscience?

In the spring of 1964, Billy Graham held a news conference in Atlantic City. He was discussing his personal support for a constitutional amendment to alter the First Amendment in order to allow Bible reading and organized prayer in public schools. Waxing eloquent on the need for moral influence in the schools, Graham saw it resulting from "nonsectarian" prayer and praise. Pressed by a reporter on his own exclusivistic view of Christianity, he admitted that Jews had to believe in Jesus as God in order to be saved. Graham was then asked what God, by his definition, would be equally acceptable to Jew and Christian, thus qualifying as nonsectarian. Flustered, he replied, "Do you mean the God up there or the God in Christ?"[27] The reporter responded, "I didn't know there were two!" Flustered even further, Graham turned to other questions. Of course Graham is no dualist, but his answer makes it clear that, no matter how vaguely defined, prayer is inevitably sectarian.

In spite of the Justice Department's believer's brief, the Constitution protects all consciences, including those of the irreligious. But the Rehnquist doctrine is fatally flawed on a second count. Any state promotion of religion, no matter how inoffensive it is perceived to be, will offend some tender religious consciences. Indeed, the government brief understands the need for the "inoffensive" when it closes its argument with the assertion that the prayers at the school ceremony "were plainly *mere* acknowledgements of a belief in God." But the *Weisman* argument is profoundly anchored in the conviction that the lowest common denominator religion, nonsectarianism, is a gloss allowing a plural establishment to flourish at the expense of the dispossessed minority, religious and nonreligious alike. It was Madison's great fear that common cause among the major Protestant Christian religions in Virginia might establish a tyranny of the majority in matters of faith. In those days, Catholics were excluded.

The astounding bias of the Justice Department in defining what it calls the "country's religious heritage" drives it to create a second-class citizenship for the minority. On the one hand, the government attorneys assure the Court that the graduation ceremony is so important to the majority that the school must not "refuse to acknowledge their beliefs through some brief, symbolic act such as Rabbi Gutterman's invocation and benediction." Indeed, the government uses strong words to condemn any denial of this acknowledgement: it "would be to falsify their experience and fundamentally distort the meaning of the ceremony." Obviously graduation ceremonies are perceived to be critically important for parents and children alike, at least for the majority. The government then offers its double standard. On the other hand, what is left for those for whom prayers "distort the meaning" of graduation? The government tells Ms. Weisman, "Don't go!" Suddenly a ceremony so important that it dare not falsify experiences or distort meanings, is construed to be totally unimportant to the offended minority. To be specific, "a decision not to be present for a graduation invocation and benediction does not demonstrate the existence of coercion."

The Justice Department lists an array of historical compromises with the First Amendment principles, seeking thereby to justify current efforts to violate the consciences of minorities. But even on its own argument, one that I have challenged on the basis of history, that both religion clauses of the First Amendment focus on religious liberty, it seems clear that the government endorses a radical denial of that very liberty in its advocacy of a dual citizenship.

If the Justice Department is genuinely concerned for the many for whom "religion provides a framework that gives coherence and meaning to the search for knowledge," it should be equally concerned for the many others for whom other frameworks provide that coherence. And the solution is so very simple. Celebrate the First Amendment at graduation. Have clergy and nonbelievers alike join in praising the human spirit that fostered democracy and freedom. Invoke the tradition of free exercise in all its diversity and inclusiveness. Such a ceremony would be far more substantial than the "mere acknowledgements" of deity.

On behalf of believers in one tradition, how dare the government propose to deny the most important ceremony in many a child's life to those young citizens who do not share that particular religious heritage? The advocates of nonpreferentialism seem to believe that if they can convince the nation that opposition to their views is infinitesimal, that fact alone justifies violating their rights. And while even a single oppressed conscience is unacceptable, the fact is that the president has created a false dichotomy between religion and irreligion. Large numbers of religious people join their nonbelieving neighbors in support of the natural rights of conscience.

In his effort to portray this false image of the giant and the gnat, the Bush administration turns a deaf ear to the millions of Christians and Jews in this country who convey, through their representatives, support for the *Lemon* test.* It is not as if all Christians agree on this matter. A case in point is the Southern Baptist Convention. President Bush addressed that organization's annual meeting in June of 1991. In praising their resolutions on church-state matters he ignored a huge minority in that body who support vigorously the decisions of the Warren Court. Justice lawyers distort facts when they operate as if all Christians were singlemindedly pitted against a pitiful handful of the irreligious. This is patently unfair to the millions of religious citizens who understand and support separation of church and state.

If the Court accepts the argument of the Justice Department in the *Weisman* case it will dismantle the *Lemon* test, a formula that enunciated the principles upon which the Court has been acting at least since 1940.

Competent Court observers expect a close vote. Such a split might convince the Rehnquist coalition, were it to prevail, to restrict themselves to the narrow issue of public ritual events. In a worst case scenario a majority could overturn the *Lemon* test, thereby seriously eroding precedents respecting separation.

Justice Rehnquist may feel a sense of satisfaction with his potential majority on the subject of establishment, based, as it is, upon a perverse reading of history. He and his supporters may believe they have returned to "original intent"; but as has been noted earlier, the game of original intent is merely

---

*See p. 85, n. 2

another way of confirming one's own sentiments. And it is those sentiments that require challenge, not an exchange of eighteenth-century quotations. On the other hand, the spirit espoused by Williams, Jefferson, and Madison is indisputable. Their expansive visions may be trapped, for a time, by constricting theory. Freedoms may suffer, principles may be ignored in the short term. But the democratic vision could not be contained by the founders and it will not long endure incarceration by those who miss Jefferson's dream. In December 1786, he wrote to Madison from Paris, "It is honorable for us to have produced the first legislature who has had the courage to declare that the reason of man may be trusted with the formation of its own opinions."

NOTES

1. Robert S. Alley, *James Madison on Religious Liberty* (Buffalo, N.Y.: Prometheus Books, 1985), p. 332.

2. Leonard Levy, *Original Intent and the Framers' Constitution* (New York: Macmillan, 1988), p. 395.

3. *Chambers* v. *Florida*, 1990.

4. Ralph Ketcham, *James Madison* (Charlottesville: University of Virginia Press, 1990), p. 38.

5. Letter to William Bradford from James Madison, January 24, 1774, in Alley, *James Madison on Religious Liberty*, p. 48.

6. James Madison, *Memorial and Remonstrance*, in Robert Rutland and William M. E. Rachel, eds., *The Papers of James Madison* (Chicago: University of Chicago Press, 1973), 8: 298–304.

7. Gaillard Hunt, ed., *The Writings of James Madison* (New York: G. P. Putnam's Sons, 1900), 3: 41.

8. Letter from James Madison, Jr., to James Madison, Sr., January 6, 1785, in *The Papers of James Madison*, 3: 217.

9. James Madison, *The Debates in the Federal Convention of 1787* (Buffalo, N.Y.: Prometheus Books, 1987), 1:181–82.

10. Ibid.

11. In Justice Black's opinion in *Adamson* v. *California*, 1947.

12. Ibid.

13. Ibid.

14. Levy, *Original Intent and the Framers' Constitution*, p. 342.

15. Ibid., p. 392.

16. Leonard Levy, *The Establishment Clause* (New York: Macmillan, 1986), p. 91.

17. Michael Malbin, *Religion and Politics: The Intentions of the Authors of the First Amendment* (Washington, D.C.: The American Enterprise Institute, 1978), p. 16.

18. In Robert S. Alley, *The Supreme Court on Church and State* (New York: Oxford University Press, 1988), p. 251.

19. In Joseph Tussman, *The Supreme Court on Church and State* (New York: Oxford University Press, 1962), p. 4.

20. Letter to Jasper Adams from James Madison, spring 1833, in Alley, *James Madison on Religious Liberty,* p. 87.

21. Ibid., pp. 87–88.

22. Daniel L. Dreisbach, "Thomas Jefferson and Bills Number 82–86 of the Revision of the Laws of Virginia, 1776–1786: New Light on the Jeffersonian Model of Church-State Relations," *The North Carolina Law Review* 69, no. 1 (November 1990): 177.

23. Richard John Neuhaus, "Contending for the Future: Overcoming the Pfefferian Inversion," *National Symposium on the First Amendment Religious Liberty Clauses and American Public Life,* Charlottesville, Va., April 11–13, 1988, p. 186.

24. *United States* v. *Lee,* 1982, 263.

25, In Edward P. Humphrey, *Nationalism and Religion in America, 1774–1789* (New York: Russell & Russell, 1965), p. 404.

26. Brief for the United States as Amicus Curiae in the case of *Lee* v. *Weisman,* October 1990.

27. In Robert S. Alley, *So Help Me God* (Richmond, Va.: John Knox Press, 1972), pp. 14–15.

5

Applying Coercion:
The Latest Element of Establishment

T. Jeremy Gunn

> If a constitutional theory has no basis in the history of the amendment it seeks
> to interpret, is difficult to apply, and yields unprincipled results, I see little use
> in it. (Associate Justice William Rehnquist, 1985)[1]

In 1986, Professor Michael W. McConnell of the University of Chicago Law
School proposed that the *Lemon* test, which long has been used to guide
interpretation of the Establishment Clause of the Constitution, be replaced
by a new "coercion" test.[2] In a short article titled "Coercion: The Lost Element of Establishment," Professor McConnell argued, in opposition to a long
line of Supreme Court decisions, that "compulsion is not just *an element,*
it is the *essence* of an establishment."[3] If one looks at eighteenth-century
evidence, he asserted, "[i]t is difficult to see . . . how an establishment could
exist in the absence of some form of coercion."[4] In just five years, Professor
McConnell's coercion-centered approach has become the dominant topic in
the establishment clause debate.

T. Jeremy Gunn, who holds a Ph.D. in religion from Harvard University, is an attorney
with the firm of Covington & Burling in Washington, D.C., and is Of Counsel for
the National Coalition for Public Education and Religious Liberty.

THE EMERGENCE OF THE TERM "COERCION"

Prior to the publication of Professor McConnell's 1986 article, the modern debate over the meaning of the establishment clause had largely been shaped by two Supreme Court decisions of the late 1940s. In *Everson* v. *Board of Education*, 330 U.S. 1 (1947), and *McCollum* v. *Board of Education*, 333 U.S. 203 (1948), the Supreme Court, asserting that its interpretation of the establishment clause was based on the historical origins of the clause, declared that the Constitution had erected a "high and impregnable" wall of separation between church and state.[5] Although referring to the wall, the *Everson* Court nevertheless held that a school board's subsidy of transportation costs for parochial and public school students did not violate the establishment clause. The next year, in *McCollum*, eight justices agreed that the establishment clause prohibited the widespread "released time" programs that permitted religious groups to come into public school classrooms to provide religious instruction for students.[6]

Justice Reed, in a solitary dissent in *McCollum*, became the first member of the Court to repudiate this "separationist" interpretation of the establishment clause. Using the now-familiar reasoning and examples of those who argue that government may accommodate and support religion, Justice Reed argued that neither history nor eighteenth-century practices supported an interpretation of the clause that would require the separation of church and state.[7] He concluded his dissent by asserting that "the history of past practices is determinative of the meaning of a constitutional clause. . . ."[8]

Edward S. Corwin, the preeminent constitutional scholar of his generation, applauded Justice Reed's dissent and wrote a scathing criticism of the Court and its new-found separationist ideology. Professor Corwin believed that history supported Justice Reed and not the majority of the Court.

> The historical record shows beyond peradventure that the core idea of "an establishment of religion" comprises the idea of *preference*; and that any act of public authority favorable to religion in general cannot, without manifest falsification of history, be brought under the ban of that phrase.[9]

Professor Corwin's judgment that the Court falsified history was joined by one of the preeminent theologians of the day, John Courtney Murray. Father Murray argued that "historical evidence does not yield the absolute *Everson* conclusion."[10] Separationist writers, relying principally on statements by Jefferson and Madison, argued that virtually all governmental aid to religion was unconstitutional.[11] Accommodationists, on the other hand, citing the founders' use of legislative prayers, chaplains, presidential proclamations of days of thanksgiving and prayer, and presidential inaugural prayers, argued that such precedents revealed that the founders had no objection to governmental support for religion. Accommodationists generally assumed that practices long in effect were presumptively constitutional. They seemed to suggest that the only relevant factor for striking down statutes on establishment clause grounds was whether the statute actually created an official establishment, such as the one existing in eighteenth-century England. Thus, the accommodationists at root argued that the Clause merely prohibited the creation of an official church.

During the thirty years following *Everson*, the Supreme Court was guided for the most part by the separationist ethos. The Court struck down school prayers, Bible reading, the posting of the Ten Commandments in schoolrooms, and most forms of aid to parochial schools.[12] But as the more liberal justices left the Court,[13] and as Presidents Nixon, Reagan, and Bush nominated more conservative justices,[14] the "wall of separation" metaphor and the *Lemon* test fell into increasing disrepute. The last time that the wall metaphor was cited favorably in a majority opinion was in *Larkin* v. *Grendel's Den, Inc.,* 459 U.S. 116, 123 (1982).

With the benefit of hindsight, we can identify four events during President Reagan's first term of office that signaled a quickening transformation in establishment clause thinking: (1) In 1982, Professor Robert Cord published an influential accommodationist history of the establishment clause.[15] (2) In 1983, the Supreme Court decided that legislative prayers offered by chaplains were constitutional, largely on the basis of the historical precedent of the practice. *Marsh* v. *Chambers*, 463 U.S. 783 (1983). (3) In 1984, the Supreme Court held that a city's Christmas nativity display was constitutional. *Lynch* v. *Donnelly*, 465 U.S. 668 (1984). (4) Justice Rehnquist published a dissenting opinion in *Wallace* v. *Jaffree*, 472 U.S. 38, 112 (1985), that adopted, albeit without attribution, Professor Cord's historical interpretation of the establishment clause. These four events both exemplified and perpetuated a more conservative approach to interpretation of the clause.

Despite this emerging accommodationist influence on the high court, and the dwindling support for separationism, the basic terms of the debate between accommodationists and separationists nevertheless had remained largely unchanged since the 1940s. Accommodationists still believed that all but preferential aid was permissible. Separationists still believed that no aid was permissible.

But a swift and remarkable transformation of the establishment clause debate began with Professor McConnell's brief nine-page article in 1986. Despite the fact that the Supreme Court had repeatedly and explicitly declared that coercion was *not* an essential element of an establishment clause violation,[16] McConnell's thesis that coercion was the "essence" of an establishment clause violation followed a rapid path to celebrity. The year after the article was published, former University of Chicago professor and now federal judge,

Frank H. Easterbrook, cited McConnell's article in a dissenting opinion and argued that "compulsion [w]as the central concern of the religion clauses. . . ." in *American Jewish Congress* v. *City of Chicago*, 827 F.2d 120, 135 (7th Cir. 1987) (Easterbrook, J., dissenting). Judge Easterbrook's formulation of the coercion argument was immediately thereafter put forward by some litigants in the *Allegheny County* case, which was then pending before the Supreme Court.[17] In an opinion joined by Chief Justice Rehnquist and Justices Scalia and White, Justice Kennedy agreed that the establishment clause was designed not to erect a wall of separation, but only to prevent governmental coercion. *Allegheny County*, 492 U.S. at 655-79 (Kennedy, J., concurring in part and dissenting in part). Since *Allegheny County* was decided, Justices Brennan and Marshall, who had opposed the new coercion test, resigned from the Court and were replaced by Justices Souter and Thomas.

In *Lee* v. *Weisman*, the recent graduation prayer case, the Solicitor General of the United States and the petitioners urged the Supreme Court to abandon the *Lemon* test and to supplant it with the "coercion" test.[18] The justices on the Supreme Court showed much greater interest in the coercion standard than in the *Lemon* test during oral argument, and they grilled the attorneys appearing before them about the relationship between governmental coercion and the establishment clause.[19] Coercion has become the key element of establishment clause analysis.

COERCING HISTORY

The advocates of the new coercion test assert that their interpretation of the establishment clause derives from the founders' original intent.[20] Justice Kennedy, speaking for four members of the Court in 1989, wrote that "the meaning of the clause is to be determined by reference to historical practices and understandings."[21] The Solicitor General of the United States has declared that "[a] proper theory of the establishment clause must . . . embrace the validity of [the founders'] practice and its modern counterparts. . . ."[22] The advocates of a coercion standard have been especially harsh on the Supreme Court's past inquiries into establishment clause history. "[T]he damage wrought by the brief writers' law office histories pales into insignificance when compared to the law office history of the United States Supreme Court."[23] Because the proponents imply that their interpretation derives from a better reading of history, it is important to ascertain whether the historical evidence in fact supports the conclusions they have drawn.

Everyone agrees, of course, that the founders believed that governments should not coerce religious practices or beliefs. The burden of those favoring a coercion standard is to prove something more. They must show that the founders believed that coercion was the "central concern" of the establishment clause[24] and hence was the "essence,"[25] a "necessary element,"[26] the "touchstone,"[27] the "hallmark,"[28] or the sine qua non[29] of an establishment clause violation. Thus the question is not whether the establishment clause prohibits coercive actions, but whether the founders understood coercion to be the central concern of the establishment clause. Therefore, the new standard would make coercion a necessary condition, whereas heretofore it has been only a sufficient condition of an establishment clause violation.

The proponents cite essentially two types of evidence in support of their position: first, they assert that Madison and Jefferson believed that the clause prohibited only coercion, and second, they assert that certain practices adopted during the founders' generation suggest that the founders themselves assumed a coercion standard.

Did Madison and Jefferson Adhere to a Coercion Standard?

The proponents of the coercion standard argue that Madison and Jefferson, "the architects of our principles of religious liberty,"[30] believed that religious liberty would be guaranteed if government was prevented from coercing religious beliefs or practices.[31] The proponents thus imply that if Madison and Jefferson—hitherto reputed to be the authors of the separationist standard—in fact believed that coercion was the exclusive harm resulting from governmental interference with religion, then a fortiori none could object to noncoercive governmental religious practices. The proponents principally rely on four texts by these "architects" in order to justify their interpretation: two statements by Madison interpreting the establishment clause, and statements made by Madison and Jefferson pertaining to the Virginia Bill Establishing Religious Liberty.

Madison on the Establishment Clause

The proponents of the coercion standard most frequently justify their position by quoting Congressman Madison's interpretation of the establishment clause during the First Congress debates. Commenting on the draft text before Congress on August 15, 1789, Madison

> apprehended the meaning of the words to be, that Congress should not establish a religion, and enforce the legal observation of it by law, nor compel men to worship God in any manner contrary to their conscience.[32]

Professor McConnell interprets these words of Madison as explaining that "compulsion is not just an element, it is the essence of an establishment."[33]

Charles Cooper, the author of the Petitioners' Brief in *Lee* v. *Weisman*, believes that "Madison's comments make clear . . . that the purpose of the proposed amendment was to protect against government *coercion* of religious observance or support."[34]

It is curious, for several reasons, that the proponents of the coercion standard should choose these words from the establishment clause debates. First, Madison did *not* say that coercion is the "essential element" or the "only element" of an "establishment." Indeed, he said that "Congress should not establish a religion" before he even mentioned coercion. Thus, Madison may be understood as explaining the version of the establishment clause then pending to mean that: (a) Congress should not establish a religion, *and* (b) Congress should not enforce an establishment. These observations could suggest that the creation of an establishment by itself is a violation separate and distinct from the legal enforcement of an establishment. Second, Madison was not even interpreting the establishment clause as finally approved, but was commenting upon a draft version. The version under consideration at the time Madison spoke provided that "no religion shall be established by law, nor shall the equal rights of conscience be infringed."[35] The final text prohibits not only an establishment, but "laws respecting an establishment." Consequently, the language to which the proponents refer is not applicable to the amendment as ratified. Third, shortly before Madison spoke, Congressman Daniel Carroll, a Catholic from Maryland, observed that "[a]s the rights of conscience are, in their nature, of peculiar delicacy, [they] will little bear the gentlest touch of [the] governmental hand. : . ."[36] Congressman Carroll was most certainly not assuming that coercion was the appropriate standard, for he believed that religious rights should be protected from even the "gentlest touch." Thus, the interpretation attributed to Madison by the coercion proponents was not the only possible interpretation of the draft amendments. Finally, even if we adopt the proponents' reading of Madison, and thereby conclude that he and Carroll were in disagreement, we must assume that Madison's view was repudiated by Congress. For almost immediately after Madison spoke, Congress rejected the version of the clause addressed by Madison and voted for a new version written by Congressman Livermore that incorporated Carroll's concern. The version of the establishment clause that Congress adopted on August 15 read: "Congress shall make no laws *touching religion* or infringing the rights of conscience."[37]

It is, therefore, not at all apparent that Madison meant what the proponents of the coercion standard say that he meant. But even if he did say that coercion should be the standard, Congress immediately thereafter *rejected* that version and adopted another that accorded with the sentiments of Congressman Carroll. There is no reliable evidence that Madison or the drafters intended the establishment clause to preclude only state coercion. Thus Judge

Easterbrook's conclusion—that "Madison did not suggest that the establishment clause put government out of the business of suasion; neither did anyone else in 1789"[38]—is simply inaccurate.

The proponents of the coercion test also turn to Madison's "Detached Memoranda," a collection of notes that he wrote after retiring from public office.[39] Judge Easterbrook reads the "Detached Memoranda" to suggest that Madison himself believed that governmental religious proclamations were constitutionally permissible because they are "merely recommendatory,"[40] and that Madison's "approach to interpretation would have led him to conclude that . . . the many thanksgiving proclamations of Presidents Washington and Adams, were dispositive on the strictly legal point."[41]

Unfortunately, Judge Easterbrook used an abridgment of the "Detached Memoranda" that omitted passages expressly repudiating his interpretation.[42] For example, Madison stated, in a passage not contained in the abridgement, that promotion of religion was a matter for the churches and not for the government.

> But reason and the principles of the [Christia]n religion require that [if] all the individuals composing a nation even of the same precise creed & wished to unite in a universal act of religion at the same time, the union ought to be effected thro' the intervention of their religious *not of their political representatives*. In a nation composed of various sects, some alienated widely from others, and where no agreement could take place thro' the former, *the interposition of the latter is doubly wrong*.[43]

In fact, not only did Madison repudiate the conclusion that such proclamations were "permissible," he believed that they were harmful. "The practice, if not strictly guarded, naturally terminates in a conformity to the creed of the majority and a single sect, if amounting to a majority."[44] Not only do such proclamations merely buttress the religion of the majority, they cause an "increase of party animosities."[45]

But, in any case, Madison's "Detached Memoranda" repeatedly spoke of the establishment clause as doing more than simply prohibiting governmental coercion. He believed that the Constitution "[s]trongly guarded . . . the separation between Religion & Gov[ernmen]t . . ." (p. 555), that "[t]he Constitution of the U.S. forbids everything like an establishment of a national religion" (p. 558), and that the "establishment of the chaplainship to Cong[res]s is a palpable violation of equal rights, as well as of Constitutional principles. . . ." (ibid.). Presidential proclamations regarding religion are "no part of the trust delegated to political rulers" (p. 560). Madison's "Detached Memoranda" simply cannot properly be enlisted to support the interpretation proffered by the proponents of the coercion standard.

The Virginia Bill Establishing Religious Liberty

The proponents of the coercion test also assert that the events surrounding Virginia's adoption of Jefferson's Bill for Establishing Religious Liberty in 1785 also support their interpretation of the establishment clause.[46] They argue that both the text of the Bill and Madison's *Memorial and Remonstrance Against Religious Assessments*,[47] written in opposition to Patrick Henry's Assessment Bill that was designed to fund religious education, revealed that the "architects of our religious liberty" were concerned about governmental coercion rather than governmental endorsement of religion. Having assumed that the Virginia Statute Establishing Religious Liberty reflected Jefferson's viewpoint, Judge Easterbrook observed that it "does not protest government use of persuasion on matters religious; it is concerned with compulsion alone."[48] Apparently unaware that Jefferson's version of the Bill differed from the one ultimately adopted by the House of Delegates, the proponents of the coercion standard do not quote Jefferson's draft language that did not survive the legislative cuts:

> The opinions of men are not the object of civil government, nor under its jurisdiction.[49]

This deleted passage reflects Jefferson's own position: religion is outside government's domain. The use of force *exacerbates* the wrong; it is not the basis of the wrong.

It is also inaccurate to imply that Madison's *Memorial and Remonstrance* criticized only coercive practices. Rather, Madison criticized the state for subjecting citizens to the task of rendering insincere homage or for involving itself in matters outside its proper realm.

> It is the duty of every man to render to the Creator such homage and such only as he believes to be acceptable to him.[50]

The issue is not whether Madison believed that religious coercion was wrong—he most certainly did. The passages cited by the proponents are eloquent statements of just such a position. The issue here is whether coercion was the only evil of establishments that Madison criticized; the evidence shows that it was not.

Ultimately, the proponents of the coercion standard have been unable to quote *any* founder who said that coercion was anything like the "essence," the "central concern," a "necessary element," the "touchstone," or the sine qua non of an "establishment." These words are those of the modern-day proponents of the coercion standard, not those of the founders' generation. Indeed, the founders' silence is resounding.

ARE THE FOUNDERS' PRACTICES A PROPER GUIDE FOR INTERPRETING THE CONSTITUTION?

The proponents of the coercion standard argue that we understand what the establishment clause means by examining not only the words of the founders, but their practices as well. Justice Kennedy rejected an alternate test for interpreting the clause because, "if applied with consistency, [it] would invalidate long-standing traditions [and thus] cannot be a proper reading of the clause," and because "the meaning of the clause is to be determined by reference to historical practices and understandings."[51] In support of their interpretation, the proponents of the coercion standard list several practices that suggest that governmental support for religion is constitutional: congressional chaplains, aids to religion provided in the Northwest Ordinance, presidential proclamations in support of days of thanksgiving and prayer, Indian treaties that provided aid to religion, and others.[52] The Solicitor General urges that the establishment clause be interpreted by reference to these practices.[53] And Charles Cooper, arguing on behalf of litigants before the Supreme Court, asserts that the "conduct of the founders reflected their intentions concerning the establishment clause. . . ."[54]

In arguing that constitutional rights should be interpreted in light of the practices of the founders' generation, proponents of the coercion test essentially are seeking to resuscitate the same method of constitutional interpretation that was employed in the *Dred Scott* decision to legitimize human slavery.[55] Such a method of interpretation is justified neither by history nor by logic.

Writing for the Court in *Dred Scott*, Chief Justice Taney dismissed the argument that blacks were included within the phrase "all men are created equal" because

> if the language, as understood in that day, would embrace them, the conduct of the distinguished men who framed the Declaration of Independence would have been utterly and flagrantly inconsistent with the principles they asserted. (*Scott* v. *Sanford*, 60 U.S. at 410)

Finding it inconceivable that the men who founded our nation could have acted inconsistently with their own principles, the *Dred Scott* Court looked to the conduct of the founders' generation to interpret the meaning of the law.

> [T]he men who framed this declaration were great men—high in literary acquirements—high in their sense of honor, and incapable of asserting principles inconsistent with those on which they were acting.[56]

Thus, in the reasoning of the *Dred Scott* decision, "negroes" are not "men" within the phrase "all men are created equal" because the "great men" who ratified that phrase were slaveholders. For the *Dred Scott* Court it was easier to deny the humanity of blacks than to contemplate the possibility that the founders failed to adhere to their own principles.

The founders, unlike their modern admirers, fully recognized that conduct was an unreliable measure of principle. John Jay, the first Chief Justice of the United States and co-author of the *Federalist*, candidly admitted the shortfalls of his contemporaries' conduct. Writing in the month that the Constitution was ratified, Jay acknowledged that many of the principles of his generation were "more generally admitted in theory than observed in practice."[57] Jay believed, for example, that slavery was a violation of the fundamental law of his country and of the rights of his fellow human beings. Writing in 1819, Jay admitted that slavery was

discordan[t] with the principles of the Revolution; and [was] repugnant to the . . . Declaration of Independence. . . .[58]

Chief Justice Jay observed that his contemporaries acted inconsistently with these fundamental principles:

That Men should pray and fight for their own Freedom and yet keep others in Slavery is certainly acting a very inconsistent as well as unjust and perhaps impious part, but the History of Mankind is filled with Instances of human Improprieties.[59]

Thus, what Chief Justice Jay labeled the founders' "improprieties," modern-day jurists should not blithely assume to be controlling precedents.[60]

Slavery is but one conspicuous example that reveals the inappropriateness of looking to eighteenth-century practices to guide the interpretation of American fundamental law. For example, the founders frequently criticized the states for violating their own bills of rights. "In Virginia," Madison declared, "I have seen the Bill of Rights violated in every instance where it has been opposed to a popular current."[61] Madison explicitly repudiated interpreting the establishment clause consistently with the practices of his generation. In rejecting chaplainships, he argued from principle, not practice.

The object of this establishment [of chaplains] is seducing; the motive to it is laudable. But is it not safer to adhere to a right p[r]inciple. . . .[62]

Thomas Jefferson similarly rejected the argument that the quasi-religious practices of the administration of President Washington were relevant for determining their constitutionality. Addressing the question of the constitutionality of state-endorsed prayers, President Jefferson first considered Washington's example. Although "aware that the practice of my predecessors may be quoted,"[63] Jefferson ultimately rejected that precedent. "[C]ivil powers alone have been given to the President of the United States, [who possesses] no authority to direct the religious exercises of his constituents."[64]

Madison also rejected the precedential value of Washington's use of prayer proclamations, and ultimately disavowed his own use of such proclamations as well. Madison maintained that presidents all-too-frequently use the issue of prayer to further their immediate political interests and could, under the guise of furthering morality or religion, seek to enhance themselves politically. According to Madison, Washington's first proclamation "was issued just after the suppression of the Insurrection in Penn[sylvani]a and at a time when the public mind was divided on several topics. . . ."[65] Madison's own proclamations were issued when his popularity was waning during the War of 1812.[66] Thus even the founders cited by the proponents rejected the very method of constitutional interpretation that is now being advanced in their name.

Although arguing that the Constitution should be interpreted in light of the practices of the founders, the proponents of the coercion test offer no principled basis for distinguishing among the founders' varying practices. They do not, of course, propose that we should follow Jefferson's refusal to promulgate days of thanksgiving and prayer. But, as Professor Herbert Wechsler has observed,

> the main constituent of the judicial process is precisely that it must be genuinely principled, resting with respect to every step that is involved in reaching judgment on analysis and reasons quite transcending the immediate result that is achieved.[67]

The proponents of the coercion test simply cite those practices of which they approve, and ignore those practices that are inconsistent with their preferred outcome.

THE COHERENCE OF COERCION

The proponents of the coercion test also criticize past Supreme Court establishment clause decisions for being incoherent. Justice Rehnquist asserted that the *Lemon* test "is difficult to apply and yields unprincipled results. . . ."[68] The Solicitor General has condemned the "confusion," "division," and "demonstrated shortcomings of the *Lemon* test."[69] It would seem that these critics of *Lemon*, who believe that they have an interpretation of the clause that is mandated by history, would be able to present a consistent and coherent explanation of how the coercion test would operate. But we find, upon asking even the most basic questions, that the discussions of the coercion test are vague, uncertain, and inconsistent with each other.

There are three "coherence" questions that the coercion proponents should be capable of answering: First, is governmental coercion a *necessary* element of an establishment clause violation, or is it one among other possible factors to be considered? Second, what is the definition of the term "coercion"? Third, what type of evidence is relevant for proving the existence of coercion?

1. *Is governmental "coercion," under the new test, a necessary element of an establishment clause violation?* Since *Engel* v. *Vitale,* the Supreme Court has held that although governmental coercion is sufficient to constitute a violation of the establishment clause, coercion is not a necessary element.[70] Thus it is clear under *Lemon* that the establishment clause may be violated even in the absence of coercion. But the proponents of the coercion standards are inconsistent on whether coercion is in fact a necessary element, and, if it is not, what other elements might be sufficient to constitute an establishment clause violation.

Professor McConnell criticized *Engel* v. *Vitale* for having introduced the erroneous "notion" that "the establishment clause does not involve an element of coercion."[71] Such a criticism implicitly suggests that coercion is a necessary element. Indeed, he found it "difficult to see . . . how an establishment could exist in the absence of some form of coercion" and that "legal compulsion . . . would seem to be the essence of an establishment."[72] History, McConnell believed, supported his position because "noncoercive supports for religion were not within the contemporary understanding of an establishment of religion."[73] But McConnell's position may not be as clear as these statements suggest. Elsewhere he suggested that official preference for one religion may, by itself, constitute an establishment clause violation. "Along with the prohibition of religious coercion, the 'clearest command of the establishment clause is that one religious denomination cannot be officially preferred over another.' "[74] One element or two?

The Solicitor General's Brief in *Lee* v. *Weisman* is ambivalent as to whether coercion is a necessary element. On the one hand, the Solicitor General did not explicitly state that coercion was the "only" means of violating the establishment clause, although he referred to coercion as the "touchstone."[75] But sometimes he referred to coercion as if it were the only element. Like Professor McConnell, he criticized the *Engel* Court and its progeny for concluding that proof of coercion was unnecessary. "The Court, we submit, should reconsider isolated statements in some later decisions to the effect that 'proof of coercion' is 'not a necessary element of any claim under the establishment clause.' "[76] Once again the implication is that coercion is necessary. The Solicitor General opines that "*compelled* taxation and *forced* religious observance were the dangers to religious liberty that the establishment clause was intended to avert."[77] But in his oral argument before the Supreme Court, the Solicitor General backtracked and acknowledged that there were two alternate elements of an establishment clause violation: coercion *or* governmental preference for one sect.[78] One element or two?

Judge Easterbrook, for his part, suggested that there was one other way in addition to governmental coercion by which the establishment clause could be violated: governmental financing of religion. "[F]orce or funds are essential ingredients of an 'establishment.' "[79] Those who joined Justice Kennedy in *Allegheny County* also assume that coercion is only one of two possible means of violating the establishment clause. They find that the second violation is not "funding," but providing "benefits" to religion to such a degree that a religion is established.

> Our cases disclose two limiting principles: government may not coerce anyone to support or participate in any religion or its exercise; and it may not, in the guise of avoiding hostility or callous indifference, give direct benefits to religion in such a degree that it in fact "establishes a [state] religion or religious faith, or tends to do so." These two principles, while distinct, are not unrelated, for it would be difficult indeed to establish a religion without some measure of more or less subtle coercion, be it in the form of taxation . . . or governmental exhortation to religiosity that amounts in fact to proselytizing.[80]

We are not told whether "direct benefits" is identical to "funding," nor at what "degree" the providing of benefits becomes an "establishment." In any case it certainly sounds tautological to say: "The establishment clause prohibits giving direct benefits to religion to such a degree that the benefits tend to establish a state religion."[81]

It would be only fair to require the proponents of the coercion test—who vehemently criticized the "confusion" in *Lemon*—to state clearly and precisely whether coercion is a necessary element of an establishment clause violation. And, if it is not a necessary element, what other elements are sufficient to trigger a violation of the establishment clause? We are not given an answer.[82]

2. Do the proponents explain or define the meaning of the term "coercion"? Certainly we should expect that those who wish to supplant the longstanding *Lemon* test with a coercion test would be able to articulate exactly what they mean by "coercion." Although it is not difficult to imagine that the physical punishment of citizens who refuse to adopt the majority religion would be unconstitutional under the coercion tests, it may be more difficult to see how the test would play itself out in other less obvious circumstances.

Judge Easterbrook candidly acknowledges that it may be difficult to define "coercion" in the religious context. "That line is one demarcating force (forbidden) from suasion (tolerable, even if unwelcome). It may be hard to draw. . . ."[83] Professor McConnell similarly sees definitional difficulties. He admits that his standard does

> not answer all questions. For example, it obviously would not answer the question, "What is coercion?" Enormous variance exists between the persecutions of old and the many subtle ways in which government action can distort religious choice today.[84]

On the other hand, the Solicitor General apparently thinks that working out the parameters of the meaning of "coercion" is not a problem preventing prompt adoption of the coercion standard—although he does not even attempt to provide a definition himself.[85]

Justice Kennedy's *Allegheny County* dissent is a peculiar opinion inasmuch as, while Kennedy asserts that he is applying the *Lemon* test to the facts before him, he is also attempting to revise establishment clause jurisprudence. In passages quite similar to those of Easterbrook, the dissenters argue that governmental use of religious symbolism could violate the establishment clause in an "extreme case"[86] or in "some circumstances."[87] But we are given no clear guidance for recognizing when either might be present.[88] The only guidance for determining when symbolic endorsement too closely approximates an establishment apparently is found in popular practices.[89]

The clearest attempt to link "coercion" to "establishment" was made by Judge Easterbrook. Without immediate citation to any authority, he states that a "threat of penalty" is inherent in the definition of "establishment."

> But without taxes, test oaths, appointments of ministers, or other acts backed by threat of penalty, it is impossible to speak of "establishment." The use of governmental force and funds is exactly what people meant in 1789 by the word "establishment."[90]

Judge Easterbrook is simply incorrect in stating that the concept of "coercion" is inherent in the definition of "establishment." In the eighteenth century, "establish" or "establishment" denoted "setting up" or "making permanent."[91] In fact, Judge Easterbrook himself should recognize that the term means something different, for in the paragraph immediately following his definition he refers to "Jefferson's Bill for *Establishing* Religious Liberty." Certainly

Jefferson did not intend to apply "force and funds" in his bill to establish religious liberty. Indeed, the Constitution itself uses the root term "establish" seven times prior to its appearance in the First Amendment, and each time it suggests "setting up" rather than "force."[92]

The problem of what constitutes "coercion" generally has stimulated a profound philosophical and jurisprudential debate.[93] The proponents of the coercion test—who apparently are oblivious of the complexity of the issues they raise—ignore the entire debate. Similarly, the proponents of the new standard do not explain how the establishment clause, under a coercion test, differs from the free exercise clause.[94] Thus, we are told that the coercion test should be adopted, but we are provided only vague notions of what the standard actually would be.

3. *What type of evidence is necessary to prove the existence of coercion?* If a coercion test were adopted, litigants who sought to challenge a law would need to know what kind of evidence would be appropriate to prove that there had been coercion. Unfortunately, the advocates of the coercion test provide only limited—and even then inconsistent—guidance on what would be relevant. Suppose, for example, that a variation on the *Engel* v. *Vitale* school prayer case were to come before the court. What kind of evidence would the Supreme Court want the trial court to hear? The testimony of schoolchildren that they felt coerced or that they enjoyed the prayers? The testimony of child psychologists describing how impressionable schoolchildren are?

We also should be told whether courts ought to examine coercion from the "reasonable person" standpoint or whether the courts may consider the testimony of people who are particularly sensitive to what they deem to be offensive religious displays. Justice Kennedy apparently eschews the reasonable person standard in establishment clause adjudication.[95] Judge Easterbrook apparently thinks that we *should* analyze coercion based upon the reasonable person standard.[96] The Solicitor General thinks that coercion should be evaluated not from the perspective of what the government has done, but by looking to the "autonomy of the observers of the practice."[97] But would the Solicitor General's autonomy test find a violation of the establishment clause whenever a religious minority honestly feels coerced? Or perhaps no evidence will be necessary. In *Allegheny County* Justice Kennedy asserted—without citation of the record—that "no one was compelled" to look at, and people were "free to ignore," the religious displays.[98] Is this "judicial notice" sufficient to resolve constitutional issues?

CONCLUSION

The year after Justice Rehnquist criticized any interpretation of the establishment clause that has "no basis in the history of the amendment it seeks to interpret [and] is difficult to apply," Professor McConnell offered a new coercion-centered interpretation. Although the new coercion standard has had a meteoric rise to prominence, it nevertheless fails to satisfy the very criteria that Justice Rehnquist announced. We must, therefore, conclude that "there is little use in it."

NOTES

1. *Wallace v. Jaffree*, 472 U.S. 38, 112 (1985) (Rehnquist, J., dissenting).
I would like to offer thanks to my colleagues Kenneth Doroshow and John Jenab for their particularly helpful suggestions.

2. The *Lemon* test derives from the Supreme Court decision *Lemon* v. *Kurtzman*, 403 U.S. 602 (1971). This tripartite test asks whether governmental actions: (a) had the purpose of aiding religion; (b) had the primary effect of aiding religion; or (c) caused unnecessary entanglement with religion. If the governmental action violated any of *Lemon's* three prongs the action would be deemed unconstitutional.
The establishment clause provides that "Congress shall make no law respecting an establishment of religion. . . ." U.S. Constitution Amendment 1.

3. Michael W. McConnell, "Coercion: The Lost Element of Establishment," *William & Mary Law Review* 27 (1986):933, 937 (emphasis added). In an article published the previous year, Professor McConnell discussed the issue of coercion, although less directly than in his subsequent article. Michael W. McConnell, "Accommodation of Religion," *Supreme Court Review* 1985:1-59, esp. 35-39. For the line of Supreme Court precedents, see note 16 below.

4. McConnell, "Coercion," p. 938.

5. *Everson*, 330 U.S. at 18; *McCollum*, 333 U.S. at 212.

6. Justice Frankfurter, writing separately, estimated that in 1947, almost two million American schoolchildren participated in "released time" religious instruction of the type prohibited by the Court. *McCollum*, 333 U.S. at 224–225 (Frankfurter, J.).

7. Justice Reed referred favorably to "the many instances of close association of church and state in American society [that] are so much a part of our tradition and culture. . . ." Ibid., 239 (Reed, J., dissenting).

8. Ibid., 256.

9. Edward S. Corwin, "The Supreme Court as National School Board," *Law and Contemporary Problems* 14 (1949):3–22. "In a word, what the "establishment of religion" clause of the First Amendment does, and *all that it does, is to forbid Congress to give any religious faith, sect, or denomination a preferred status.*" Ibid., p. 10 (emphasis in original). Corwin also stated that the Fourteenth Amendment made this prohibition of preferential treatment for religious sects applicable to the states as well. Ibid.

10. John Courtney Murray, "Law or Prepossessions?" *Law and Contemporary Problems* 14 (1949):25.

11. See, for example, Leo Pfeffer, *Church, State, and Freedom*, rev. ed. (Boston: Beacon Press, 1967) and Leonard W. Levy, *The Establishment Clause: Religion and the Constitution* (New York: Macmillan, 1986).

12. *Engel* v. *Vitale*, 370 U.S. 421 (1962) (prayer); *Abington School District* v. *Schempp*, 374 U.S. 203 (1963) (Bible reading); *Stone* v. *Graham*, 449 U.S. 39 (1980) (posting Ten Commandments); *Committee for Public Education* v. *Nyquist*, 413 U.S. 756 (1973) (school aid); and *Lemon* (school aid). Ironically, the conservative Chief Justice of the United States, Warren E. Burger, wrote *Lemon* v. *Kurtzman*, 403 U.S. 602 (1971), the opinion that shaped the general contours for establishment clause analysis.

13. Warren (1969), Fortas (1970), Black (1972), Douglas (1975), Brennan (1989), and Marshall (1991).

14. Burger (1969), Rehnquist (1972), O'Connor (1981), Scalia (1986), Rehnquist as Chief Justice (1986), Kennedy (1989), Souter (1990), and Thomas (1991).

15. Robert L. Cord, *Separation of Church and State: Historical Fact and Current Fiction* (New York: Lambeth Press, 1982).

16. *Engel* v. *Vitale*, 370 U.S. 421, 430 (1962); *Abington School District* v. *Schempp*, 374 U.S. 203, 222–23 (1963); *Committee for Public Education* v. *Nyquist*, 413 U.S. 756, 786 (1973); *Allegheny County* v. *Greater Pittsburgh ACLU*, 492 U.S. 573, 597–98 n.47 (1989).

17. Ibid.

18. *Lee* v. *Weisman*, No. 90–1014. Brief for the United States as Amicus Curiae (hereinafter "Solicitor General Brief"); Brief for the Petitioners, written by Attorney Charles Cooper (hereinafter "Cooper Brief").

19. *Lee* v. *Weisman*, Oral Argument, November 6, 1991.

20. For discussions of "original intent" jurisprudence, see, for example, Paul Brest, "The Misconceived Quest for the Original Understanding," *Boston University Law Review* 60 (1980): 204–38; H. Jefferson Powell, "The Original Understanding of Original Intent," *Harvard Law Review* 98 (1985): 885–948; Charles A. Lofgren, "The Original Understanding of Original Intent?" in Jack N. Rakove, ed., *Interpreting the Constitution: The Debate over Original Intent* (Boston: Northeastern University Press, 1990).

21. *Allegheny County*, 492 U.S. at 670.

22. Solicitor General Brief, 7.

23. McConnell, "Coercion," p. 933. "[I]t seems only right to call time out to reexamine those holdings of the Court that were products of faulty history. . . ." Ibid., p. 934.

24. "This emphasis on compulsion as the central concern of the religion clauses has a solid footing." *American Jewish Congress*, 827 F.2d at 135. McConnell refers to the "centrality of coercion" in establishment clause interpretation. McConnell, "Coercion," p. 940.

25. "[C]ompulsion is not just an element, it is the essence of an establishment." McConnell, "Coercion," p. 937.

26. Cooper Brief, 14, 34.

27. Solicitor General Brief, 7.

28. Cooper Brief, 16 n.13.

29. "Absent coercion, the risk of infringement of religious liberty by passive or symbolic accommodation is minimal." *Allegheny County,* 492 U.S. at 662.

30. *American Jewish Congress,* 827 F.2d at 132; Cooper Brief, 14.

31. "[T]o Jefferson, like Madison, the essence of an establishment of religion was some form of legal coercion . . . ." Solicitor General Brief, 18.

32. James Gales and W. W. Seaton, eds., *Annals of Congress* 1:730 (Washington, D.C., 1834). This passage is cited in *American Jewish Congress,* 827 F. 2d at 136; *Allegheny County,* 492 U.S. at 660; McConnell, "Coercion," pp. 936-37; and Cooper Brief, 24.

33. McConnell, "Coercion," p. 937.

34. Cooper Brief, 24.

35. *Annals of Congress,* 1:729.

36. Ibid., p. 730.

37. Ibid., p. 731 (emphasis added).

38. *American Jewish Congress,* 827 F.2d at 136.

39. James Madison, "Madison's 'Detached Memoranda,' " Elizabeth Fleet, ed. *William and Mary Quarterly* 3 (1948):554 ff.

40. *American Jewish Congress,* 827 F.2d at 132.

41. Ibid., 136.

42. The abridgment was published in Philip B. Kurland and Ralph Lerner, eds., *The Founders' Constitution* (Chicago: University of Chicago Press, 1987), 5:103-105.

43. Madison, "Detached Memoranda," pp. 560–61 (emphasis added).

44. Ibid., p. 561.

45. Ibid. The "Detached Memoranda" is also cited in support of the proponents' position that the founders' *practices* are a proper guide for interpreting the Constitution. This issue will be discussed below.

46. McConnell, "Coercion," pp. 937-38; Solicitor General Brief, 10 n.6.

The Virginia Bill Establishing Religious Liberty was written by Thomas Jefferson in 1777. It was presented to the Virginia House of Delegates in that same year, but was defeated. In 1785, in an attempt to use the Commonwealth's taxing power to raise money for teachers of Christianity, Patrick Henry introduced an Assessment Bill calling for tax support for teachers of religion. Madison wrote his famous *Memorial and Remonstrance Against Religious Assessments* against Henry's bill and ultimately coordinated the legislative battle to defeat it. Taking advantage of the momentum of this victory, Madison in 1785 reintroduced Jefferson's bill into the House of Delegates and guided it successfully to enactment. See generally Thomas E. Buckley, *Church and State in Revolutionary Virginia, 1776-1787* (Charlottesville: University Press of Virginia, 1977), and Merrill D. Peterson and Robert C. Vaughan, eds., *The Virginia Statute for Religious Freedom* (New York: Cambridge University Press, 1988).

47. See James Madison, *The Papers of James Madison,* Robert A. Rutland, ed. (Chicago: University of Chicago Press, 1973), 8:295–306.

48. *American Jewish Congress,* 827 F.2d at 135. "Jefferson believed coercion to be a necessary element of a First Amendment violation." Cooper Brief, 34.

49. See Thomas E. Buckley, "The Political Theology of Thomas Jefferson," in *The Virginia Statute for Religious Freedom*, p. 88.

50. *Memorial and Remonstrance*, p. 299.

51. *Allegheny County*, 492 U.S. at 670. Kennedy says the only relevant practices are those of the federal government, not the states. Ibid. Justice Kennedy was criticizing Justice O'Connor's "endorsement" test that she put forward in *Lynch* v. *Donnelly*, 465 U.S. at 687–94 (O'Connor, J. concurring).

52. See, for example, McConnell, "Coercion," p. 939; *American Jewish Congress*, 827 F.2d at 133; *Allegheny County*, 492 U.S. at 671.

53. See, e.g., Solicitor General Brief, 7 ("A proper theory of the establishment clause must therefore embrace the validity of this practice [of devotional exercises] and its modern counterparts rather than treating them as anomalies"). Without citing any authority, the Solicitor General declares that "[t]he Founding Fathers . . . saw no inconsistency between ceremonial acknowledgments of the country's religious heritage and the establishment clause." Ibid. Similarly, from the premise that "[t]he Founders encouraged civic recognition of the Nation's religious heritage," it is concluded that such practices "therefore did not implicate the prohibition embodied in the establishment clause." Ibid., 9. See also ibid., 18–19.

54. Cooper Brief, 31.

55. *Scott* v. *Sanford*, 60 U.S. (19 How.) 393 (1857).

56. Ibid.

57. Letter from John Jay to the English Antislavery Society (June 1788), in Henry P. Johnston, ed., *The Correspondence and Public Papers of John Jay* (New York: G. P. Putnam's Sons, 1890–1893), 3:340.

58. Letter from John Jay to Elias Boudinot (November 17, 1819), ibid., 4:431.

59. Letter from John Jay to Richard Price (September 27, 1785), ibid., 3:168.

60. During the Constitutional Convention in Philadelphia, delegates similarly were made aware of the inconsistency between the principles of the Declaration of Independence and the Constitution's deference to the practice of slaveholding. Gouverneur Morris, a firm supporter of the Constitution, told his fellow delegates that slavery was "a nefarious institution," a "curse of heaven," and a "sacrifice of every principle of right, of every impulse of humanity." Slavery existed only "in defiance of the most sacred laws of humanity." Max Farrand, ed., *The Records of the Federal Constitutional Convention* (New Haven, Conn.: Yale University Press, 1966), 2:221–22.

61. *The Papers of James Madison*, Robert A. Rutland, ed. (Chicago: University of Chicago Press, 1977), 11:297–98. Elbridge Gerry, the conservative Antifederalist from Massachusetts, acknowledged that his own state had "abused" the right to assemble that was guaranteed in the Constitution of 1780. *Annals of Congress*, 1:732. Aedanus Burke condemned the actions of the South Carolina legislature that were so "irregular" that "the very name of a democracy, or government of the people, now begins to be hateful and offensive." Aedanus Burke, *Considerations on the Society or Order of the Cincinnati* 13 (1783). Although Georgia's Constitution of 1777 established procedures for amendments, the state legislature repeatedly ignored them during the 1780s. Gordon S. Wood, *The Creation of the American Republic* (New York: W. W. Norton & Co., 1969), p. 274.

62. Madison, "Detached Memoranda," p. 559.

63. Letter from Thomas Jefferson to Rev. Mr. Millar (January 23, 1808), in *The Writings of Thomas Jefferson,* H. A. Washington, ed. (Washington, D.C.: Taylor & Maury, 1853), 5:237.

64. Ibid., pp. 237–38.

65. Madison, "Detached Memoranda," p. 561.

66. We should not forget that domestic responses to foreign wars are not good sources for a heightened appreciation of our civil liberties. See, for example, the World War II Japanese internment case, *Korematsu* v. *United States,* 323 U.S. 214, 223 (1944) (the "military urgency of the situation demanded that all citizens of Japanese ancestry be segregated").

67. Herbert Wechsler, "Toward Neutral Principles of Constitutional Law," *Harvard Law Review* 73 (1959):15.

68. *Wallace* v. *Jaffree,* 472 U.S. at 112.

69. Solicitor General Brief, 6, 24.

70. In *Engel,* The Supreme Court held that:

> The establishment clause, unlike the free exercise clause, does not depend upon any showing of direct governmental compulsion and is violated by the enactment of laws which establish an official religion whether those laws operate directly to coerce nonobserving individuals or not.

Engel v. *Vitale,* 370 U.S. 421, 430 (1962). See also cases cited in note 16 above.

71. McConnell, "Coercion," p. 936.

72. Ibid., p. 938.

73. Ibid., p. 939.

74. McConnell, "Accommodation of Religion," p. 39. Professor McConnell also has been quoted as saying that "[c]eremonial acknowledgment of highly ecumenical styles of prayer amounts to establishment of a civil religion, and that's a problem." Marcia Coyle, "Not Just a Prayer," *National Law Journal,* November 11, 1991, 26, col. 4. But if this is McConnell's position, he did not make it clear in his pathbreaking article. There are other examples in his article where coercion is treated as the only relevant element: "[C]ourts are wasting their time when they draw nice distinctions about various manifestations of religion in public life that entail no use of the taxing power and have no coercive effect." McConnell, "Coercion," p. 939.

75. Solicitor General Brief, 7.

76. Solicitor General Brief, 19 n.18 (citation omitted).

77. Solicitor General Brief, 16 (emphasis added).

78. Oral Argument in *Lee* v. *Weisman,* November 6, 1991.

79. *American Jewish Congress,* 827 F.2d at 137. Later, Judge Easterbrook defines "establishment" as "a term with meaning, denoting a relationship characterized by public funding and legal penalties." Ibid., 140.

It is not necessarily clear that Judge Easterbrook sees "funding" as entirely distinct from "coercion," or whether for him it is simply one manifestation of coercion. McConnell referred to the taxing power, but apparently considered it part of "coercion." Spending, of course, raises issues different from taxing for a specific program. Presumably, both McConnell and Easterbrook would consider a tax levied for the specific purpose of financing religion to be unconstitutional. But Judge Easterbrook, to some extent, would also consider funding religion from general revenues to be problematic constitutionally whereas McConnell, at least as far as his article suggests, would see funding religion as a political and not a constitutional issue.

80. *Allegheny County*, 492 U.S. at 659–60 (citations omitted).

81. It is somewhat similar to interpreting the free press clause to say that Congress may not enact a statute that tends to abridge freedom of the press.

82. Perhaps only Charles Cooper is clear on this point. In his brief to the Supreme Court in *Lee* v. *Weisman*, Cooper rejected the rule of *Engel* v. *Vitale* and argued that "government coercion of religious conformity is a necessary element of an establishment clause violation." Cooper Brief, 14 (capitalization altered). Cooper asserted that this doctrine derived from the founders.

> The Founders did not fear *expression* of religious values by public officials; they feared *coercion* of religious values by public officials. The First Amendment was designed by the Framers to protect only against the latter.

Ibid. As has been shown, other proponents of the coercion standard have been less clear.

83. *American Jewish Congress*, 827 F.2d at 137. Unfortunately, Judge Easterbrook does not explain what he means by "coercion." We are told, however, that there are two things that are *not* coercion: governmental speech and governmental use of symbolism. "Speech is not coercive; the listener may do as he likes." *American Jewish Congress*, 827 F.2d at 132. The government may choose to make pronouncements on religious questions if it so desires. The reason is that governmental speech does not coerce.

> When the government expresses views in public debates, all are as free as they were before; that these views may offend some and persuade others is a political rather than a constitutional problem.

Ibid., 133. "All speech may offend. There is no hackler's veto." Ibid., 134. Judge Easterbrook recognized that there might be a special problem when the governmentally sponsored religious speech is delivered either to young people or to a captive audience. Ibid., 134. But, not finding such problems in the case before him, the Judge did not consider the matter further. He also acknowledged that "[o]ne can imagine governmental speech so pervasive that it impinges on freedom of thought even if the listener is not 'captive.' " Ibid. (citation omitted). "Some governmental speech will offend in itself; other speech will mobilize to action and so be more offensive still; yet none is forbidden. The absence of coercion is why. The government may encourage what it may not compel." Ibid.

84. McConnell, "Coercion," p. 941. Professor McConnell provides only hints of the scope of "coercion" under his test. On the one hand, practices with a long historical tradition probably are permissible; McConnell, "Coercion," pp. 938–39, and "liberty enhancing accommodations of religion" are permissible, including statutes that prohibit employers from firing workers who refuse to work on their Sabbath. The refer-

ence is to *Estate of Thornton* v. *Caldor,* 472 U.S. 703 (1985). McConnell does not discuss why the state can coerce employers to respect the religious preferences of their employees. But although the government can specifically single out Sabbatarians for favorable treatment, McConnell nevertheless believes that governmental financial aid cannot be targeted to religious schools. The reason such aid is impermissible is because it "has the purpose and effect of coercing or altering religious belief or action." McConnell, "Coercion," p. 940.

85. He suggests that the interpretation of a coercion standard would not need to be developed *ab initio* because "coercion" has previously been "raised in many areas of constitutional law." Solicitor General Brief, 22 n. 21 (citing *Arizona* v. *Fulminante,* 111 S.Ct. 1246 [1991] and *Schneckloth* v. *Bustamonte,* 412 U.S. 218 [1973]). Even if we ignore the extraordinary implications of the Solicitor General's attempt to analogize religious rights to the rights of suspected felons undergoing police searches and interrogations, the fractured opinions in the very "coercion" cases he cites do not suggest that this "coercion test" is likely to lead us away from "confusion" and "division." Five separate opinions were filed in *Schneckloth*, and four were filed in *Fulminante.*

86. *Allegheny County,* 492 U.S. at 661.

87. Ibid.

88. Justice Kennedy, like McConnell and Easterbrook, never provides a working definition of "coercion," although he does offer a few examples:

> Forbidden involvements include compelling or coercing participation or attendance at a religious activity, requiring religious oaths to obtain government office or benefits, or delegating government power to religious groups.

Allegheny County, 492 U.S. at 660 (citations omitted).

89. Justice Kennedy apparently believes that widespread practices, if noncoercive, are necessarily constitutional.

> Noncoercive government action within the realm of flexible accommodation or passive acknowledgment of existing symbols does not violate the establishment clause unless it benefits religion in a way more direct and more substantial than practices that are accepted in our national heritage.

Ibid., 662–63.

90. *American Jewish Congress,* 827 F.2d at 135.

91. For a detailed discussion of the use of these terms in the eighteenth century, see chapter 4 of my work, T. Jeremy Gunn, *A Standard for Repair: The Establishment of Religion Clause of the United States Constitution* (New York: Garland Press, 1992).

92. See the following constitutional provisions:

> We the people of the United States, in order to form a more perfect union, *establish* justice . . . do ordain and *establish* this Constitution for the United States of America. (Preamble)

> To *establish* an uniform rule of naturalization. . . . (Art. I, § 8)

To *establish* post offices. . . ." (Art. I, § 8)

[Governmental offices] which shall be *established* by law. (Art II, § 2)

. . . inferior courts as the Congress may, from time to time, ordain and *establish*. (Art. III, § 1)

The ratification of the conventions of nine states, shall be sufficient for the *establishment* of this Constitution. . . . (Art. VII)

93. See, for example, J. Roland Pennock and John W. Chapman, eds., *Coercion* (Chicago: Aldine, 1972); Alan Wertheimer, *Coercion* (Princeton University Press, 1987); Peter Westen, " 'Freedom' and 'Coercion'—Virtue Words and Vice Words," *Duke Law Journal* 1985 (1985):541–90; Robert Nozick, "Coercion," in *Philosophy, Science, and Method: Essays in Honor of Ernest Nagel*, Sidney Morgenbesser, Patrick Suppes, and Morton White, eds. (New York: St. Martin's Press, 1969), pp. 440–72; Harry G. Frankfort, "Coercion and Moral Responsibility," in *Essays on Freedom of Action*, Ted Hoderich, ed. (London: Routledge & Kegan Paul, 1973), pp. 65–86.

94. "Congress shall make no law respecting . . . the free exercise [of religion.]" U.S. Constitution Amendment 1. Scott J. Ward has explicitly suggested that "the establishment clause, like the free exercise clause, should focus on governmental coercion affecting religious choice." See Scott J. Ward, "Reconceptualizing Establishment Clause Cases as Free Exercise Class Actions," *Yale Law Journal* 98 (1989):1739.

95. Referring to Justice O'Connor's "endorsement" test, the *Allegheny County* dissenters wrote:

The notion that cases arising under the establishment clause should be decided by an inquiry into whether a "reasonable observer" may "fairly understand" government action to "sen[d] a message to nonadherents that they are outsiders, not full members of the political community," is a recent, and in my view a most unwelcome, addition to our tangled establishment clause jurisprudence.

492 U.S. at 668 (quoting majority opinion).

96. "The question under *Lynch* is not whether, as an initial matter, the members of this panel see this crèche as part of an integrated secular display, but whether reasonable people could see it so." *American Jewish Congress*, 827 F.2d at 130.

97. Solicitor General Brief, 22.

98. *Allegheny County*, 492 U.S. at 664.

6

"Civilizing" Native Alaska:
Federal Support of Mission Schools, 1885–1906
Michael J. Oleska

FEDERAL EDUCATIONAL POLICY PRIOR TO 1870

National interest in civilizing the American Indians surfaced as early as 1776, when the Continental Congress approved a resolution affirming that "friendly commerce between the people of the United Colonies and the Indians, and the propagation of the gospel, and the cultivation of civil arts among the latter, may produce many and inestimable advantages for both." Congress also directed officials living among the various tribes to find suitable places for ministers and teachers to reside. During the Washington administration, the suggestion that the government should appoint missionaries to live among the Indians and be supplied with the necessary tools for introducing agriculture received a favorable response. The president asked Congress for funds to support Indian agents that they might live among the various friendly tribes and encourage them to take up farming, but rejected the idea that these agents should be evangelists.[1]

During the Jacksonian era, all attempts to civilize were abandoned in favor of relocation. The tribes that had, in fact, made the most progress toward

Rev. Michael J. Oleska, Th.D., is an Orthodox parish priest at St. Nicholas Church in Juneau, Alaska. He ministers to Native American communities throughout the state.

93

assimilation were the very ones forced to leave their ancestral homes in Georgia, Tennessee, Alabama, and Mississippi and resettle in the "Indian Territory" of present-day Oklahoma. The literate and articulate Cherokee, not unlike the Aleuts a half century later, protested the violation of their treaty rights, and actually won a significant appeal to the United States Supreme Court, which the administration, nevertheless, refused to enforce.[2]

While coveting the Indians' land, intruders were in constant conflict with both the Indians and the federal authorities charged with defending Indian treaty rights. State governments, on the other hand, insisting that their sovereignty extended to Indian lands, denied federal jurisdiction. The Jackson administration believed the only solution was removal of the Indians to a remote region where their sovereignty could be practically maintained, rather than the creation of a sovereign Indian political entity within the several states, which would find itself (especially with runaway slaves a constant issue) in continuous conflict with state authorities, slave owners, and squatters. Consequently, federal Indian policy focused on removal until the 1849 goldrush demonstrated that this, too, had become impractical. The issue of slavery dominated the next decade, so that it was not until after the Civil War that the country could seriously attend to the Indian problem.

INDIAN POLICY REFORM: 1867–1887

The Bureau of Indian Affairs, initially established by the Secretary of War in 1824, was transferred to the Department of the Interior in 1849.[3] The army, however, continued for decades to demand the return of the Indian office to its jurisdiction. Considering the Indians a military problem, the army also argued that it could more efficiently execute policy directives than the cumbersome, underpaid, and often incompetent bureaucrats whom the Interior Department had assigned to manage the various Indian agencies. Indeed, serving far from the centers of society, poorly paid, and poorly supervised, politically appointed agents had become notoriously corrupt and inefficient by the time General Grant was elected president. But civilian philanthropists and humanitarians opposed returning the Indian office to the jurisdiction of the army, fearing that military control would inflict further injustices on Native Americans. The House of Representatives, anxious to participate in the formation of federal Indian policy, regularly supported the army's position, while the Senate, managing Indian affairs through its treating-ratifying powers, sought more popular alternatives.[4]

The Episcopal Church had proposed that a commission of citizens be appointed to formulate a new federal Indian policy in 1862, but Congress did not appropriate funds for such an undertaking until 1869, when nine men were alloted $25,000 to constitute the Board of Indian Commissioners. While this body would deliberate, however, the Grant administration proceeded with changes of its own, seeking to find a way to provide the Indian office with decent, dedicated agents without surrending to the army's demands. Several senators had suggested that religious leaders be invited to participate in the 1867 Indian Peace Commission, established by Congress to conclude peace with hostile Plains tribes and persuade them to relocate to reservations. Most denominations, however, were initially reluctant to follow suit, partly because of the essentially political nature of the Indian situation and partly because they lacked confidence in the government's ability to "educate and civilize," but primarily because they doubted that the government would sustain such a policy for more than a few years. The churches, too, lacked the funds and personnel for such a task, and their constituencies were not particularly interested in Indian affairs. Only the Society of Friends, the Quakers, enthusiastically welcomed this opportunity to influence federal policy. This enticed President Grant to experiment with placing several Indian agencies under Quaker direction in 1869.[5]

The outcome of the Quaker experiment sufficiently impressed the White House that on December 5, 1870, President Grant reported to Congress:

> The act of Congress reducing the Army renders army officers ineligible for civil positions. Indian agencies being civil offices, I determined to give all the agencies to such religious denominations as had heretofore established missionaries among the Indians, and perhaps to some other denominations who would undertake the work . . . as missionary work. The societies selected are allowed to name their own agents, subject to the approval of the Executive, and are expected to watch over them and aid them as missionaries to Christianize and civilize the Indian.[6]

The first report of the Board of Indian Commissioners supported this policy, advising that removal to reservations should be accelerated so that the process of civilizing and Christianizing might also be expedited.

> Schools should be established and teachers employed by the government to introduce the English language in every tribe. . . . The teachers employed should be nominated by some religious body having a mission nearest to the location of the school. The establishment of Christian missions should be encouraged, and their schools fostered. The pupils should at least receive the rations and clothing they would get if remaining with their families. . . .[7]

By 1872, these recommendations had been implemented on the majority of reservations, as the Commissioner of Indian Affairs reported to Congress:

The Hicksite Friends have in their charge 6 agencies with 6,598 Indians; Orthodox Friends, 10 agencies, with 17,724 Indians; Baptists, 5 agencies with 40,800 Indians; Presbyterians, 9 agencies with 38,069 Indians; Christians, 2 agencies with 8,287 Indians; Methodists, 14 agencies with 54,473 Indians; Dutch Reformed, 5 agencies with 8,118 Indians; Congregationalists, 3 agencies with 14,476 Indians; Episcopalians, 8 agencies with 26,929 Indians; Unitarians, 2 agencies with 3,800 Indians; Lutherans, 1 agency with 273 Indians.[8]

Problems inevitably erupted with this arrangement. The Lutherans, for example, felt neglected and protested their tiny portion of the large Indian mission field, complaining to the government in 1875,

We ask and believe that you will and can give us an agency now, as well as in the future. If there is no vacancy at present, it would not take long to make one. We are not asking that you do any more for us than you have done for other churches. You have assigned agencies to others without their sending missionaries to the tribe, and can do so in our case, if you desire. On the authority of the Lutheran Church, we insist on an agency being assigned to us.[9]

THE PROPAGATION OF CHURCH-RUN SCHOOLS IN ALASKA

Alaska remained so exotic and remote that any denominations not included in its division into spheres of influence were hardly noticed—with one notable exception. The Russian Orthodox Church, active in the region since 1784, had established churches and schools at Kodiak, Sitka, Unalaska, Atka, Nushagak, Russian Mission, and the Pribilof Islands, and later at Killisnoo, Juneau, Nutchek, Belkovsky, St. Michael, Chuathbaluk, and Afognak. Had the original policy of assigning agencies to the church already serving the area been applied in the Alaskan case, the entire southern half of the territory would have been alloted to the Orthodox, but instead their educational program was ignored. Due precisely to the predictable problems that this provoked, a substantial published record of interdenominational conflicts, dividing both families and communities, survives, chiefly from the newspaper *American Orthodox Messenger*, which followed Alaskan events closely from its New York editorial office. On one side were American Protestant missionaries, funded and supported by the U.S. federal government, whose policies were consistent with those established by the Rev. Dr. Sheldon Jackson, a Presbyterian minister who was appointed federal Commissioner of Education for Alaska in 1885, a post he held for twenty-three years. The U.S. federal position being that fluency in English was synonymous with civilization, the established policy of these federal/mission schools was to use the English language exclusively and suppress all others, and to convert native Alaskans to Protestant Christianity. On the other side were native Alaskan and Slavic Orthodox clergy, most of them receiving some funds from the Orthodox Missionary Society in Russia, which was dedicated to fostering literacy in native Alaskan languages, Russian, and, after the transfer of Alaska, English as well. For them, multilingualism and literacy in several languages were the marks of citizenship.

THE ORTHODOX SCHOOLS

The first Alaskan schools were founded by Orthodox lay monks who taught the "four R's" (reading, 'riting, 'rithmetic, and religion). Saint Herman, assisted by several Aleuts, operated an orphanage and school on Spruce Island, near Kodiak, in 1816, and ran it for over twenty years. Hieromonk Gideon founded a bilingual school at Kodiak even earlier, teaching over a hundred Creole and native students to read and write in their indigenous Alutiiq tongue, as well as in Russian. As the colony gradually expanded, schools were established in major settlements and a curriculum was developed to prepare natives to assume responsibility for the more important leadership positions within the Russian American Company, which bore the costs of this educational effort.

The principal architect of Aleut bilingual education in Alaska was Saint Innocent (Father John Veniaminov). Shortly after his arrival in Unalaska in 1824, Father John began his collaboration with the Aleut chief, Ivan Pan'kov, to devise a suitable writing system for the Fox Island dialect, and to translate Holy Scripture into Unangan, as the local language was called by its speakers. Within three years, Father Veniaminov had translated an Orthodox catechism into Aleut and proposed that it be published, together with the original, "since many Aleuts understand Russian."[10] Almost a century of Russian and Siberian contact had produced dozens of intermarriages and hundreds of bicultural, bilingual offspring. Later, as Bishop Innocent, Veniaminov's greatest contribution to Alaska was the development of a school system whose curriculum prepared students to become the middle management for the company. Courses in geometry, trigonometry, navigational science, astronomy, and accounting, as well as Russian, catechism, church history, mathematics, and six years of Alaska native languages, three years of Latin, Slavonic, and medicine were offered at Sitka.

By 1867, most of the schools financed by the Russian American Company and the Orthodox Mission were staffed by Aleut and Creole graduates of Bishop Innocent's schools. During the next thirty years, Aleut Orthodox priests and laymen established more schools in southwestern Alaska. Both the education system and the Russian Orthodox Church became vital symbols of the Aleut cultural identity.[11]

One Atkan Creole, whose Russian father and Unangan Aleut mother had raised him to be bicultural and bilingual, became a respected priest as well as a renowned educator among his people. Father Iakov (James) Nets-vetov attended seminary at Irkutsk, in Siberia, and, after returning to his home village, opened another Aleut bilingual school, and probably developed an impressive dictionary of his native language. He also painted the first icons for the Atka church. Father Netsvetov was transferred to the Yukon Delta in 1842, where he learned Yup'ik Eskimo, and developed a writing system for it based on the Cyrillic alphabet. He founded the first Alaskan Eskimo bilingual school.

By the time the Alaskan colony was sold to the United States in 1867, there were Aleut sea captains, navigators, ship builders, musicians, priests, teachers, storekeepers, accountants, metal smiths, explorers, cartographers, and even one Major General in the Russian military. Sitka, the territorial capital, was 55 percent Aleut; the second largest settlement, Kodiak, 90 percent Aleut. The colony depended on the Creole and Aleut professionals as the foundation of its social and economic life, since they far outnumbered the fewer than 800 Russians who, at the zenith of czarist imperial rule, lived in Alaska.

THE FEDERAL/MISSION SCHOOLS

Recognizing the extent of such powerful native forces in Alaska, a 1900 editorial in the *Orthodox Messenger* summarized the mission's educational philosophy in this way:

> Our foreign missions . . . do not have a cultural character. They do not understand their tasks in the sense of propagating European culture. The reason for this, of course, is that European culture and civilization are by no means . . . wholly the outgrowth of Christianity. It owes to Christianity only the little that is really noble and lofty in it. If we go into particulars, we shall find that it is in direct opposition to it.

The stage was being set for a conflict in philosophies and values in the remote villages of the Alaskan frontier. Dr. Jackson and fellow Presbyterian missionary, S. Hall Young, assumed a radically different attitude toward native languages and culture. The latter boasted in his autobiography:

> One strong stand, so far as I know I was the first to take, was the determination to do no translating into any of the native dialects. I realized . . . that the task

of making an English-speaking race of these natives was much easier than the task of making a civilized and Christian language out of the native languages. We should let the old tongues with their superstitions and sin die—the sooner the better—and replace these languages with that of Christian civilization and compel the natives in all our schools to speak English and only English.[12]

Jackson had been active in Alaska since 1877, and had determined that federally supported mission schools, operating as "Protestant Forts," could protect the natives from abuses of the military, sourdoughs, and bootleggers.[13] Bilingualism was never considered as an option. While maintaining an office in Washington, and keeping in close contact with influential religious and political leaders, Jackson influenced the course of Alaskan culture for many decades. He had close ties with President Benjamin Harrison, William Cleveland (President Cleveland's brother), and John Eaton, the Federal Commissioner of Education. The Presbyterian Church, in fact, paid Jackson's salary through 1907.

Sheldon Jackson orchestrated the educational effort by combining church and federal support, as had been done since the Grant administration in the lower Forty-Eight. He believed that only missionaries could be attracted to serve in such remote communities for such nominal salaries. The major American Protestant denominations accepted Jackson as the coordinator for mission strategy in Alaska.[14] Baptists were given Kodiak; the Methodists, the Aleutian Islands; the Episcopalians, the Interior; the Quakers, the Kotzebue region; the Moravians, Bristol Bay and later the Kuskokwim Delta; Swedish Covenant, Nunivak Island; and the Presbyterians, the Southeast Panhandle and Northslope regions. There would be no competition between denominations, Jackson reasoned, if each had its own separate sphere of influence.

In Alaska, boarding schools were established by federally funded missions to "recreate" the young native in the "likeness" of white men. Education aimed primarily, as one superintendent wrote, at training them to become laborers, miners, teamsters, and agricultural workers. Jackson's mission may be summed up in the following statements:

We have a full right by our own best wisdom and then even by compulsion to dictate terms to them; to use constraint and force . . . without consulting to any troublesome extent the views of the Indians whom we are to manage.[15]

We have no higher calling in the world than to be missionaries to those people who have not yet achieved the Anglo-Saxon frame of mind.[16]

THE CONFLICT

When the American missionary teachers encountered the Aleuts and Orthodox Tlingits, many of their stereotypes were shattered. They had come to
teach Alaska natives to read and write, although they already could—in two
languages. But these were viewed as the wrong languges. The Americans had
come to bring the Christian gospel to the heathen, but these claimed already
to be Christian, to have their own churches, with their own clergy, worship-
ping in their own languages. But, from the perspective of the newly arrived
missionaries, this was the wrong church, the wrong Christianity. Because they
were funded by the government, then, the teachers acted as agents of the
federal government in suppressing and persecuting another faith.

In Kodiak, for example, the Baptist Mission and the public school teacher
resorted to forcing their way into Aleut homes and compelling parents to
relinquish custody of their children. The North American Commercial Company then transported the children to nearby Woody Island, where the Baptist
mission school had been erected. The native children remaining in Kodiak
were taught "to pray according to the Protestant custom and to sing Protestant hymns" at the public school. Only after the Orthodox priest complained
that such a violation of the principle of separation of church and state was
illegal, did this practice end.

One violation of the First Amendment guarantee of religious freedom
led to another. But unlike the suppression of Native American religious traditions on reservations in the forty-eight contiguous states, the persecution
of Eastern Orthodoxy in Alaska represented federal discrimination against
an articulate Christian population who were well aware of their rights and
protested their violation.

Mrs. Olga Shamkov filed suit in Kodiak in 1894 against the Baptist Mission
for the kidnapping of her son, and although the court ordered him returned
to his mother, the abductor, a Mr. Roskor, went unpunished for seizing the
boy.[17]

At Nushagak, in March 1896, the Orthodox priest requested permission
from the boarding school operated by the Moravian Church to visit the mission
and administer Holy Communion to the Orthodox children residing there,
if they would not be allowed to return home for Easter. The administrator
of the school replied: "Such which attend the mission cannot go, neither can
you come here to administer the Holy Sacrament. This is in accordance with
the rules of the government, and the direct request of the ex-governor of
Alaska."[18]

A few years later, an Orthodox Tlingit woman died at Sitka. Her husband
and two of her four sons were also Orthodox, while the other two had been
raised at the Presbyterian mission school. Apparently at the instigation of

the local teacher and missionary, Rev. A. E. Austin, the territorial governor, James Sheakley, and the federal marshal, W. E. Williams, came to the home, seized the body, removed it from its original coffin, and took it to a neighboring home. This sparked a long series of court appeals, resulting in the woman being buried in two coffins—one Orthodox, one Presbyterian. When the headmistress of the school attempted to coerce the widower to transfer custody of his younger sons to the government/mission school, the local Orthodox priest intervened to prevent it.[19]

This incident provoked an anti-Presbyterian backlash in Sitka, and resulted in a long petition to the Russian ambassador in Washington, D.C. The 482 Aleut and Tlingit signators complained that the czar had not handed them over to American rule without some guarantee that their property, civil, and religious rights would be honored, and that under what they considered "Presbyterian rule," they could never get a fair hearing. "We are," they asserted, "subjected to vexations of every description" and cannot obtain redress in the courts or "other official places where Presbyterian influences reign supreme." The signators asked if the Russian government could possibly appoint a representative to reside at Sitka as an inspector, serving as a watchdog to assure that continuing injustices were not committed against native Alaskans who had formerly been citizens of the Russian empire.

The local Tlingit chiefs, writing in Russian, petitioned President McKinley to end sectarian control of Alaska, specifically insisting that the federal government establish impartial law enforcement and close "American saloons." They charged that twenty-eight natives had been killed but no arrests had been made in any of these cases, although the names of the murderers were well known. They feared that the next Presbyterian governor, John Brady, would create unbearable conditions, since he had already illegally obtained a right of way through the Tlingit Indian village and cleared a road through their ancestral burial ground, ". . . and with the bones of some he banked his ground, and some he threw into the water [harbor]."[20] The Tlingit chiefs stated flatly,

> We do not want American saloons. We beg the government to close them. We understand now that whiskey is poison to us. . . . We do not want the civilization that not only does not stop saloons but encourages them.

Not without sarcasm, they wrote of American "civilization" and "education," emphasizing,

> We do not want the education by which our daughters are torn from their homes and alienated, taught the English language only to give them an easier scope and advantage to practice prostitution. . . . We do not imagine . . that the dance

halls and dives of Juneau and Sitka must necessarily be filled with our educated daughters.[21]

These pleas were reiterated by Orthodox Bishop Nicolai who wrote to the president in 1898, asking that Alaska be "delivered" from Dr. Sheldon Jackson's control. The bishop alleged that Jackson's policies had introduced conflict and strife where before there had been none, and he accused the government of trying to "drive out the Orthodox Church by every possible means, lawful and unlawful," although its record in providing free, quality education had been exemplary.[22]

At Unalaska, in the Aleutian Islands, an Aleut student at the Methodist-operated Jesse Lee Home suddenly died in the boarding school dormitory and was secretly buried in the Orthodox cemetery. The federal government had assigned local children to the school with the promise that the children's religious tradition would be respected. When the native community became aroused, the school administrators asserted that the girl's father, an American Protestant, had instructed them to convert all three of his children to Methodism. The following spring, however, when he returned to the village, the Orthodox priest asked the girl's father if he had, in fact, issued such instructions. He not only denied doing so, but removed his remaining children from the home.

The parish priest, Father Alexander Kedrofsky, initiated a correspondence with Mrs. Agnes Newhall, the matron of the Methodist home, expressing his resentment that his faith was being denigrated by a government-supported agency:

> If there is a "Russian" or "American" religion, I know no such religions. I know only that there is a Christian religion, to our misfortune divided in two. . . . If you happen to address someone with a question about religion, do not ask "Do you want to have a Russian or American religion?"[23]

To this, in keeping with current federal policy, the matron replied:

> We assume complete charge of the children under our care. As for religious instruction, it is wholly under the direction of the home management and according to the Protestant faith. Your request to visit the home for religious instruction cannot be granted. . . . No children are allowed to attend the Greco-Russian Church. . . . In the case of death, services and burial are conducted by home management, except in such cases as we shall decide otherwise. Interference in these respects shall not be tolerated.[24]

As early as 1873, six years after the transfer of Alaska to American rule, an Aleut father was arrested by the federal treasury agent, a Mr. McIntyre, on St. Paul Island. The man, who had refused to enroll his son in the "American" school, was handcuffed, locked in a cellar, and fed only bread and water for four days. The boy was shut in a closet and fed the same diet for the same period.[25] The government agents imposed fines on resistant parents and attendance gradually improved, although the Aleuts continued to support their local bilingual Aleut-Russian school until about 1912, when the U.S. government forcibly closed it.

Long after 1906, when the federal government abandoned its policy of financial support for American mission schools, anti-native, anti-Orthodox prejudices continued to influence both official and unofficial attitudes, policies, and actions of civilian and military personnel in Alaska. During Prohibition, federal authorities reportedly promised to release or mitigate the punishment for Orthodox natives accused of manufacturing "homebrew" if they would join the Presbyterian church in Juneau. During the Second World War, Aleuts—but not white Americans—were evacuated from the Aleutian Islands and interned in abandoned mining camps in southeastern Alaska. Their homes and churches were ransacked during their three-year absence by the soldiers sent to their villages to defend them. One fourth of the population, mostly the elderly, died in camps that were totally unfit for human occupancy.

Not only were irreplaceable icons stolen from private homes, but at Port Heiden, the military decided to use the Orthodox chapel as a supply shed. The church at Atka, with treasures dating from the time of Father Netsvetov, was burned by the U.S. Navy, and the chapel at Eagle Harbor, on Kodiak Island, was shelled during target practice. The magnificient cathedral of the Holy Ascension, Father Veniaminov's original parish, was saved the indignity of being transformed into the officer's club, complete with bar and dance floor, only by the threat that at least one Aleut man would commit suicide on its front steps if his church was desecrated.

Nearly fifty years after these violations of religious liberty, the Aleuts have yet to receive so much as an apology. As recently as 1968, the federal government, against the unanimous wishes of the Aleut population, invited the Assembly of God to establish a mission on St. Paul Island, for the "religious diversification of the Aleuts."[26] Forced assimilationism is far from dead.

CONCLUSION

Although precedent for federal support of sectarian schools can be found as early as 1776, cooperation between the government and Christian churches as a general principle of American Indian policy was not widely accepted until the 1870s, the decade following the Alaska Purchase. As the national policy toward Native Americans shifted from extermination to relocation and, finally, to assimilation after the Civil War, Alaska was spared the trauma of violence, warfare, and relocation that had characterized federal relations with indigenous peoples in the "lower Forty-Eight"; but it became, therefore, the primary testing ground for the new, putatively more humane, assimilationist policy that was to be executed by federally supported missionaries, whose twin goals were to educate and baptize the indigenous people of Alaska.

The program was widely resented among literate, bilingual Tlingits and Aleuts who had accepted Eastern Orthodox Christianity during the Russian colonial period, and who had been educated in both Russian and their native language. They were thus able to protest the violation of their civil and religious rights in letters and petitions to the Alaskan Territorial officials, the Imperial Russian ambassador, and the president of the United States himself. Decades after the policy of support had been officially abandoned, however, Orthodox individuals and communities in Alaska were still subjected to discrimination and outright persecution.

By violating the provisions, in both letter and spirit, of the Bill of Rights, the federal government became involved in sectarian disputes and social injustices the First Amendment had been written to preclude. Whenever federal officials attempt to support one denomination at the expense of another, the protective wall of separation between church and state collapses, with disastrous consequences for all concerned. Religious tolerance and good will is destroyed, and the relationship of trust between the national government and its citizens is poisoned. The suspicion and anxiety, the sense of injustice and indignation, which the collusion of federal and church leadership a century ago produced among Orthodox Alaskans will require decades more to heal.

NOTES

1. Francis P. Prucha, *American Indian Policy, 1790–1834* (Lincoln: University of Nebraska Press, 1962), p. 214.

2. *Worcester* v. *Georgia,* 1832, in Ronald N. Satz, *American Indian Policy in the Jacksonian Era* (Lincoln: University of Nebraska Press, 1975), pp. 47–49.

3. Francis P. Prucha, *Documents of United States Indian Policy* (Lincoln: University of Nebraska Press, 1978), p. 80.

4. Loring B. Priest, *Uncle Sam's Stepchildren* (Lincoln: University of Nebraska Press, 1968), p. 17.

5. Ibid., p. 29.

6. Prucha, *Documents of United States Indian Policy,* p. 135.

7. Ibid., p. 133.

8. Ibid., p. 143.

9. Priest, *Uncle Sam's Stepchildren,* p. 32.

10. Paul D. Garrett, *St. Innocent* (Crestwood, N.Y.: St. Vladimir's Press, 1978), p. 74.

11. Dorothy K. Jones, *A Century of Servitude* (Fairbanks: University of Alaska Native Language Center, 1980), p. 153.

12. Michael E. Krauss, *Alaska Native Languages* (Fairbanks: University of Alaska Native Language Center, 1980), p. 23.

13. Richard L. Dauenhauer, *Conflicting Visions in Alaskan Education* (Fairbanks: University of Alaska Center for Cross-Cultural Studies, 1980), p. 12.

14. Ibid., p. 18.

15. Priest, *Uncle Sam's Stepchildren,* p. 242.

16. Dauenhauer, *Conflicting Visions in Alaskan Education,* p. 19.

17. *Documents Relative to the History of Alaska* (Fairbanks: University of Alaska Microfilm), reel 3: 74.

18. Ibid., p. 174.

19. *American Orthodox Messenger* 6, no. 12 (1894): 224.

20. Rev. Michael J. Oleska, *Alaskan Missionary Spirituality* (Mahwah, N.J.: Paulist Press, 1987), p. 325.

21. Ibid.

22. Ibid., p. 327.

23. Oleska, *Alaskan Missionary Spirituality,* p. 330.

24. Ibid., p. 4.

25. Jones, *A Century of Servitude,* p. 28.

26. Ibid., p. 152.

7

Prayer in School:
Why It Does Religion No Favor

William F. Schulz

For all of my elementary school years I attended a nonsectarian private school. During several of those years our daily classroom work was preceded by a reading from the Bible. Sometimes the teacher would select the passage and sometimes a student would be given the privilege of both choosing the Scripture of the day and presenting it.

It is often presumed by those who advocate public prayer or Bible reading in the schools that the practice, if not a cure for the moral decay of modern culture, can at the very least do no harm. I want, however, to testify to the contrary. Not only did Bible reading not save me from whatever moral quagmires I may over the years have tumbled into; it deposited in me a lode of prejudices which took more than fifteen years to overcome.

The harm that this superficially innocuous ritual inflicted was not of the type imagined by the Supreme Court when it ruled that neither official government-composed prayers (*Engel* v. *Vitale,* 1962) nor Bible readings or the Lord's Prayer (*Abington* v. *Schempp,* 1963) could be ritually recited in the public schools. Though I was raised a Unitarian, I did not feel myself reli-

Rev. William F. Schulz, D.Mn., D.D., is President of the Unitarian Universalist Association of Congregations, and a member of the National Advisory Council of Americans United for Separation of Church and State and the National Advisory Board of Americans for Religious Liberty.

giously oppressed by the school practice (although, had I known more at the time about religious pluralism, I might have felt differently). Indeed, I remember that the opportunity to choose and read a scriptural passage to my classmates was an occasion of some pleasure—not, I should say, because I was religiously inclined but for the opportunity it gave to show off my declamatory skills!

The damage I suffered was not, self-evidently, to my religious freedom but to my religious sensibilities. From the daily recitation of Bible passages, I learned that (a) the Bible (and, implicitly, all religious expression) was something to get out of the way before the real work of the day began; (b) the Bible was boring (unless you yourself picked the passage and liked to orate); (c) the Bible was incomprehensible (even *if* you yourself picked the passage and liked to orate); (d) the only exceptions to (b) and (c) were the Biblical passages having to do with sex (a discovery I made the day one of my classmates chose to read the verses in Leviticus which prohibited sleeping with a menstruating woman); (e) adults thought Bible reading was good for you (but did they know about Leviticus?); and (f) adults thought Bible reading was good for everybody (regardless of a person's religious tradition or lack of one). This was not a set of insights designed to endear the Bible to me or me to religion. I required almost two more decades of maturity, a stint in theological school, and a few years in the ministry to overcome these misconceptions.

While many solid legal and Constitutional reasons exist for keeping religious ritual and public education separate, there is an ecclesiastical reason as well: to do otherwise is the surest way to corrupt and desiccate religion.

LEGAL SAFEGUARDS AGAINST PUBLIC SCHOOL PRAYER

The two landmark Supreme Court decisions on public prayer and Bible reading in the public schools came in the early 1960s, the heyday of the Warren Court. In *Engel* v. *Vitale* (1962), the Court ruled 6–1 that public recitation of the so-called Regents' Prayer—"Almighty God, we acknowledge our dependence upon Thee and we beg Thy blessings upon us, our parents, our teachers, and our country"—composed by the New York State Regents for use in the public schools of that state was unconstitutional. "It is no part of the business of government," the Court declared, "to compose official prayers for any group of the American people to recite. . . ."[1]

A year later, *Abington* v. *Schempp* reached the Supreme Court. High school student Ellory Schempp objected to the daily Bible readings broadcast over the public-address system each morning at his Abington, Pennsylvania, high school. "At least ten verses from the Holy Bible shall be read, without comment, at the opening of each public school on each school day," read the Pennsylvania law that mandated Abington's practice. In this case the Court ruled 8–1 that such exercises "prescribed as part of the curricular activities of students who are required by law to attend school" were in violation of the establishment clause of the Constitution. Mr. Justice Clark, speaking for the Court, elaborated:

> The place of religion in our society is an exalted one, achieved through a long tradition of reliance on the home, the church, and the inviolable citadel of the individual heart and mind. We have come to recognize through bitter experience that it is not within the power of government to invade that citadel, whether its purpose or effect be to aid or oppose, to advance or retard. In the relationship between man and religion, the State is firmly committed to a position of neutrality.[2]

These two cases (and *Schempp*'s companion case, *Murray* v. *Curlett*,[3] brought by the outspoken atheist Madalyn Murray O'Hair on behalf of her son, William, who in later years became a devoted fundamentalist and denounced his mother's views) created a firestorm of public controversy which continues to smolder to this day.

Americans consistently support "prayer in school." A 1988 survey by the Princeton Religious Research Center, for example, revealed that 68 percent of respondents favor an amendment to the Constitution that would allow prayer in the public schools with only 26 percent opposed. When asked, "Do you think that a small percentage or a large percentage of the public would be offended if prayer were permitted in the public schools?" 18 percent replied a "large percentage" and 71 percent a "small."[4]

And yet, despite these opinions; despite the fact that "returning God to the classroom" was high on the social agenda of the Religious Right throughout the 1970s and 80s; despite Ronald Reagan's endorsement of a prayer amendment to the Constitution; and despite the "Reaganization" of the Supreme Court, the fundamental principles of *Engel* v. *Vitale* and *Abington* v. *Schempp* still stand. Indeed, in 1985, the Court reaffirmed those principles in *Wallace* v. *Jaffree*, ruling 6–3 that an Alabama statute calling for a one-minute moment of silence in all public schools "for meditation or voluntary prayer" violated the establishment clause.[5]

On the face of it, a moment of silence would seem innocuous enough to pass constitutional muster, and, in fact, the Reagan administration, in an *amicus* brief on behalf of Alabama, argued that during that moment "the student may pray but is equally free to meditate or daydream or doze."[6] But, as most teachers know only too well, the state hardly needs a statute authorizing students to daydream or doze. The whole point of legally codifying one particular minute of the schoolday for silence is to encourage religious reflection. This was made amply clear in the testimony to the District Court of the Alabama state legislator who had originally introduced the legislation. The sole reason for the legislation, its sponsor affirmed, was to "return voluntary prayer" to the public schools. And that was enough to convince the majority of the Supreme Court that the legislation "had *no* secular purpose."[7]

THE BENEFITS OF GOVERNMENT RELIGIOUS NEUTRALITY

That legislation need have a "secular purpose" in order to be constitutional means not only that government may not favor the interests of one religion over another—only the most unreconstructed believer in America as a "Christian nation" would dispute that—but also that it may not seek to advance the interests of religion in general. A respect for pluralism requires a respect both for diverse religions and the areligious among us as well.[8] This is one reason why the Regents' Prayer—though it presents itself as nonsectarian—and a moment of silence for "meditation or voluntary prayer"—empty of prescribed content though that moment be—are both unconstitutional.

And yet, while it may appear that the secular purpose requirement is inimical to the interests of religion, the fact remains that the consequences for religion of strict government neutrality in this regard, far from being adverse, are in fact felicitous. No one recognized this more readily than James Madison, who called any political use of religion "an unhallowed perversion of the means of salvation"[9] and argued that "religion flourishes in greater purity without [rather] than with the aid of government."[10] Specifically with regard to the use of the public schools to promote religion, Madison said:

> [It is] to weaken in those who profess this religion a pious confidence in its innate excellence, and the patronage of its author; and to foster in those who still reject it a suspicion that its friends are too conscious of its fallacies to trust it to its own merits.[11]

Religion that is imposed upon its recipients turns out to engender either indifference or resentment. Most American religious leaders have recognized that persuasion is far more powerful than coercion when it comes to promoting one's religious views.

Not surprisingly, then, large numbers of religious leaders have supported the Supreme Court in its prayer decisions. That a Unitarian Universalist should applaud the Court's tenacity is not unexpected, for, despite the fact that Unitarian Horace Mann introduced Bible reading into the curricula when he founded the first public school system,[12] it was another Unitarian [Universalist]—namely, Ellory Schempp—who tossed it out.

But sympathy for the Court among the religious has extended well beyond Unitarian Universalism. Within a year after the *Schempp* ruling, leaders of the Baptists (including the Southern Baptists), Disciples of Christ, Episcopalians, Lutherans, Methodists, Presbyterians, and the United Church of Christ had joined the Board of the National Council of Churches and the leadership of Orthodox, Conservative, and Reform Judaism in backing the Court.[13] The reasons are not hard to come by. They have to do with the nature of God, prayer, morality and ritual, and the changing face of American religion.

To hold the notion, for example, as some of the Court's opponents have done, that God could be "tossed out" of the public schools by the action of a court is to entertain a cramped and paltry concept of God. Whatever God may be, He or She is not subject to the legislative or judicial tempers of the age; any child who wishes to invoke God's help in school—and, as God well knows, many, many have!—is more than welcome to do so privately.[14] The more serious opponents of the Court, however, have argued that to eliminate prayer and Bible reading from the schools is to eliminate the teaching of morality. There is no question, of course, that the maxims of conventional morality are transmitted to students through the public schools ("Now, Sarah, we don't hit Johnny!"). Nor is there any doubt that some of those maxims have been derived from the Judeo-Christian traditions of our majority culture. But morality is taught through modeling, explanation, dialogue, and discipline; it is a mystification of language and a misunderstanding of prayer to think that moral values are inculcated through the stupefied repetition of words. After all, in pre-World War II Germany, children from the ages of six through eighteen were all required to recite a prayer at the beginning of each school day, and the consequences were hardly morally auspicious.[15] There is a difference, too, between teaching generally accepted moral standards ("Now, Sarah . . ."), regardless of their religious origins, and invoking the rituals of the traditions from which those standards have been derived.

Be this as it may, at the heart of the religious objection to public prayer and Bible reading in public schools is a recognition of the sacral nature of ritual. The bottom line is that for those of us who revere ritual—whether it be the uttering of a prayer or the presentation of Scriptures—two factors determine its power: its context and its voluntariness.

Prayer may be equally meaningful in the middle of battle or the quiet of the sanctuary, but where it loses its power to touch and move and transform is in the rushed and raucous context of a public school classroom. In this venue prayer or Bible reading cannot help but be an afterthought or time-filler. As one teacher said of the Bible reading practice, "Most of the time the reading was droned out like the reading of a phone book."

Furthermore, prayer or Bible reading in the schools, unlike on the battlefield or in the sanctuary, is a prescribed, not a voluntary, exercise. Religious ritual depends for its meaning upon the willingness of its participants to receive the rite and the affectional posture in which they do so. To force religion on those not prepared for or receptive to it is to do both them and religion a disservice. As one of *The New Yorker's* "Talk of the Town" correspondents has said, "I have come to be embarrassed by prayer in general [because] I associate public prayer with dishonest preachers and cynical politicians . . . and with an unctuous, Nixonian tone of voice I would be glad never to hear again."[16] It is exactly because we so respect religious ritual and want it to be received in a context and spirit of respect, that many of us in religious leadership seek to keep it out of the public schools.

For these theological reasons, then, many religious leaders support the Court. And in more recent years an additional factor has come into play; for while in 1962, it might have been possible to convince ourselves of such a thing as a "nondenominational prayer" respecting all the households of faith represented in the United States—wrong though we would have been even then—that is surely not true today. With growing percentages of our population calling themselves Buddhists, with Islam an increasingly more powerful claimant on American religious fealty, and with Native American rituals spreading in influence, neither the Regents' Prayer nor reading from the Hebrew or Christian Scriptures can any longer be considered a religiously neutral expression. America is a far more religiously diverse nation than most of us have ever imagined.

One final word and a caveat.

Although I have argued here on both legal and religious grounds for the exclusion of religious ritual from the public schools, there remains, when all the arguing is through, one thing about which the Court's opponents are right. On some level, what they have sensed is a retreat on the part of our culture as a whole from a recognition of anything sacred or awe-inspiring and of the role that religion has played in shaping our history. While prayer and Bible reading are not the ways to address this deficit in our collective consciousness, the deficit itself is real enough.

When the Court's early decisions first came down, they were heralded by their supporters as providing an unparalleled opportunity for the schools, now liberated from the religiously banal, to get on with the business of teaching seriously about religion. The comments of legal scholar Paul Freund, writing in 1965, were typical:

> The school prayer decisions are more important for the doors they leave open than for those they shut. The study of religious traditions, training in moral analy-

sis, and the cultivation of sensibilities beyond the intellectual are all left open and beckoning.[17]

The problem is that almost thirty years later, they still beckon. Frightened by the Court's decisions, many publishers of American history textbooks, for example, have removed all reference to the religious motivations of the Puritans and the Pilgrims, Susan B. Anthony and Martin Luther King, Jr. The renowned church historian Martin Marty has observed that "in typical textbooks and curricula in high schools one can go for years and hear *no* references, none at all, to religion or Christianity."[18]

This is a patent absurdity and accounts in large measure for the religious illiteracy of the present generation of students. The Court never intended to proscribe teaching *about* religion. Indeed, in his majority opinion in *Schempp*, Mr. Justice Clark wrote explicitly:

> We do not agree . . . that this decision in any sense [creates a "religion of secularism"]. In addition, it might well be said that one's education is not complete without a study of comparative religion or the history of religion. . . . It certainly may be said that the Bible is worthy of study for its literary and historic qualities. Nothing we have said here indicates that such study of the Bible or religion, when presented objectively as part of a secular program of education, may not be effected consistent with the First Amendment.[19]

Fortunately this problem is now being addressed by such organizations as the Research Foundation of Americans United for the Separation of Church and State and the National Education Association which, along with twelve other organizations, have established principles for delineating the academic study of religion from the devotional.[20]

For those of us who do care about prayer, Scripture, and religion, the challenge, then, is clear: to encourage in our public schools the cultivation of religious sensibilities without violating religious freedom; to respect both the Constitution and the impact of religion upon America. To dishonor either would be tragic. Tragic and entirely unnecessary.

NOTES

1. David E. Engel, ed., *Religion in Public Education* (New York: Paulist Press, 1974), p. 15.

2. Ibid., p. 19.

3. Ibid, pp. 12–19.

4. "Emerging Trends," Princeton Religion Research Center, 10, no. 1 (January 1988): 5.

5. *Wallace* v. *Jaffree*, 105 S. Ct. 2479 (1985), p. 2480.

6. Robert F. Drinan, "Those Moments of Silence," *America*, October 6, 1984, p. 185.

7. *Wallace* v. *Jaffree*, pp. 2480–81.

8. This despite the claim of theologians like Paul Tillich that all persons are religious to the extent that they are preoccupied with matters of "ultimate concern."

9. Garry Wills, *Under God: Religion and American Politics* (New York: Simon and Schuster, 1990), p. 376.

10. Ibid., p. 379.

11. Donald W. Shriver, Jr., "A Religious Argument Against School Prayer," *USA Today*, May 1984, p. 60.

12. "Our system," Mann wrote, "earnestly inculcates all the Christian morals; it founds its morals on the basis of religion; [and] it welcomes the religion of the Bible. . . ." Horace Mann, *Twelfth Annual Report of the Board of Education* [of Massachusetts], (Boston: Dutton and Wentworth, 1846), pp. 116–17.

13. Arlene and Howard Eisenberg, "Why Clergymen are Against School Prayer," *Redbook*, January 1965, p. 35.

14. As an eminent Baptist put it: "They [supporters of school prayer] sloganeer with things like 'Let's put God back into the schools' as though the Almighty were some kind of pencil sharpener. . . . The God who brought the Hebrew people through the Red Sea and the God who raised Jesus Christ from the dead is not subject to government action of any kind." Ibid., p. 98.

15. Ibid., p. 97.

16. In Martin Marty, "Context," *The New Yorker* 23, no. 3 (February 1, 1991): 1.

17. Paul A. Freund, *Religion and the Public Schools* (Cambridge, Mass.: Harvard University Press, 1965), p. 23.

18. Marty, "Context," p. 2.

19. Engel, *Religion in Public Education*, p. 18.

20. See, for example, "Religion in the Public School Curriculum," a pamphlet published by the American Academy of Religion and thirteen other organizations.

8

From Equal Access to Distribution of Religious Materials

August W. Steinhilber

The Equal Access Act became law on August 11, 1984 (20 U.S.C. 4071-74). Succinctly stated, this law provides that if a public secondary school permits any noncurriculum-related student group to meet during noninstructional time, then it must permit all student groups to meet during noninstructional time regardless of religious, political, or philosophical persuasion. (Please note that the previous sentence was precisely constructed and the words chosen carefully: the law's coverage of secondary schools does not extend to elementary schools; if all groups are curriculum-related the Act does not apply; the meetings must be student-initiated; and the Act applies only to noninstructional time. What a school does during instructional time is its own concern.[1])

Many religious groups, however, have never considered the Equal Access Act anything more than a stepping stone to their real goal—namely, an opportunity to proselytize or evangelize those children in school who are not of their religious persuasion. Soon after the U.S. Supreme Court ruled the Equal Access Act constitutional in *Westside Community Board of Education* v. *Mergens*, 110 S. Ct. 2356 (1990), those of us in public education began seeing the publication *A Field for the Harvest*, produced by Christian Advocates Serving Evangelism (CASE). The pamphlet declares: "God has opened a huge mission field. Our missionaries to this field must be our high school students."

August W. Steinhilber is General Counsel of the National School Boards Association.

114

It must be emphasized at this juncture that the opinion of the U.S. Supreme Court in the *Mergens* case was relatively narrow in that it held the Equal Access Act to be constitutional, and then defined what was required of school districts under the Act. The court did *not* announce or proclaim any new constitutional rights for students as has been suggested by some of the pamphlet's writers.

Furthermore, the pamphlet declares: "Students have the right to pass out Christian papers and tracts to their peers on campus. As long as the students do not disrupt school discipline, school officials must allow them to be student evangelists." Another publication, *First Amendment Guidelines for Public Schools*, written for Student Action for Christ, Inc., proclaims: "Can students distribute religious literature at school? Yes!"

It was not long thereafter that school officials began seeing students distributing Christian pamphlets such as *Issues and Answers*. Attempts to restrict the distribution of religious and other materials have been met with legal action, some claiming that the students involved believed it to be part of their spiritual duties to propagate the Gospel of Jesus Christ by distributing religious materials during school hours on school property. Thus, the argument is made by student representatives that the denial of the opportunity to evangelize is a denial of their free exercise rights under the First Amendment. They contend that the Constitution's only restriction on barring the distribution of religious materials in school is contained in the establishment clause of the First Amendment, which restricts only the government, not individuals, from distributing religious material.

The school district will be confronted with a myriad of legal arguments by religious groups and their legal defense funds. School boards must be prepared to handle each of their arguments:

- The state cannot constitutionally restrict speech on the basis of the content of that speech. Furthermore, the constitutional prohibition is especially true if the speech in question is a religious speech and thus, covered by the free exercise clause of the First Amendment.

- Religious speech may not be censored simply because some individual may find it offensive, object to the speech, or wish to disrupt it. Constitutionally protected freedom of speech is designed to protect against such objections.

- The appeal to fairness and equal treatment, while not a constitutional argument, is an appeal to be reasonable. Often, those who wish to distribute religious material invoke the Equal Access Act and the *Mergens* decision even though neither applies specifically to the distribution of religious material.

- The government sends a discriminatory message whenever religious groups are restricted, the inference being that nonreligious speech enjoys a higher degree of protection than religious speech. The message sent to students, therefore, is that the government is antireligious.

- The establishment clause applies only to restrictions of government speech and does not restrict private speech. The distribution of religious material, being an exercise of private speech, is, thus, protected by the free exercise clause. No government coercion is involved; the private distribution of religious materials lies outside of the scope of the establishment clause.

- Even if a school district has the right to restrict speech, using the time, place, and manner concepts embodied in the cases involving First Amendment constitutional law, the government can restrict speech only in the least restrictive manner; therefore, students have the absolute right to distribute material in common meeting places.

- School board policies on time, place, and manner restrictions applying on all material will be attacked as overly broad because students always pass notes and other materials among themselves. (This is a point well taken, which will be discussed in this essay.)

What can a school board do under these circumstances? Despite these arguments, however, school districts may restrict the distribution of religious materials in schools, provided they do so properly. Since religious discussion and worship are forms of speech and association, school boards must first look to what restrictions on free speech are permitted under the First Amendment.[2]

According to the U.S. Supreme Court in *Cornelius* v. *NAACP Legal Defense and Education Fund*, 473 U.S. 788, 799 (1985), "protected speech is not equally permissible in all places and at all times." The courts have drawn distinctions on whether the place in question is a public forum (e.g., a street or park), a limited public forum, or a nonpublic forum. While the state may not prohibit all communication activities, it can, however, restrict certain content-based expression provided there is a compelling state interest and the restriction is narrowly drawn.[3] This standard is, indeed, high and, fortunately, schools have not been deemed public forums. They are either limited public forums or nonpublic forums.

Again, it must be emphasized that the constitutional basis for restricting speech has nothing to do with the Equal Access Act and the U.S. Supreme Court opinion in *Westside Community Board of Education* v. *Mergens*. The majority opinion specifically stated that the Court was not deciding the case on the basis of the free speech and free exercise clauses. The Act does not grant students the right to distribute religious material.

Returning to the constitutional issue, the state may open public property in whole or in part and, if it does open the property, it need not do so indefinitely. Moreover, that open portion can still be restrictive on the time, place, and manner; the protected speech may be curtailed as long as those restrictions are content-neutral. In addition, the government, in a limited public forum, can confirm the activity within the forum to that which is compatible with the intended use.[4] Furthermore, in a nonpublic forum, the state may exclude all speech; control the subject matter of speech, as long as it is not viewpoint-biased; or limit the activity that is compatible with the intended use.

Clearly, advocates for religious groups will contend that schools are limited public forums—an argument that may have some validity in some secondary schools, but one with little, if any, validity in elementary schools. Thus, there can be a total ban on the distribution of religious materials at the elementary school level and a similar ban in those secondary schools that do not provide a limited open forum. Even if a school were to be determined under specific circumstances to be a limited open forum under the constitutional criteria used in *Widmar* v. *Vincent*, 454 U.S. 263, not those criteria established by the Equal Access Act, certain communications can still be banned *in toto*, such as:

- indecent, vulgar, or lewd material or obscenity using the standard of minors, not adults
- libelous material
- material that invades the privacy of others
- material that promotes unhealthy activities
- material that promotes illegal activities for minors
- material that infringes upon someone's copyright
- advertising or commercial material
- all materials from nonstudent-sponsored organizations.

Materials not covered by this in the list can be restricted in other ways. First and foremost is the restriction commonly referred to in constitutional law as *time, place, and manner*.

Students normally pass notes or other information to other students. Any restriction on *time, place, or manner* should not be placed on distribution of six or fewer copies. Beyond that number, a school district can:

- require that a student notify the principal in advance of his or her intent to distribute material and have the material reviewed to make sure that it is not contrary to any of the written restrictions;

- prohibit distribution in hallways because of its adverse effect on maintaining order, since it could result in a roadblock restricting the free flow of student movement;

- limit the time of day and the number of days that materials can be distributed;

- require that all materials from all organizations be placed on specific tables in specific rooms;

- hold students responsible for cleaning up materials left on the floor and on the table; and

- require that the distribution be in an orderly manner and not coercive.

NOTES

1. For a more complete description of the law, the reader is referred to *The Equal Access Act and the Public Schools—Questions and Answers*, published by the Americans United Research Foundation in 1991.

2. *Widmar* v. *Vincent* 454 U.S. 263 (1981).

3. *Perry Education Association* v. *Perry Local Educators' Assn.*, 460 U.S. 37 (1983).

4. *Cornelius* v. *NAACP Legal Defense and Education Fund*, 473 U.S. 788 (1985).

9

The Battle over "Secular Humanism" in the Public Schools

James E. Wood, Jr.

For more than two decades, the public schools of America have largely come to be perceived by the New Religious Right as dominated by "secular humanism." Writing more than a decade ago, United States Senator Jesse Helms of North Carolina expressed a view that is still widely shared: "When the U.S. Supreme Court prohibited children from participating in voluntary prayers in public schools, the conclusion is inescapable that the Supreme Court not only violated the right of free exercise of religion of all America; it also established a national religion in the United States—the religion of secular humanism."[1]

In the seventies and eighties, "secular humanism" gradually became a code word for all the evils in American society, largely replacing "communism" as the greatest threat facing America and its democratic institutions in the fifties and sixties. "Godless communists" and "their fellow travelers" of only a few decades ago were now labeled "secular humanists." In the words of Tim LaHaye, one of the founders in 1979 of the now-defunct Moral Majority, "secular humanism" is "the world's greatest evil."[2]

In a series of widely distributed books on "secular humanism," LaHaye charged that most of the evils in the world today can be traced to "secular humanism," which he saw as having taken over the government, the media,

James E. Wood, Jr., is Director of the J. M. Dawson Institute of Church-State Studies at Baylor University.

and education in America.[3] Similarly, Pat Robertson contended that "secular humanists" have stolen the government, the courts, and the public schools from America's God-fearing majority, and it is up to Christians to win back these institutions.[4] The allegedly pervasive influence of "secular humanism" was seen by its foes as constituting a new form of religious establishment.[5]

I

Without defining "secular humanism," the New Religious Right perceives it as being widespread throughout American society. The focus of the movement's crusade against "secularism humanism" is directed at the public schools.[6] That is where, it is charged, the "immoral indoctrination" of impressionable minds is occurring. The charge is twofold: contrary to the United States Supreme Court decisions on religion and the public schools, the public schools are teaching a religion to children that is antithetical to "Judeo-Christian values"; and the religion being taught is "secular humanism." To its adversaries, "secular humanism" embodies anti-moral and anti-Christian ideas that undergird the liberal educational and political philosophy that has come to control America in recent decades.[7] Opposition to "secular humanism" in the public schools has expressed itself in censorship of public school textbooks; objection to the teaching of evolution; and widespread disapproval of various courses in the public school curriculum, particularly in social studies. "Secular humanism" is blamed for progressive education, the exclusion of religion from the public schools, the decline of ethical and moral values, sexual promiscuity, the rise of drug abuse, and the waning of respect for authority.[8]

Special blame for the triumph of "secular humanism" is placed on the United States Supreme Court. In the words of Pat Robertson, the Court's decisions on religion and the public schools made "atheism the only acceptable religion for America's schoolchildren."[9] Charging that the public schools have suffered "an inculturation of values totally contrary to the Judeo-Christian tradition," Robertson singled out the public schools as being "so fallen that they have become jungles."[10] Almost a decade ago, he predicted that in the next twenty years all schools in America would be private.[11] In his book *The Battle for the Public Schools,* LaHaye charged that "public schools have become conduits to the minds of our youth, training them to be anti-God, anti-moral, anti-family, anti-free enterprise, and anti-American." "Public education," he wrote, "is controlled by elitists with an atheistic, humanistic viewpoint."[12] In a similar vein, Jimmy Swaggart declared, "The public school system, gutted by secular humanism, is literally attacking the home, the family, the structure of this country."[13] "I don't have any good words about the public school system. If it weren't for the Christian school system, this country would have gone to Hell in a handbasket."[14] The charge is repeatedly made that the Supreme Court's decisions outlawing public school-sponsored religious education classes, prayer, and devotional Bible reading officially established "secular humanism" in the public schools. Thereby, it is said, the Supreme Court joined atheists and agnostics in considering traditional religion irrelevant. "Secular humanism" is perceived to be the established religion of the public schools, which some have called "government seminaries of secular humanism."[15]

In recent years, most of the battles over public school textbooks, often resulting in the adoption of strict guidelines of censorship, have centered on the broad charge of the incorporation in these books of the teachings of "secular humanism."[16] By and large the courts have not been willing to uphold parental grievances against the public school curriculum and public school textbooks. In 1975, in one of the most widely publicized censorship cases, a West Virginia federal district court rejected the charges of some parents that a series of English textbooks undermined their religious beliefs and established the religion of "secular humanism" in the public schools. The district court ruled that it would take "a complete loosening of the imagination" to conclude that the inclusion of allegedly godless and profane books in the public schools constitutes an establishment of the religion of "secular humanism."[17] The West Virginia decision was consistent with a New York case some years earlier, in which that court denied the appeal of parents to ban certain classics in English literature (e.g., *Oliver Twist* by Charles Dickens and the *Merchant of Venice* by William Shakespeare) that were found to be offensive on religious grounds.[18] Similarly, the Michigan Appellate Court ruled against curriculum grievances based upon the religious views of the plaintiffs.[19]

In the 1980s, legislation was introduced in several states to disallow those subjects in the public school curriculum that were viewed to be incompatible with basic Christian teachings.[20] On the local level, book banning and book censorship took place in public schools throughout the country. This nationwide movement has been led and supported by a variety of organizations, such as Pat Robertson's National Legal Foundation, the National Association of Christian Educators, Phyllis Schlafly's Eagle Forum, and Beverly LaHaye's Concerned Women for America. In Lake City, Florida, the school board removed Geoffrey Chaucer's "The Miller's Tale" and Aristophanes' *Lysistrata* from the high school curriculum; in Newport News, Virginia, Alice Walker's Pulitzer Prize-winning novel, *The Color Purple,* was removed from a high school library because of its "objectionable language"; in Omaha, Nebraska, the showing of a film version of Shakespeare's *Romeo and Juliet* was canceled because parents complained that the play "romanticizes teenage suicide"; and in South Umpqua, Oregon, the school board rejected a seventh-grade textbook, *Introduction to Social Science,* after a Christian group alleged that it contained "concepts that are controversial and inappropriate."

The alleged establishment of "secular humanism" in the public schools is seen not only as antithetical to Judeo-Christian values but also as a violation of the establishment and free exercise clauses of the First Amendment. In pursuing this argument, however, the New Religious Right finds itself in an incongruous position: while raising objections regarding government neutrality toward religion and church-state separation in the matter of "secular humanism," it is not willing to apply this principle of separation to the inculcation of Judeo-Christian teachings and values in the public schools. If the establishment clause prohibits the teaching of the "religion of secular humanism," must it not also prohibit the teaching of the tenets and values of Christianity? Ironically, the claim that the teaching of "the religion of secular humanism" in the public schools violates the rulings of the U.S. Supreme Court on the establishment clause is generally made by those very antagonists who are most prone to deplore the Court's decisions themselves.

In the past, litigation directed against the public schools has been based primarily on specific issues, whereas now there is evidence of a much broader effort being made to challenge the entire public school curriculum. On the one hand, considerable effort is being given to the support of the Christian day school movement throughout the country and, on the other, attempts are being made to compel the public school curriculum to accommodate the fundamentalist beliefs of parents of pupils in the public schools. The charge that "secular humanism" is the religion taught in the public schools is deeply rooted in the notion that public school neutrality toward particular religious faiths or traditions constitutes the teaching of "secular humanism" as a philosophical worldview. The very term "secular humanism" has come to be identified by the New Religious Right with everything taught in public education that does not reenforce its own religious biases and beliefs. The assumption is that, since public school teachers may not teach courses such as biology, history, government, or English from a religious (e.g., Christian, Jewish, Muslim, or Buddhist) point of view, public school educators are inevitably engaged, whether consciously or not, in espousing a philosophy of secularism in which moral and religious values are trivialized and/or denied.[20]

II

For more than half a century, a campaign has been waged to prohibit, or at least to restrict, the teaching of evolution. During the twenties, anti-evolutionary bills were introduced in numerous state legislatures, including statutes outlawing the use of "evolutionary" textbooks, although the vast majority of these were either never passed or, as in Oklahoma, repealed. In the *Scopes* trial of 1925, biology teacher John Scopes met with defeat when he challenged Tennessee's law prohibiting the teaching of evolution. The United States Supreme Court's unanimous decision in *Epperson* v. *Arkansas* in 1968, however, clearly invalidated state laws prohibiting the teaching of evolution in the public schools.[22] In its decision, the Court declared, "There can be no doubt that Arkansas sought to prevent its teachers from discussing the theory of evolution because it is contrary to the belief of some that the Book of Genesis must be the exclusive source of doctrine as to the origin of man. . . . It is clear that fundamentalist sectarian conviction was and is the law's reason for existence."[23] Faced with the Supreme Court's ruling that legislation aimed at prohibiting the teaching of evolution in the public schools is unconstitutional, anti-evolutionists adopted a new tactic in the 1970s. Their purpose was no longer to promote anti-evolution legislation, which they now recognized as hopeless, but rather to argue for the inclusion of "scientific creationism" along with evolution in the public school curriculum. The strategy thus shifted from efforts aimed at prohibiting the teaching of evolution in the public schools to one of advocacy for the teaching of "scientific creationism" (in effect, the Genesis account of creation). Thus, for creationists, the strategy became one of demand for "equal time" rather than for substituting the Genesis account of creation for evolution.

After the *Epperson* decision, legislation mandating the teaching of "scientific creationism" on an equal basis with evolution was introduced in more than twenty states, including Arkansas, California, Colorado, Florida, Georgia, Illinois, Indiana, Iowa, Louisiana, Maryland, Michigan, Mississippi, South Carolina, and Texas.[24] Following the national swing to the right in the 1980 elections and with strong support by the New Religious Right, local school districts, as well as state legislatures, were under considerable pressure to enforce the teaching of "scientific creationism" in the public schools.

Arkansas became the first state, in March 1981, to enact an equal time bill into law, followed four months later by Louisiana, which enacted an almost identical law. The Mississippi senate, minutes after it convened, overwhelmingly voted to enact a similar law within hours after the Arkansas "creation science" law was struck down by United States District Judge William R. Overton, who ruled that it violated the establishment clause.[25]

Despite well-organized local and state efforts and well-orchestrated legislative proposals, "scientific creationism" met with resistance from some education agencies and particularly in the courts. In 1975, a Tennessee law mandating the inclusion of theories of creation in textbooks dealing with origins of man and the world was declared unconstitutional by the Sixth Circuit Court of Appeals.[26] Following the action in 1975 by the Indiana Commission on Textbook Adoption approving a creationist biology textbook, a state court ruled that the commission's action "both advanced particular religious preferences and entangled the state with religion," and therefore violated both the state and federal constitutions.[27] In California, a judge denied the claims of creationists that evolution was taught dogmatically and that its inclusion in the curriculum constituted an infringement of the free exercise of religion rights under the Constitution.[28]

Following passage of an equal-time creation bill in Louisiana in 1981, the State Department of Education and the Board of Elementary and Secondary Education delayed implementation of the act until an appropriate court with jurisdiction could rule on its constitutionality, since the commission indicated that it believed the act violated both the establishment and the free exercise clauses of the federal Constitution. The commission's action was later sustained by a federal district court's ruling.[29] In Maine, "scientific creationism" was ruled unconstitutional by the Commissioner of Education. A Maryland House committee overwhelmingly defeated a bill requiring the teaching of "scientific creationism" in the public schools. In Minnesota, a senate bill requiring the teaching of creationism alongside the "theory" of evolution was defeated by the Committee on Education. A resolution opposing the teaching of creationism in the public schools was also passed by the Michigan State Board of Education.

The creationist movement suffered its greatest setback, however, in June 1987, when the United States Supreme Court, in *Edwards* v. *Aguillard,* struck down by a vote of seven to two the Louisiana law.[30] "A government intention to promote religion is clear," the Court opined, "when the State enacts a law to serve a religious purpose. This intention may be evidenced by promotion of religion in general . . . or by advancement of a particular religious belief." In fact, the Court concluded, "The preeminent purpose of the Louisiana legislature was clearly to advance the religious viewpoint that a supernatural being created humankind" and to provide persuasive advantage to a particular religious doctrine that rejects the factual basis of evolution in its entirety. The Court found "creation science" to be a term embracing a particular religious doctrine held also by those responsible for the legislation.

According to the Court, the law was further flawed because it "does not serve to protect academic freedom, but has the distinctly different purpose of discrediting evolution by counterbalancing its teaching at every turn with the teaching of creation science." Thus, fairness was not advanced, the Court noted, since the Act clearly provided for discriminatory preference for the teaching of "creation science" and against the teaching of evolution. While school boards were prohibited from discriminating against anyone's choosing to be a "creation scientist" or teaching "creationism," no similar protection was provided for those choosing to teach evolution or some other non-creation science theory or who simply refused to teach "creation science."

In Louisiana, as elsewhere, the argument for legislation mandating the teaching of "creation science" in the public schools has been based on academic freedom, since it proposes to offer an alternative view to the theory of evolution. In *Aguillard,* the Court categorically rejected the argument as being without merit. "The Act actually serves to diminish academic freedom," the Court said, "by removing the flexibility to teach evolution without also teaching creation science, even if teachers determine that such curriculum results in less effective and comprehensive science instruction." Teaching a variety of scientific theories about the origins of humankind, the Court reasoned, might be valid where there is a clear secular intent, but the primary purpose of the Louisiana law is to advance a particular religious belief and, in so doing, it "seeks to employ the symbolic and financial support of government to achieve a religious purpose."

The Court noted that for some decades it had been particularly vigilant in reviewing compliance with the establishment clause in elementary and secondary schools. Quoting Justice Felix Frankfurter in the case of *McCollum* v. *Board of Education* over forty years ago, which denied the constitutionality of providing religious education classes in the public schools, the Court noted that it has done so because "the public school is at once the symbol of our democracy and the most pervasive means for promoting our common destiny. In no activity of the State is it more vital to keep out divisive forces than in its schools."[31]

Writing in dissent for himself and Chief Justice William A. Rehnquist, Justice Antonin Scalia charged that there is "ample evidence that the majority is wrong" in this decision. According to Justice Scalia, the Louisiana statute was designed to protect academic freedom by ensuring that "students would be free to decide for themselves how life began, based upon faith and balanced presentation of scientific evidence." In concluding his dissent, Justice Scalia went a step further by calling into question the validity of the "secular purpose" test and urging its abandonment.[32]

The *Aguillard* decision was praised by a wide range of organizations of civil libertarians, educators, scientists, and religious groups, including the American Civil Liberties Union, Americans United, the American Jewish Committee, the National Association of State School Boards, the National Council of Churches, the National Education Association, the National Science Teachers Association, the National Association of Secondary School Principals, and the Committee for Public Education and Religious Liberty (PEARL). The ruling was deplored by a variety of conservative organizations and religious groups, among them Concerned Women for America, the National Association of Evangelicals, the Rabbinical Alliance of America, the Catholic Center, and the Free Methodist Church of North America.

The *Aguillard* decision has far-reaching implications, by affirming, in effect, that the public school curriculum is not to be used for the advancement of religious ideas or to be tailored to the religious beliefs of parents. The decision also gives support to the right of the public schools to include secular concepts and ideas in the curriculum, even if they are in conflict with some religious beliefs.

Meanwhile, "creation science" or "scientific creationism" continues to vie for classroom legitimacy and time in the public schools, but since the *Aguillard* decision, greater resistance to this pressure has come from those involved with public education and the courts. During the past year, in response to attempts to mandate the teaching of creationism as a science, the Curriculum Development Commission of the California Board of Education stated that creationism does not belong in science classes and recommended that the board not purchase any textbooks that put forth any theories concerning origins which are not based on factual evidence. The California Curriculum Committee ruled that theories of creation could be taught in social studies and in English literature courses, but not in science classes. In Texas, the State Board of Education voted in November 1990 to adopt eleven general science and biology textbooks which emphasize evolution in biological science and avoid discussion of creationism or other alternatives to standard scientific theories of origins. In the same month, the Seventh United States Circuit Court of Appeals upheld a lower court's ruling that teaching "creation science" amounts to teaching religion and that the school district in New Lenox, Illinois, has the right to prohibit a social studies teacher from teaching "scientific creationism" who based his claim to do so on "academic freedom."[33]

III

In August 1987, the New Religious Right suffered another setback in the battle over "secular humanism" in the public schools; the United States Court of Appeals for the Sixth Circuit, in *Mozert* v. *Hawkins County Board of the Education,* overturned a lower court decision which held that the Hawkins County, Tennessee, public schools had violated the Constitution by requiring fundamentalist Christian children to use textbooks that offended their religious beliefs.[34] The reading of such textbooks, the circuit court reasoned, is appropriate since the students are not obligated, let alone required, to accept or deny any religious beliefs to be found in the readings. The three-judge appellate court also rescinded District Judge Thomas G. Hull's order that the public schools pay private school tuition and other costs to the parents as a result of the students' expulsion for refusing to use the textbooks assigned them. The parents had charged that the public school textbooks, namely the Holt Reader Series, promoted "anti-Christian" themes, including feminism, humanism, pacifism, the equality of all religions, and "one-world government."

The three-judge panel ruled that to find certain concepts or ideas in public schools textbooks to be objectionable is not in and of itself an infringement of a constitutional right such as is embodied in the free exercise clause. In the *Mozert* case, the circuit court found that the district court erred in applying the decision made by the United States Supreme Court in *Sherbert* v. *Verner*[35] and *Thomas* v. *Review Board of Indiana Employment Security Division*,[36] since in each of those cases the burden on the plaintiff's free exercise of religion consisted of "being required to perform an act which violated the plaintiff's religious convictions or forego benefits." Quoting the United States Supreme Court in *Bowen* v. *Roy*,[37] the three-judge panel in *Mozert* noted: "The free exercise clause affords an individual protection from certain forms of governmental compulsion; it does not afford an individual a right to dictate the conduct of the Government's internal procedure." "What we do hold," the Court said, "is that the requirement that public school students study a basal reader series does not create an unconstitutional burden under the free exercise clause when the students are not required to affirm or deny a belief or engage or refrain from engaging in a practice prohibited or required by their religion."[38]

The appeals court made a distinction between a public school's requiring children to take part in a religious ritual, saluting the flag, or requiring students to affirm or deny a religious belief and requiring them to read and listen to differing views and discuss them. The court found "no evidence that the conduct required of the students was forbidden by their religion. . . . There was no proof that any plaintiff student was ever called upon to say or do anything that required the student to affirm or deny a religious belief or to engage in or refrain from engaging in any act either required or forbidden by the student's religious convictions." While witnesses testified that the textbooks "could" or "might" lead the students to come to conclusions that were contrary to the parents' religious beliefs, the court found that this was "not sufficient to establish an unconstitutional burden."

There is some justification in arguing that the primary issue in the Tennessee case was not so much one of religion as it was one of tolerance and the integrity of public education. One of the plaintiffs, Vicki Frost, specifically stated that she objected to readings that develop "a religious tolerance." "We cannot be tolerant in that we accept other religious views on an equal basis with ours." In citing a 1986 Supreme Court decision that public schools serve the purpose of teaching fundamental values "essential to a democratic society," which "include tolerance of divergent political and religious views,"[39] the court of appeals acknowledged that tolerance of religious views, as referred to by the Supreme Court, is "a *civil* tolerance, not a religious one."

As Circuit Judge Danny J. Boggs aptly noted in his concurring opinion, there is an important difference to be noted between "teaching civil toleration of other religions, and teaching religious tolerations of other religions." Both religion clauses of the First Amendment are to ensure the equality of all religions before the law; i.e., all religions are to enjoy the same civil and political rights and, therefore, the state may *not* advance the view that all religions are but different paths to God or ultimate truth. At no time, however, was it found that the Hawkins County public schools advocated or sought to impose the viewpoint that "all religions are merely different roads to God," as the plaintiffs charged was implied in some of the reading selections in the Holt Reader Series.[40]

Religious objections per se to public school textbooks cannot be made the basis of a violation of the establishment clause. The circuit court cited Justice Robert H. Jackson's concurring opinion in *McCollum*, in which Justice Jackson declared, "If we are to eliminate everything that is objectionable to any of these warring sects or inconsistent with any of their doctrines, we will leave public education in shreds. Nothing but educational confusion and a discrediting of the public school system can result from subjecting it to constant lawsuits."[41] The court summarily dismissed the idea that the textbooks were anti-religious or that students should be protected from information and views which they or their parents may find contrary to their own religious beliefs. Education requires exposing students to ideas and information that may well lie beyond the sheltered world from which they may come, since education by its very nature involves exploration of knowledge and preparation for living in a free and pluralistic society.

In a concurring opinion, Judge Cornelia G. Kennedy observed that a "principal educational objective is to teach the students how to think critically about complex and controversial subjects." This, Judge Kennedy maintained, is essential preparation for citizenship. Indeed, Kennedy wrote, the state has a compelling interest in seeing that parents not be allowed to pull their children out of these discussions in the public schools simply because the parents hold differing views, for public schools serve as a great integrative force in a highly heterogeneous society.

The court reasoned that government actions which merely offend or cast doubt on religious beliefs are not in themselves in violation of the establishment clause. Rather, the state may not advocate a religious or anti-religious viewpoint. Furthermore, "an actual burden on the profession or exercise of religion is required." Here, again, the court drew a distinction between those actions that may require or result in exposure to ideas that are at odds with one's own religious beliefs and those governmental actions that actually interfere with the free exercise of religion.

IV

Still another major defeat for the New Religious Right in the battle over "secular humanism" in the public schools came on August 26, 1987, in *Smith v. Mobile County Board of School Commissioners,* in which a three-judge panel of the United Court of Appeals for the Eleventh Circuit unanimously reversed United States District Judge W. Brevard Hand's ruling of March 1987 banning forty-four textbooks allegedly promoting the "religion of secular humanism"[42] from public schools in Mobile County, Alabama. At issue in this case was the effort by parents to force the public school curriculum to conform to their own religious views.[43] The plaintiffs, supported by Pat Robertson's National Legal Foundation, alleged that "secular humanism" is a religion and that teaching it in the public schools breaches the First Amendment. While strongly supported by many religious fundamentalists, Judge Hand's decision was widely deplored by civil libertarians and educators alike, as being not only a blow to religious liberty but also "in fact a blow for ignorance."

The appellate court declared that Judge Hand had erred in his controversial ruling that the history, home economics, and social studies textbooks were in violation of the First Amendment ban on government establishment of religion. There was no question, the court said, that the purpose behind using the textbooks under attack was clearly secular, not religious, and that there was no evidence of excessive government entanglement with religion in this case. Therefore, the court centered on the test of primary effect, i.e., whether the use of the textbooks in question had the primary effect of either advancing or inhibiting religion. The appeals court had suspended the book ban shortly after Judge Hand's decision of March 4, 1987, while the appeal process was under way.

In ruling in favor of the Mobile County Board of Education and against the 624 fundamentalist Christian parents, the court went out of its way to explain its application of the test of "primary effect," as enunciated by the United States Supreme Court, and to affirm that the subject in question (i.e., the textbooks under review) "neither advances nor inhibits religion." Upon examination of the contents of these textbooks, including the passages charged with being offensive, the court found that "the message conveyed is not one of endorsement of secular humanism or any religion . . . nor do these textbooks evidence an attitude antagonistic to theistic belief." Rather than advancing or inhibiting religion, the court concluded that the use of the textbooks conveys information that is essentially neutral in religious context to the school-children who utilize the books.[44]

Quoting from the United States Supreme Court *McCollum* decision barring setting aside a portion of each day for religious instruction by representatives of various faiths, the appeals panel noted that " 'the place of religion in our society is an exalted one, achieved through a long tradition of reliance on the home, the church, and the inviolable citadel of the individual heart and mind,' and not hostility towards religion."[45] Neutrality toward religion is not to be equated with hostility, the court declared. Unfortunately, the court charged, District Judge Hand had construed the constitutional mandate of government neutrality on religion "into an affirmative obligation to speak about religion." Nor has the "omission of certain facts regarding religion from these textbooks of itself constituted an advancement of secular humanism or an active hostility towards theistic religion," both of which are prohibited by the First Amendment.

The fact that the appellees found some of the material in these textbooks offensive is also "not sufficient to render use of this material in the public schools a violation of the establishment clause." Given the diversity of religion in this country, if the criterion were merely one of incompatibility with the beliefs of a particular community of faith there would be very little that could be taught in the public schools. The court also made clear that it was not ruling on the educational adequacy of the textbooks themselves, since "the wisdom of an educational policy or its efficiency from an educational point of view is not germane to the constitutional issue of whether that policy violates the establishment clause."[46]

V

The response of the plaintiffs in both the *Mozert* and *Smith* cases was that they would appeal the circuit court decisions all the way to the United States Supreme Court. The *Mozert* case was appealed, but the Supreme Court refused to review the appellate decision; the Court did so without comment and without recorded dissent. The plaintiffs in *Smith* later decided not to appeal the circuit court's decision to the Supreme Court because they feared that the Court would not hear it. In all three cases cited here relating to the battle over "secular humanism" in the public schools, the central issue was religious censorship of public school textbooks. As stated earlier, there is nothing new about censorship. It has a long history and has frequently cropped up in the United States, aimed particularly at books in public libraries and public schools. The present censorship movement, however, which is primarily aimed at the public schools, holds a twofold significance that warrants special concern. First, there is the phenomenal rise in the incidents of attempted censorship of public school textbooks during the past two decades, and second, there has been a shift away from a focus on a particular book or literary work to a broad assault on the public school curriculum.

Today, few would question that censorship of public school textbooks is on the rise, and has, indeed, become a national problem. Recently, Arthur Kropp, president of People for the American Way, reported that there is an explosion of censorship created by religious bigotry, specifically aimed at removing certain textbooks from the public school curriculum. One recent study of the 1986–1987 academic year reported 156 censorship incidents, constituting a 22 percent increase over the previous year.[47] Reports of organized efforts by parents and organizations to censor public school textbooks have become commonplace throughout the country. Another recent study has documented a 160 percent increase in incidents of censorship during the past five years.[48] At least half of these incidents are reported to be aimed not at single books or specific library materials, but at a broader agenda involving not only individual courses but also virtually the entire curriculum of the public schools. In the 1989–1990 school year, some 244 incidents took place, while in the preceding year only 172 efforts were made to withdraw public school texts from classroom use.[49]

Many local groups of parents, encouraged and supported by outside organizations such as Pat Robertson's National Legal Foundation, Mel and Norma Gabler's Educational Research Analysts, Phyllis Schlafly's Eagle Forum, Beverly LaHaye's Concerned Women for America, the California-based Traditional Values Coalition, the Christian Educators Association International (CEAI), the National Christian Educators Association (NACE), and Citizens for Excellence in Education (CEE), are pressuring school boards and state legislatures to adopt restrictive measures for the selection of public school textbooks and the development of the public school curriculum. Failure to accomplish censorship through these measures is met with threats of legal suits against public school administrators, teachers, and school boards. All of these groups seek, in effect, to introduce sectarian religion into the public school classroom.

Robert L. Simonds, who founded both the NACE and the CEE in 1983, has asserted in written statements that his goal was to encourage fundamentalist teachers and school administrators to "take dominion" over the public schools.[50] The former (NACE) encourages teachers to "model what they believe" and to "emphasize moral and spiritual values" in their instruction, while the latter (CEE) encourages the formation of groups to promote fundamentalist Christians as school board candidates.

The recent wave of censorship of public school textbooks is primarily directed at imposing a sectarian Christian viewpoint on the public schools and wresting them from the concept of the secular public school. In the words of Mel and Norma Gabler, who have waged campaigns on censorship of public school textbooks throughout the country as well as in their home state of Texas, "acceptable textbooks should be passed on high morality, fixed values, Christian concepts, and a proper portrayal of our nation's great heritage."[51] Similarly, CEE's stated goals are "to bring public education back under the control of Christians" and "to change the atheist-dominated ideology of secular humanism in our schools' texts, curriculum, and teachers' unions."[52]

Government neutrality toward religion in the public schools has come to be viewed by many as government hostility toward religion. In a series of decisions bearing on religion and the public schools, the United States Supreme Court has frequently addressed this issue, but for many the assurances of the Court have been of no avail. Over forty years ago in the *McCollum* case, the Court went out of its way to make the point as follows: "To hold that a state cannot consistently with the First and Fourteenth Amendments utilize its public school system to aid any or all religious faiths or sects in the dissemination of their doctrines and ideas does not . . . manifest a government hostility to religion or religious teachings. A manifestation of such hostility would be at war with our national tradition as embodied in the First Amendment's guaranty of the free exercise of religion."[53]

The assault on the public schools not only continues, but also has greatly accelerated during the past decade. So great is the assault that in the thinking of some observers, the American public school may well be on the way to becoming "an endangered species." While the public schools are subjected to a wholesale indictment for their neutrality toward religion, nonpublic schools, the vast majority of which are religious, have come to be described, according to one study of the movement, as "the most rapidly expanding segment of formal education in the United States."[54]

The battle over "secular humanism" in the public schools is dangerous because, while "secular humanism" remains largely undefined by fundamentalists, it is assumed that the term is somehow to be equated with secular*ism*, and, therefore, must be destructive of all religious and moral values. The truth is that nonreligious or secular humanism does not mean, let alone require, the rejection of Judeo-Christian religious and moral values. To be sure, whenever and wherever Judeo-Christian or other traditional religious values are denigrated in the public schools, it should be condemned as incompatible with the secular character of American public education and the guarantees of the First Amendment.

Unfortunately, the attack on "secular humanism" in the public schools is all too often but a thinly veiled attack on the public schools themselves—both on their academic freedom and their academic integrity. Much of the myth of "secular humanism" has been perpetrated by those who seek to Christianize the public schools, to make them more responsive to their own particular or sectarian religious views, rather than let them remain schools in which a secular or nonreligious approach to the study of history, science, government, and literature prevails. The study of humankind, human experience, and human values is quite properly the focus of·the public schools, while inculcation of religious beliefs, religious experiences, and religious values is the focus of religious education that is rooted in the home and the church or synagogue.

Parochial or church schools and programs of religious education have their own reason for being and should not be defended by indicting the public schools for being secular in their teaching. America's public schools are necessarily committed to *human* values, *human* achievements, and *human* capabilities, in which the activities, interests, and historical development of humankind are made central in education. It is for this reason that public schools enjoy the support of public funds while parochial or church schools which are committed to a particular religious worldview are denied public funds. While public schools are not to be committed to any religious worldview as such, the secular public school cannot fulfill its role without giving serious consideration to the place of religion in the life of humankind and society. As the United States Supreme Court declared almost thirty years ago, "It might well be said that one's education is not complete without a study of comparative religion or the history of religion and its relationship to the advancement of civilization."[55]

Admittedly, religion continues to receive short shrift in the public school curriculum. Several recent studies of American history textbooks, for example, reveal that very little attention is given to the role of religion. This phenomenon cannot be ignored and cannot be justified, but this fact alone does not warrant the charge that the public schools are hostile toward religion or that "secular humanism" has become the established religion in the public schools. In spite of the earnest efforts of a variety of educators to establish institutes and to provide curriculum resources aimed at giving greater attention to the teaching *about* religion in the public school curriculum and the categorical assertion by the U.S. Supreme Court that "one's education is not complete without a study of . . . religion,"[56] it must be acknowledged that far too little attention is given to the study about religion in the public school curriculum.

Again, an explanation of this neglect of religion studies in the public school is not to be found in the unwarranted claim of a hostility toward religion on the part of the public schools or the courts. Rather, the reasons for this lack of attention to religion are to be found in the very problems associated with teaching about religion in the public school curriculum, among which are fears of controversy on the part of public school officials and public school administrators, widespread disagreement as to what should be taught concerning religion, an already crowded curriculum, and the lack of trained teachers and teacher education programs to carry out lesson plans of religion studies within the existing curriculum requirements of the public schools. The fact remains, however, that teaching about religion is integral to education, and that to omit the role of religion in history, society, and the world at large is not a complete education.

The place of study about religion in public education has come to be recognized by a wide range of educational and religious groups. During the past two decades various national organizations have analyzed and observed the neglect of study about religion in the public school classroom. Several years ago, the eight thousand-member Association for Supervision and Curriculum Development published a report on religion studies in the public school curriculum in which it deplored the fact that public school textbooks "virtually ignore religion." Paul Vitz of New York University, in his study, sponsored by the National Institute of Education, of sixty representative social studies textbooks, found that none of them "contain one word referring to any religious activity in contemporary life."[57] A wide range of religious denominations— Catholic, Protestant, and Jewish—have urged the implementation of religion studies in the public schools and participate, along with many professional educational organizations, in the National Council on Religion and Public Education. Recently, a broad coalition of sixteen religious and educational groups published a pamphlet titled "Religious Holidays in the Public Schools" with the purpose of helping teachers to deal with basic issues surrounding the celebration and appreciation of religious holidays. The sponsoring organizations included, among others, the American Association of School Administrators, the American Academy of Religion, the American Federation of Teachers, the American Jewish Committee, the National Association of Evangelicals, the National Council of Churches, the National Council for Social Studies, and the National Education Association.

It should also be noted that a variety of programs aimed at the inclusion of religion in the public school curriculum have been initiated in such states as Florida, Indiana, Kansas, Minnesota, North Carolina, and Pennsylvania. During the past year the National Endowment for the Humanities issued a grant to North Dakota State University and the North Dakota Department of Public Instruction to develop and implement a training program for the inclusion of teaching about religion in the public school curriculum. In November 1990, the Georgia State Board of Education approved a program to encourage and to train public school teachers to teach about religion in the public schools. Sponsored by the First Liberty Institute of George Mason University in Virginia, the program selected Georgia as the national pilot for the implementation of the program. The Institute hopes to serve as a national teacher-training and resource center for public school curriculum development in this area.[58]

In spite of these hopeful signs, publishers of public school textbooks continue to feel pressure to avoid controversial subjects and to bow to the will of organized groups whose aim is to censor public school textbooks. Thereby, out of economic considerations, publishers are inclined to surrender their free-dom to cover significant educational issues simply because they are contro-versial. Well-organized and repeated efforts toward religious censorship of public school textbooks inevitably have had, and continue to have, a chilling and inhibiting effect on public school administrators and classroom teachers in dealing with the phenomenon of religion. Fortunately, because of recent court decisions, including those of the United States Supreme Court and lower courts, and at the urging of various educational and religious groups, publishers are becoming more willing to review their textbooks with regard to the place given to the role of religion. For those educators who are easily intimidated, the result can be one of accommodation to the pressures of religious censorship to the point that the academic integrity of the public school and the public school educator is eroded and substantially weakened. While the battle over "secular humanism" in the public schools is far from over, the pejorative use of "secular humanism" as the established religion of the public schools needs to be seen as unfounded and unjustified, largely made by persons who seek to make the public schools more responsive to their own sectarian religious views.

NOTES

1. Jesse Helms, "Introduction," in Homer Duncan, *Secular Humanism: The Most Dangerous Religion in America* (Lubbock, Tex.: MC International Publication, 1979), p. vi.

2. Tim LaHaye, *The Battle for the Mind* (Old Tappan, N.J.: Fleming H. Revell Co., 1980), p. 57.

3. Ibid., p. 9.

4. *Newsweek,* October 14, 1985.

5. Writing more than a decade ago, Trafford P. Mahor, S.J., of St. Louis University made the charge that " 'secular humanism' is *the* established religion of the United States today," and contended that "secular humanism" can be traced back to Thomas Jefferson, the father of American public education. For more detailed treatments of this thesis, see John W. Whitehead and John Conlan, "The Establish-ment of the Religion of Secular Humanism and Its First Amendment Implications," *Texas Tech Law Review* 10, no. 29 (1978/1979): 46–56 and, similarly, Paul James Tascano, "A Dubious Neutrality: The Establishment of Secularism in the Public Schools" *Brigham Young University Law Review* (1979):184.

6. See, for example, Tim LaHaye, *The Battle for the Public Schools* (Old Tap-pan, N.J.: Fleming H. Revell Co., 1983); Duncan, *The Religion of Secular Humanism and the Public Schools* (Lubbock, Tex.: MC International Publications, 1983); *"Had It?"* (Nashville, Tenn.: Thomas Nelson, Inc., 1974); and Cannaught Coyne Marshner, *Blackboard Jungle* (New Rochelle, N.Y.: Arlington House Publishers, 1978).

7. See James E. Wood, Jr., *Secular Humanism in the Public Schools* (New

York: Education in the Society Unit of the National Council of Churches, 1986), pp. 5–9.

8. LaHaye, *The Battle for the Mind,* pp. 9, 26.

9. Pat Robertson, Freedom Council fund-raising letter, August 5, 1985. With the Supreme Court's decision, "Morals based on Judeo-Christian ethics have been completely excluded from the public schools on the grounds that it is unconstitutional to teach such," see Duncan, *The Religion of Secular Humanism and the Public Schools,* pp. 82–83.

10. *The Washington Post,* February 8, 1986.

11. Quoted in David Ballier, "The Witch Hunt Against 'Secular Humanism,' " *The Humanist* 44 (September/October 1984): 18.

12. LaHaye, *The Battle for the Public Schools,* p. 14.

13. Quoted in J. Charles Park, "Education Attacked from the Right in Dangerous Theater of the Absurd," *Social Education* 49 (May 1985): 350.

14. Address by Jimmy Swaggert delivered at the National Religious Broadcasters Convention, February 6, 1986, widely reported by television and in the press.

15. Whitehead and Conlan, "The Establishment of the Religion of Secular Humanism," p. 56. This phrase is often used by Mel and Norma Gabler, founders of Educational Research Analysts, who, since 1962, have carried on a battle to remove objectionable textbooks reflecting ideas of "secular humanism" from the public schools.

16. See James C. Hefley, *Textbooks on Trial* (Wheaton, Ill.: Victor Books, 1976), and Edward B. Jenkinson, *Censors in the Classroom: The Mind Benders* (Carbondale: Southern Illinois University Press, 1979).

17. *Williams* v. *Board of Education of the County of Kanawha,* 388 F.Supp. 93 (1975); see also *Censoring Textbooks: Is West Virginia the Tip of the Iceberg?* (Washington, D.C.: Institute for Educational Leadership, 1974).

18. *Rosenberg* v. *Board of Education of City of New York,* 92 N.Y.S 2d 344 (1949).

19. *Todd* v. *Rochester Community Schools,* 200 N.W.2d 90 (1972).

20. See Martha McCarthy, "Curriculum Censorship: Actors and Interests Involved," in *Public Schools and the First Amendment* (Bloomington, Ind.: Phi Delta Kappa Educational Foundation, 1983); Nelda Cambrion McCabe, "School Board Censorship: Library Books and Curriculum Materials," in *School Law in Changing Times,* M. A. McGhehey, ed. (Topeka, Kans.: National Organization on Legal Problems of Education, 1982), pp. 78–89.

21. See Martha McCarthy, A *Delicate Balance: Church, State, and the Schools* (Bloomington, Ind.: Phi Delta Kappan Educational Foundation, 1983), p. 90.

22. *Epperson* v. *Arkansas,* 393 U.S. 97 (1968).

23. Ibid., pp. 107–08.

24. See Gerald Caplan, "Evolution and the Biblical Account of Creation: Equal Time," in *School Law in Changing Times,* p. 67, and J. Levit, "Creationism, Evolution, and the First Amendment: The Limits of Constitutionally Permissible Scientific Inquiry," *Journal of Law and Education* 14 (1985): 211, 212.

25. *McLean* v. *Arkansas,* Arkansas Board of Education, 529 F. Supp. 1255, 1264–73 (E.D. Ark. 1982).

26. *Daniel* v. *Waters*, 515 F.2d 485 (6th Cir. 1975).

27. *Hendren* v. *Campbell*, No. S577-0139 (Super. Ct. Ind. Apr. 14, 1977).

28. *Segraves* v. *State*, No. 278, 978 (Cal. Super. Ct. March 6, 1981).

29. *Aguillard* v. *Edwards*, 756 F.2d 1251 (5th Cir. 1985).

30. *Edwards* v. *Aquillard*, 482 U.S. 578 (1987).

31. *McCollum* v. *Board of Education*, 333 U.S. 203 (1948) at 231.

32. *Edwards* v. *Aguillard*, 482 U.S.578 (1987).

33. *Webster* v. *New Lenox School District*, 917 F.2d 1004.

34. *Mozert* v. *Hawkins County Board of Education*, 827 F.2d 1058.

35. *Sherbert* v. *Verner*, 374 U.S. 398 (1963).

36. *Thomas* v. *Review Board of Indiana Employment Security Division*, 450 U.S. 707 (1981).

37. *Bowen* v. *Roy*, 476 U.S. 693 (1986).

38. *Mozert* v. *Hawkins County Board of Education*, 827 F.2d 1058.

39. *Bethel School District* v. *Frazer*, 478 U.S. 675 (1986).

40. *Mozert* v. *Hawkins County Board of Education*, 827 F.2d 1058.

41. *McCollum* v. *Board of Education*, 333 U.S. 203 (1948).

42. *Smith* v. *Mobile County Board of School Commissioners*, 827 F.2d 684.

43. See " 'Humanist' Textbooks on Trial in Alabama," *The Washington Post*, October 6, 1986, A4; see also ibid., October 8, 1986, A6. In response to this case, the American Association of University Professors (AAUP), which represents fifty thousand faculty members and research scholars, through its panel on academic freedom, has expressed its grave concern over the growing evidence of textbook censorship. In its recent report, the AAUP panel declared, "We can think of no reason that is consistent with any proper concept of education in a free society for expurgating a novel, play, or poem" (*The Washington Post*, October 10, 1986, A12).

44. *Smith* v. *Mobile County Board of School Commissioners*, 827 F.2d 684.

45. *McCollum* v. *Board of Education*, 333 U.S. 203 (1948).

46. *Smith* v. *Mobile County Board of School Commissioners*, 827 F.2d 684.

47. See *Attacks on the Freedom to Learn, 1986-1987*, a report from People for the American Way.

48. "Censorship Attempts Grow: Books, Courses are Targets," *NEA Today* 6 (October 1987): 6.

49. See *Christianity Today*, pp. 64–66.

50. See "Notes on Church-State Affairs," *Journal of Church and State* 30 (Autumn 1988): 643.

51. Mel Gabler, "Have You Read Your Child's School Textbooks?" *Faith for the Family* (March–April 1974). Reprint distributed by Education Research Analysts, Longview, Texas.

52. "Censorship Attempts Grow," *NEA Today*, p. 6.

53. *McCollum* v. *Board of Education*, 333 U.S. 203 (1948).

54. James C. Carper and Neal F. Devins, "The State and the Christian Day School," in James E. Wood, Jr., ed., *Religion and the State* (Waco, Tex.: Baylor University Press, 1985), p. 211.

55. *Abington School District* v. *Schempp*, 374 U.S. 203 (1963) at 225.

56. Ibid.

57. Paul Vitz, *Censorship: Evidence of Bias in our Children's Textbooks* (Ann Arbor, Mich.: Servant Books, 1986), p. 1.

58. The curriculum materials, "Living with Our Deepest Differences: Religious Liberty in a Pluralistic Society," developed by the Williamsburg Foundation, were tested in 1990 in five states.

10

The Evolution of Creationism

Eugenie C. Scott

I recently spoke with the well-known evolutionist and writer, Stephen Jay Gould, at a scientific conference. He remarked to me, "You guys are doing pretty well now, aren't you? Creationism is about washed up, isn't it?" Last month I attended my professional (biological anthropology) meetings and was greeted by my university colleagues with, "You still working for that science education outfit? Isn't creationism dead by now?"

Not long ago, I also gave a workshop to two hundred high school science teachers in northern California, who listened with great attention and concern to my discussion of the activities of "scientific" creationists, what they are doing to teachers around the country, and what teachers can do about it.

Teachers know, even if college professors don't. I don't have to tell them that even though the creationists have lost in the courts, they are winning at the grassroots level. This religiously-based movement has profound implications for church-state separation, as well as for maintaining the integrity of science education.

"Scientific" creationism is the most recent manifestation of American anti-evolutionism, which has a long history. Current polls show that only 49 percent of Americans believe that evolution occurs, making evolutionists a minority.[1] The activist anti-evolutionists feel passionately that evolution is an

Eugenie C. Scott is Executive Director of the National Center for Science Education, Inc., a pro-evolution, nonprofit organization that provides advice and support for citizens attempting to keep "scientific" creationism out of the public schools.

idea that must be kept out of public school science classes, thinking that it leads children away from God and toward a life with no morals, ethical precepts, or divine guidance. As Henry Morris, Director of the California-based Institute for Creation Research (ICR), says:

> Evolution is the foundation of communism, fascism, Freudianism, social Darwinism, behaviorism, Kinseyism, materialism, atheism, and in the religious world, modernism and neo-orthodoxy. Jesus said "A good tree cannot bring forth corrupt fruit" (Matthew 7:18). In view of the bitter fruit yielded by the evolutionary system over the past hundred years, a closer look at the nature of the tree itself is well warranted today.[2]

The anti-evolutionists who call themselves "scientific" creationists claim that not only is the creation story of Genesis literally true (six 24-hour days, a flesh-and-blood Adam and Eve, the Flood an historical event), but that they can support these claims with scientific data. Unfortunately, members of the general public know little about science and hardly anything about evolution. Many are confused by what *sounds* like a valid, competing scientific view. After all, the "scientific" creationists rarely present their religious bias in public settings. They are more likely to discuss thermodynamics, Polonium halos in granite, the rate of oil seepage in the oceans, and how quickly coal can be made in a laboratory. They don't discuss whether there is one creation story or two in Genesis. In the literature of the faithful, however, the religiosity of the movement is clear. The May 1991 solicitation letter from the ICR reads in part,

> Greetings in the Lord from your Christian co-workers here at ICR. We trust the battle goes well on your front. Many have recently written with thankfulness for the victories provided by the creation message, both in their own personal lives as they grow in strength and depth in their own faith, and in their ministries to those in need of this liberating truth.

In my many years as a practicing scientist teaching at the university level, and in all my reading of the scientific literature, I have not once seen the teaching of evolution referred to as a "mission" or as "liberating truth." To become a member of the Creation Research Society, one must sign a "statement of belief" that all the assertions of the Bible are "historically and scientifically true," that the Flood of Noah "was an historical event worldwide in its extent and effect," and that "all basic types of living things, including man, were made by direct creative acts of God during the creation week described in Genesis." Of all the scientific societies to which I belong, not a single one requires a pledge of belief, secret handshake, or anything of the sort. It is, in fact, the opposite of the spirit of scientific inquiry to decide first what the truth is, and then go forth and, as the pledge of the Creation Research Society requires, "to reevaluate science from this viewpoint." More typical is the attitude illustrated by the motto from the Royal Society of London, "I am not bound to swear allegiance to the word of any master. Where the storm carries me, I put into port and make myself at home."

Creationists use the words of science, though not in the same way *real* scientists use them. But the general public has a lot of trouble telling the difference. When creationists say, "Neither evolution nor creationism are scientific because nobody was there to see it," your average, scientifically unsophisticated citizen says, "Hmmm. I guess he's right about that." Scientists (*real* ones, that is) know that direct observation is not the only way science is done.

Although there is no space here to discuss it, creationism has been evaluated by competent scientists and found to be factually wrong, theoretically bankrupt, and lacking in scientific rigor. There are many books and articles that analyze the creationist position, some of which are listed at the end of this chapter. Even nonscientists, when presented with the evidence, can recognize creationism as a pseudoscience. Federal District Court Judge William Overton, after hearing testimony from both creation "scientists" and evolutionists, firmly concluded that creation science was not scientific.

> While anybody is free to approach a scientific inquiry in any fashion they choose, they cannot properly describe the methodology used as scientific, if they start with a conclusion and refuse to change it regardless of the evidence developed during the course of the investigation.[3]

It is not irrelevant also to point out that the theological view of the "scientific" creationists is at variance with that of most other Protestants. A statement by the United Presbyterian Church makes this point clearly:

> . . . the imposition of a fundamentalist viewpoint about the interpretation of biblical literature—where every word is taken with uniform literalness and becomes an absolute authority on all matters, whether moral, religious, political, historical, or scientific—is in conflict with the perspective on biblical interpretation characteristically maintained by biblical scholars and theological schools in the mainstream of Protestantism, Roman Catholicism, and Judaism. Such scholars find that the scientific theory of evolution does not conflict with their interpretation of the origins of life found in biblical literature.[4]

During the last decade, the creation-evolution controversy has taken two forms: efforts to get creationism into the curriculum (to ameliorate the "evil" effects of evolution) and to get evolution out. The movement has succeeded on both counts, though anti-evolutionism has been more successful than pro-creationism. Creationism is indeed being taught in many schools, but more common is the teacher who simply does not teach evolution "to avoid the controversy." These pressures are not new, but neither have they remained the same through time.

EVIL-UTION

What is this idea of evolution that causes so much trouble? In 1859, Charles Darwin had two goals in *The Origin of Species*: to convince readers that evolution had occurred, and that the main mechanism by which evolution took place was natural selection. By evolution, Darwin meant that living things are related through common ancestry, and that change has taken place through time. His elegant phrase, "descent with modification" still remains a sound definition of evolution.

By natural selection, Darwin meant a process by which change took place through the differential reproduction of heritable variations having increased survival or reproductive value. In plain English, he suggested that organisms that have abilities or characteristics allowing them to live longer and repro-duce more offspring leave more descendants, which themselves possess those valuable abilities or characteristics. As individuals with these favored varia-tions increase or decrease through time, change (evolution) takes place in the species. In cold climates, for example, rabbits that happen to have thick coats would survive longer and reproduce more offspring than rabbits with thinner coats. Through time, with the survival and reproduction of more thick-coated rabbits each generation, the species would eventually be characterized by thick coats rather than thin ones. Natural selection would have brought about evo-lution. Given sufficient time (and other factors), this process can also produce new species. Natural selection is still considered by most scientists to be the main means by which change takes place, though other mechanisms have been added since Darwin's time.

Evolution was accepted by the scientific community more quickly than was natural selection. Between the publication of *The Origin of Species* in 1859 and the beginning of the twentieth century, a controversy developed over a supposed discrepancy between theory and observation. If natural se-lection occurred, then the variability of shape, size, and other characteristics would decrease each generation, as "unfit" members of the population (and the variations they carried) died out. Carried over hundreds or thousands of generations, this logically would mean that each species should be uni-form, rather than exhibit the wide range of variation that direct observation of nature confirmed. Theory predicted reduced variability, but observation did not confirm it.

How did variability remain in or arise in a population? Darwin didn't know; it was an admitted weakness of his theory. But the theory was otherwise so logical and powerful, that even with serious questions raised against it, it was not abandoned. Then, in the early part of the twentieth century, Gregor Mendel's genetic laws were rediscovered, showing that the process of heredity itself provides plentiful material for natural selection to work upon. The incorporation of Mendelism into biology provided the missing link in Darwin's theory, and the scientific community accepted natural selection as the preeminent mechanism for change. (It is perhaps a measure of the robustness of the theory of natural selection that even creationists accept it. Ironically, modern-day "scientific" creationists reject Darwin's proof that living things share common ancestry [evolution], but accept—as must anyone who understands it—his mechanism of natural selection; they call it "microevolution.")

But simply because the scientific establishment accepted evolution didn't mean that the general public did. To some, the evolution of the universe was a frightening thought. Did this mean that creation did not occur? Then no creator is needed. If God was not needed as Creator, was God needed at all? Does this mean that perhaps the universe might not have been specially created for mankind? Worse, if evolution did occur, then *Homo sapiens* could have evolved as well. If mankind evolved just like the rest of nature, how could humans be the pinnacle of creation? These same concerns are still raised by fundamentalists opposing evolution. They claim that Genesis is the foundation of Christianity, and, as a fundamentalist minister once explained to me, if Genesis is not true, how do you know Revelations is not true? Salvation, essential to Christian faith, is jeopardized by evolution, in this view. Either evolution is true, or the Bible. Take your pick.

Needless to say, only a biblically literalist theology has difficulty with evolution. Most Judeo-Christian theologies accommodated evolution within the first few decades after Darwin. There remained a place for both God and evolution in Christian religions, but not among biblically literalist sects. It is here that the problem of acceptance of evolution lay, and continues to lie. The creation-evolution controversy is not an argument between religion and science, but between biblically literalist religion and everyone else. Unfortunately, the majority of Protestant and Catholic clergy have not made a point of informing the laity that their theology is *not* literalist, which means many individuals on the other side of the pulpit from the seminary-trained minister or priest think that they have to make a choice between religion and evolution. This confusion is easily exploited by creationists.

In the late nineteenth and early twentieth centuries, evolution was an idea first known to the intelligentsia, which seeped gradually into the body politic through middle- and high-brow magazines like *The Atlantic* and *North American Review*. Newspapers covered Spencer and Huxley's United States lecture tours, while liberal clerics like Henry Ward Beecher accepted evolution and preached about it. The first great outcry against evolution came when large numbers of individuals came into direct contact with it through science textbooks, just before World War I. Evolution in *The Atlantic* is apparently more palatable than evolution in Johnny's textbook (which is still, unfortunately, the case).

THE EVOLUTION OF CREATIONISM

Evolution began appearing in textbooks in the early part of the century. Biology textbooks published in the late teens and early twenties placed evolution as a central organizing principle of biology, to the consternation of American fundamentalists who, like their modern counterparts at the Institute for Creation Research, viewed evolution as an inherently corrupting idea. In the early 1920s, state legislatures began passing bills banning the teaching of evolution.

A Tennessee science teacher, John T. Scopes, became in 1925 a test case for his state's anti-evolution law. Many are familiar with the story of how the press and intellectuals ridiculed the fundamentalist mindset exhibited in Dayton, Tennessee. What people forget was that Scopes, a champion of evolution, lost, and the law remained on the books for several more decades. In fact, though few laws against evolution were passed after the Scopes trial, evolution began gradually and quietly slipping out of textbooks, until by the early 1960s, coverage of this important subject had dwindled to a few carefully qualified pages or phrases—generally in the back of the book where they could be conveniently skipped. The creationists, though losing in the sophisticated big city newspaper and literary world of H. L. Mencken, were winning in the small school districts around the country (the home of most Americans), where books with "too much evolution" in them did not get purchased. Textbooks were therefore rewritten to promote sales, and so instruction about evolution declined almost to the vanishing point.

The 1962 Supreme Court decision in *Epperson* v. *Arkansas* (393 US 97, 1968) concluded that laws banning evolution were unconstitutional. Anti-evolutionists then managed to get laws passed in several states that required the Bible to be taught along with evolution. This strategy was short-lived, however, as it was a patently unconstitutional establishment of religion. Some district court decisions nullified this strategy.

The next step in the evolution of anti-evolutionism is perhaps the most interesting. When evolution could not be banned, and its "evil" effects not ameliorated by teaching the Bible alongside it, an obvious solution was to claim that the Genesis creation story could be supported scientifically, and teach it as an "alternative view" to evolution in the science classes. "Scientific" creationism was born, and with it, the "equal time" argument—a contention that exquisitely taps into long-standing American cultural values, thereby ensuring its success.

Equal Time

The American cultural tradition (regardless of how shakily practiced) values democracy, fairness, equality, universal suffrage, and giving all contenders their "day in the sun." It also has a soft spot for underdogs. Coupled with a populist suspicion of authority ("nobody is going to tell *me* what to think") this democratic tradition is made to order for the creationists.

"Equal time," the argument that since evolution is taught, it is "only fair" to teach creationism, touches on all of these ideas. "What's wrong with the kids hearing an alternate point of view?" creationists ask. "Seventy-two percent of Americans want both models taught." "Teach both creation and evolution and let the children decide," as if science were a democratic process. Recently a high school biology teacher at Chico High in Chico, California, was asked by parents at a school "open house" night what he was going to do about evolution. He answered to the effect that "since the state of California won't let me teach both views, I'm not gonna teach either!" Creationists regularly present themselves as Davids battling the "scientific establishment" giant, puny, but determined—and destined—to triumph. Ironically, the "underdog" Institute for Creation Research has a mailing list of 100,000 and a budget of $3 million, and is only one of a long list of anti-evolutionist organizations.

The answer to the "equal time" argument, of course, is that equal time makes sense only for equivalent ideas. Creationists argue that "equal time" should be given to the idea that the universe, the stars, galaxies, the solar system, and the earth and its creatures appeared suddenly, exactly as we see them today. There simply is no scientific support for this idea, and much evidence against it. The evidence shows, on the contrary, that what we see today is *not* identical to what existed in the past, and this is the essential difference between creationism and evolution.

If creationism truly were a respectable scientific idea, then it would make sense to teach it. As it is not, however, to teach it would be to give equal time to nonsense. Just because a pressure group lobbies for changing the curriculum, that doesn't mean the curriculum should be changed. Geocentrism, the idea that the sun goes around the earth rather than the converse, is supported by a minority of modern "scientific" creationists. (The former treasurer of the Creation Research Society has published papers supporting geocentrism.) These individuals support their views not only with Bible passages, but also with pseudoscientific "observations" and "theory." Most Americans would draw the line somewhere: geocentrism simply is not an idea equivalent to heliocentrism, and should not be presented to schoolchildren as a valid, competing scientific datum.

Similarly, there are Religious Right proponents who claim that AIDS is a curse from God; but does it make sense to give the demon theory of disease "equal time" with the viral theory because a pressure group wants it? Equal time makes sense only for equivalent ideas. One should not present the flat earth, geocentrism, or demons as scientific alternatives, "and let the children decide." One should present good science in science classes, not theories or suppositions that have long been proven false or that were never scientific in the first place.

Creationist Neologisms

The Supreme Court, in *Edwards* v. *Aguillard* (107 SC 2573, 1987), heard a case from Louisiana in which creation "science" was required to be taught whenever evolution was taught. This law was declared unconstitutional because it promoted religion. But creation "science" was not given a full hearing before the court; there was no opportunity for its proponents to defend their notion that theirs was an equivalent scientific view. Nonetheless, there has been since then, in the more rarified elements of creationist thought, an avoidance of the term "creationist," as the Supreme Court declared that the term "creationist" *ipso facto* implied a creator and was thus a religious concept.

Now, in some quarters, instead of "scientific creationism," we find new terms. Creationist lawyer Wendell Bird has invented the euphemism "abrupt appearance theory" to replace "scientific" creationism, and a group associated with the Texas-based Foundation for Thought and Ethics has evolved the term "intelligent design theory." Literature expressing either of these two new "theories" presents many of the same old arguments presented in earlier scientific creationist writings. Clearly, the neologisms are an attempt to avoid the tainted word "creationism" and to replace it with more neutral-sounding terms. Simultaneously, however, "old-fashioned" "scientific" creationism continues to spread around the country, much as a pebble dropped in a pond creates concentric ripples that continue far longer on the edge than in the center.

THAT OLD-TIME CREATIONISM

Creationism tends to appear when Religious Right candidates get elected to school boards. We have tracked the appearance of creationism after the election of Religious Right proponents in suburbs of Seattle, Washington; Lodi, California; Buffalo, New York; Reedville, Oregon; Mansfield, Ohio; Leesburg, Florida; and Casper, Wyoming. This variety of states and cities points out that creationism is not an issue only of concern to the "Bible Belt" South, although it does tend to appear more frequently in small to medium-sized towns and cities. In some cases, the school board or individual schools are approached by parents who want creationism instituted (as in Indianapolis, Indiana; Cannon Falls, Minnesota; and Warren, Oregon), or local citizens will begin letter-writing campaigns to "soften up" the community before approaching the school board (as in Granville, Ohio; and Madera, California). Most frequently, teachers will simply decide to teach creationism with seemingly little agitation from outside (as in Sherman, Texas; Gervais, Oregon; and Vista and San Jose, California). A letter from a parent in Sherman, Texas, clearly summarizes the situation in many schools:

> Last year my daughter was in a biology class where the instructor said he was not going to teach evolution if he could not teach creationism. He told his class if anyone had a problem with that, they should see a school advisor and drop the class.

Some of the enthusiasm for creationism has been brought about by grass-roots organizing efforts over the last couple of years by the ICR, which sponsors periodic "Back to Genesis" seminars, creationist road shows wherein ICR staff put on one- to three-day seminars in communities around the country. Local citizens are introduced to this "wonderful new science" of creationism through two days of lectures, videotapes, book, tape and filmstrip sales, and, of course, prayer. Local people, duly filled with enthusiasm after these performances, go forth and multiply the word into the community, making life miserable for teachers, of course. My organization, the National Center for Science Education (NCSE), tends to get calls for help from areas where "Back to Genesis" seminars have been very successful or particularly frequent.

And successful they are. A Connecticut seminar drew 2,700 people; a Michigan seminar, 6,000. And in Sacramento, California, 7,000 people showed up for a particularly successful "Back to Genesis" seminar. The promotion of creationism is a substantial grassroots movement that should not be taken lightly.

It Plays in Peoria

In March 1989, the ICR boasted that staffers had been invited to speak in the *science* classes in six *public* high schools in Illinois. NCSE investigated, and, after a lot of searching by Illinois members, discovered that a cluster of schools around Peoria had invited creationists to speak to students during February 1989. A particularly illuminating letter was received by an Illinois NCSE member, Ransom Traxler. Mr. Chester Dugger, director of high school programs for the Peoria district, wrote:

> Every so often a local organization will invite a staff member of the Institute for Creation Research to visit the Peoria area. When this occurs an invitation is sent to each high school principal and each science department chairman stating that the staff member will be willing to come to science classes to talk abut the "creationist" point of view. Since our science textbooks deal with the theory of evolution but do not contain information about creation science, we encourage, but do not require, science teachers to take advantage of this opportunity.

So, "equal time" strikes again.

To make a long story short, the negative publicity generated by the exposé of this affair discouraged Peoria from inviting creationists in the future. Chester Dugger was quoted in a March 1991 newspaper article as saying that ICR staff soon to present a "Back to Genesis" seminar in the area would not be invited to speak in the Peoria schools. This is progress.

The Peoria situation showed us that creationism has been taught in some communities for a long time; but until recently, no one has complained. Mr. Dugger's letter indicated that creationists had been coming to Peoria public schools for twelve years! Doubtless, creationists would have been invited into these Illinois public schools in 1991 if a fuss hadn't been raised about it. Because of the efforts of NCSE members, especially Ranse Traxler, for the first time in more than a decade, Peoria students were not taught in their science classes that humans and dinosaurs coexisted. It will be interesting to see what happens in the future. Meanwhile, similar situations have emerged in other Illinois school districts.

Fifteen Years of Creationism

Another story comes from Weed, an attractive northern California town of about 3,000 nestled against the Siskiyou mountains near Mt. Shasta. In March 1990, NCSE got a call from a resident asking for help with a creationism incident at the local elementary school. The principal had sent a letter to the parents of the seventh and eighth grade classes informing them that,

For the remainder of this week our seventh and eighth grade students will be discussing and comparing the theories of evolution and creationism. On Tuesday [of the following week] and Wednesday, our eighth and seventh grade classes, respectively, will hear a representative from the Weed Ministerial Alliance give a presentation on creation. The students will be exposed to the creation theory of life as set forth in the Bible. . . . The creationism material will be treated as one theory attempting to explain the origin of life just as the eighth grade science textbook favors the evolutionary theory of life. No attempt will be made to turn the program into one which encourages students to accept a specific religious bias.

As it turns out, there were some interesting details associated with this particular lesson. The "representative of the Weed Ministerial Alliance" happened to be the principal's own minister, a fundamentalist, and he had been making this presentation for fifteen years! Because no one had complained before, the practice continued.

With the help of materials sent from NCSE, local college professors Ken Goehring and Michael Roesch attempted to persuade the principal to cancel the presentation on the grounds that "scientific creationism" was bad science and an unconstitutional advocacy of religion. The minister's 1990 visitation was videotaped by the schools, for unknown reasons. The videotape and a handout given to the children provided the best documentation that this "scientific" activity was nothing but a poorly disguised attempt to present biblically literalist theology in the guise of science. The flyer said in part,

Many (perhaps the majority) people [*sic*] in this school district believe that the world and its inhabitants were created supernaturally in a perfect state, but that mankind disobeyed his creator, bringing death and decay into the world, but that the creator-God continues to sustain life as we see it today. I certainly hold to this bias. . . . I appreciate the leadership at Weed elementary school which gives me the opportunity to come to this science class to present a brief overview of alternative data, so you can consider each alternative, weigh the implications and consequences of each position, and then decide for yourself which is more reasonable. Your choice will make a profound difference in the way you value yourself, contribute to society, and pursue excellence in life goals. Obviously, if you believe that an all-wise Creator made you and the world, then you will sense a responsibility to this Creator. If you are the product of mechanistic chance, then life looses [*sic*] much of its meaning.

Equal time, and let the children decide, with the kicker that if you make the wrong choice, you will grow up immoral with no meaning to your life.

The eighth grade students reportedly questioned Reverend Sprunger closely. A witness says Sprunger frequently "explained" a point by saying "because the Bible says so." A Catholic student reportedly asked whether she could believe God created through evolution (the semiofficial position of the Roman Catholic church) and still be a Christian. He replied, "No."

And remember that this is in a *public* school *science* class.

The Weed story, like the one in Peoria, ended well. Information was provided to the board of education by Goehring and Roesch. State officials in the Department of Education in Sacramento sent the board references to legal decisions critical of the teaching of creationism, and reminded them that California has a very strong state curriculum guide that directs teachers to teach evolution and discourages them from teaching creationism. In the spring of 1991, the school board of Weed was persuaded that the minister's visitations should cease. Were it not for the efforts of Goehring and Roesch, Weed might have continued having fundamentalists lecture in science classes for another fifteen years—or longer.

Meanwhile, a school board in Morton, Illinois, near Peoria, distressed over "too much" evolution in new textbooks adopted for biology classes, directed the staff to develop a unit on creationism to be taught in biology the following year. This of course flies directly in the face of the 1987 Supreme Court *Edwards* v. *Aguillard* decision that prohibits requiring the teaching of creationism when evolution is taught. One is reminded that the Supreme Court does not monitor compliance with its decisions. As Andrew Jackson said about his Chief Justice, "John Marshall has made his decision. Now let us see him enforce it."

TEXTBOOKS, AGAIN

Textbooks have long been a battleground between creation and evolution. For a long time, coverage of evolution was effectively reduced in textbooks because Texas (and the states of the Southeast that follow Texas's lead) restricted evolution to a "theory" set apart from all other scientific theories. Books that had "too much" evolution were not adopted, and, responding to natural selection, textbook publishers reduced the amount of evolution coverage. Now, thanks to efforts by scientists and educators and organizations like People for the American Way and NCSE, discussion of evolution is returning to the textbooks. The 1990 "crop" of high school biology books adopted in Texas were greatly superior to their predecessors in the amount of evolution included. "The timidity with which publishers used to skirt around the "e-word" is largely gone. . . . The battle over nonsectarian science education is not over, but a significant victory has been won."[5]

Nevertheless, as can be seen in Morton, Illinois, books that treat evolution appropriately may not be adopted at all or else be adopted with controversy. The improved textbooks will be rewritten in the blink of an eye if they do not sell, and we will be back to where we were five years ago. Only if individuals take an active interest and role in monitoring local textbook choice will evolution remain in the textbooks.

Creationists have expanded their efforts to produce their own textbooks. An early effort, *Biology, a Search for Order in Complexity*, published by the Institute for Creation Research, was uninspiring and had a "homemade" look to it in contrast to the sparkling graphics and vivid pictures of the commercial textbooks against which it attempted to compete. A new venture, the Foundation for Thought and Ethics' *Of Pandas and People*, is far more slickly produced. It "looks" like a textbook, or supplement, and easily "passes" in a stack of commercially produced books. It is the main statement of the "intelligent design theory."

Creationists in Alabama tried to get *Of Pandas and People* adopted by the state textbook commission, but failed. NCSE, encouraging scientists to testify before the commission on the scientific failings of the book, persuaded a majority of members of the commission that the book should not be adopted. Being able to count, the publishers figured they didn't have the votes, and withdrew the book before the embarrassment of being turned down in a state they thought they would easily sweep. At about the same time, the book (promoting the "intelligent design theory") was quietly turned down in Idaho after NCSE provided reviews of the book to textbook committee members. On the other hand, *Pandas* was recently adopted in Gaston, Oregon, and the publisher's promotional materials claim that "volume orders" have been filled "in Florida, Alabama, Illinois, Texas, New Jersey, and California."

LEANING ON TEACHERS

Pressure on teachers not to teach evolution is usually much subtler than efforts to get creationism instituted at the school board level. It may take the form of creationist literature appearing anonymously in mailboxes at school, or proselytizing from colleagues. Sometimes parents go directly to the teacher to discourage the teaching of evolution. In Hayward, California, a kindergarten teacher presented a unit on dinosaurs to her students. A parent observer later told her that she was "shocked" that the teacher hadn't mentioned that human beings coexisted with dinosaurs. When the teacher demurred, saying that this wasn't quite what she understood to be the scientific evidence, the parent informed her that she was "behind the times" and that there was "considerable evidence" that people and dinosaurs were alive at the same time. The next day, the parent brought in a large, glossy, four-color book describing Texas's Paluxy River "mantracks" and other alleged evidence "refuting" modern geology, biology, and paleontology. This "Flintstones" view of history has both humans and dinosaurs scampering away together from the rising waters of Noah's Flood.

Much of the reluctance to teach evolution comes from perceptions that administrators will not back up teachers—and the perception is too often true. A teacher in Dallas, Texas, contemplating adopting a biology textbook strong on evolution was unusually frank. "We used to teach evolution when we had a superintendent who had some backbone. Now we have an invertebrate!"

In Mahomet, Illinois, a third grade teacher *mentioned* evolution in passing to students. The next day a parent was at the principal's office demanding the opportunity to give "equal time" to "scientific" creationism in the classroom. The principal knuckled under, and the parent lectured on the "two-model" view. This lecture included handouts showing a person riding a saddled and bridled tyrannosaurus in a discussion of "human and dinosaur footprints found together in Texas." Also handed out was a now-it-can-be-told "exposé" of the falseness of the evolutionists' view of bird evolution. Debunking the view that birds evolved from reptiles, the flyer states, "No animals have been found that have *scaly* feathers or *feathery* scales." "Scientists have found no true evidence that birds come from lizards. Complete feathers and complete scales is what we would expect to find if both birds and reptiles were made by the *Creator* at about the same time." Bird evolution is actually one of the better understood sequences in paleontology, but it is also one of the creationists' favorite hobby horses.

Incidents like this make teachers wary of teaching evolution because it leads to confrontation, and, being normal people, teachers would rather do without confrontation if they can help it. The perception or the reality of not being backed up by administrators further discourages others. Sometimes the pressure not to teach evolution comes from a teacher's colleagues, and this is perhaps the most difficult to handle. These are the people, after all, with whom you work and eat lunch, whose children play with your children, and whom you see at the grocery store. In small, homogeneous communities, the problem is exacerbated. Teachers have a difficult time upholding their professional responsibilities while still preserving and being part of the social network in which they live. Most of the sectarian pressures on schools occur in small cities and towns, with all the positive and negative elements "small town" connotes. Lest big city dwellers feel unduly smug about escaping the consequences of creationism, let them remember that almost half of our citizens live in small cities and towns. That's a lot of people.

CONCLUSION

If we judge the success of the creationism movement by whether or not it is accomplishing its aims, we must conclude that it is being quite successful. Despite the good news of evolution reappearing in some of the newer textbooks, evolution is inexorably being removed from the curriculum. In far too many places in the country, "scientific" creationism, a sectarian religious view masquerading as science, is being advocated in the public schools as the true and accurate history of the universe.

And what a shame. Evolution has revolutionized human thought more than any other human idea, except perhaps heliocentrism—and even there, it's a toss-up. Science has obviously been affected: it is difficult to find a science to which evolution does not apply. Physics and astronomy are evolutionary sciences; galaxies, stars, and solar systems evolve, and the elements that make up the universe developed in the cosmic blast furnaces within nascent stars. Chemistry is an evolutionary field: biochemistry helps us understand the foundation of life and heredity. Geology is obviously evolutionary: the landforms of the earth have evolved or changed through time. And biology? As the eminent geneticist Theodosius Dobzhansky said, "Nothing in biology makes sense except in the light of evolution." It can fairly be said that one cannot be a scientist in the twentieth century without an understanding of evolution.

But not only science has been affected. Philosophy and theology, history, literature, art, and poetry have all been affected by this idea. Emerson and the transcendental movement in general were profoundly moved by the concept of evolution:

> The subtle chain of countless rings
> The next unto the farthest brings
> And, striving to be men the worm
> Mounts through all the spires of form
> "Mayday"

Evolution provided a central organizing principle for the theology of Pierre Teilhard de Chardin, who said:

Is evolution a theory, a system, or a hypothesis? It is much more—it is a general postulate to which all theories, all hypotheses, all systems must henceforward bow and which they must satisfy in order to be thinkable and true. Evolution is a light which illuminates all facts, a trajectory which all lines of thought must follow—this is what evolution is.[6]

Removing evolution from the curriculum is tantamount to educational deprivation for our children. It must not be allowed to happen because a minority pressure group seeks to impose misinformation on the rest of us. Furthermore, we must not let our schools become forums for the teaching of sectarian religious dogma such as "scientific" creationism. Even the narrowest interpretation of the First Amendment prohibits proselytizing in school. It does neither education nor religion any good to confuse the two. Children exposed to the factual misinformation, theoretical confusion, and philosophical chaos of "scientific" creationism do *not* obtain a competent science education. Further, one can well argue that holding biblically literalist views up to scientific scrutiny is an unwarranted attack upon religion! For the sake of both education *and* religion, we must enforce a separation of church and state.

As events in places like Peoria and Weed show us, nothing will change unless an objection is raised, and people are reminded that there is a First Amendment, which protects the public schools from religious indoctrination. The National Center for Science Education, Inc., supports local efforts to keep schools free from creationist dogma, but the work done by people at the local level remains critical. The only thing necessary, to paraphrase Edmund Burke, for the triumph of anti-evolutionism and "scientific" creationism, is that good men (and women) do nothing. Some of us are trying to do something, and we need all the allies we can get! We hope *you* will join us in keeping religious advocacy out of the science classes.

NOTES

1. Gallup, George, Jr., and Frank Neuport, "Forty-Seven Percent Believe God Created Man," *Los Angeles Times Syndicate,* December 1, 1991.

2. Henry M. Morris, *The Twilight of Evolution* (Grand Rapids, Mich.: Baker Book House, 1963), p. 24.

3. *McLean* v. *Arkansas,* 529F Supp. 1255 (ED Ark, 1982).

4. In Betty McCollister, ed., *Voices for Evolution* (Berkeley: National Center for Science Education, Inc., 1989), p. 19.

5. National Center for Science Education, Inc./People for the American Way, *Biology Textbooks 1990: The New Generation* (Washington, D.C.: People for the American Way, 1990), pp. 6, 8.

6. Pierre Teilhard de Chardin, *The Phenomenon of Man,* 2d ed. (New York: Harper Torchbooks, 1965), p. 219.

For Further Reading

Eve, Raymond A., and Francis B. Harrold. *The Creationist Movement in Modern America.* Boston: Twayne Publishers, G. K. Hall and Company, 1991.

Godfrey, Laurie G., ed. *Scientists Confront Creationism.* New York: Norton, 1983.

Kitcher, Phillip. *Abusing Science: The Case Against Creationism.* Cambridge, Mass.: MIT Press, 1982.

Price, Barry. *The Creation Science Controversy.* Philadelphia: Millennium Books, 1990.

11

Religious Liberty in the 1990s:
Same Battles, Different Battleground

Oliver Thomas

The single most important church-state development in the 1990s is likely to be an institutional one. The issues that plagued us in the 1980s—school prayer, creationism, vouchers, and tuition tax credits—will remain. The forum in which these issues are debated and ultimately resolved, however, will change. It is the battlefield, not the battle, that will be different.

For decades, the federal courts have served as the arbiter of most church-state disputes. Americans long have assumed that if their constitutional rights were abridged—whether by state-sponsored prayer in public schools or by the diversion of public funds to parochial schools—they could seek redress in federal courts. Like the framers, we blithely assumed that it was the judiciary's task to enforce the constitutional rights of all, not just of the majority. In the words of Justice Jackson:

> The very purpose of a Bill of Rights was to withdraw certain subjects from the vicissitudes of political controversy, to place them beyond the reach of majorities and officials and to establish them as legal principles to be applied by the courts.

Oliver Thomas is an ordained Baptist minister and General Counsel for the Baptist Joint Committee, the public affairs office for ten Baptist conferences and conventions in the United States, with a combined membership of approximately 27 million. The committee deals exclusively with issues pertaining to religious liberty and the separation of church and state.

One's right to life, liberty, and property, free speech, a free press, freedom of worship and assembly, and other fundamental rights may not be submitted to vote; they depend on the outcome of no elections.[1]

Justice Jackson's sage advice notwithstanding, recent decisions of the United States Supreme Court belie the federal judiciary's commitment to religious and civil liberties. These decisions indicate that the Court is likely to become far less assertive in the church-state area, referring more questions to the political branches of government for final resolution. This shift in the Court's jurisprudence has been demonstrated most clearly in abortion cases[2] but recently has spilled over into the free exercise docket.[3]

Historically, the Supreme Court has accommodated the free exercise claims of minorities by creating exemptions from generally applicable laws. In *Employment Division* v. *Smith* (1990), the Court departed from this long-standing practice. The case arose when two drug rehabilitation counselors, who were fired for using peyote in Native American religious ceremonies, were denied unemployment compensation benefits. The two filed suit under *Sherbert* v. *Verner* (1963)[4] and its progeny, claiming that the free exercise clause protected their right to engage in this ancient religious practice.

The Supreme Court disagreed. A five-person majority of the Court opined that the free exercise clause was never intended to provide relief from generally applicable governmental regulations. Describing such accommodation as a "luxury" we no longer can afford, the Court went on to note that while legislatures might appropriately grant exemptions to religious organizations where free exercise concerns are present, such accommodation is not the task of the judiciary.

It may fairly be said that leaving accommodation to the political process will place at a relative disadvantage those religious practices that are not widely engaged in; but that unavoidable consequence of democratic government must be preferred to a system in which each conscience is a law unto itself or in which judges weigh the social importance of all laws against the centrality of all religious beliefs.[5]

The religious community's reaction to *Smith* was one of shock and outrage.[6] Said the American Jewish Congress: "The decision of the majority in *Smith,* which overturns thirty years of free exercise jurisprudence, is deplorable not only because of its harsh impact on a long-established Native American religion, but also because it threatens the religious liberty of all Americans and particularly those of minority faiths."[7] Dean Kelley of the National Council of Churches complained that the Court had "gutted" the free exercise clause "by no longer requiring the state to show a compelling interest for overriding an important worship practice of a recognized religion."[8]

The Supreme Court reached its decision with apparent disregard for the legislative history surrounding the enactment of the free exercise clause. Just weeks after *Smith* was decided, Professor Michael McConnell's article "The Origins and Historical Understanding of Free Exercise of Religion"[9] was published. The article demonstrates that the doctrine of judicial accommodation set forth in *Sherbert* v. *Verner* (1963) was consistent with the intent of the framers regarding the free exercise clause. This fact was brought to the Court's attention in an extraordinary petition for rehearing filed by more than fifty leading professors of constitutional law, including Professors McConnell, Laurence Tribe, Gerald Gunther, Kent Greenawalt, and Douglas Laycock. Joining the professors was a coalition of religious and civil liberties organizations ranging from the American Civil Liberties Union, People for the American Way, the National Council o Churches, and the American Jewish Congress to the Christian Legal Society, National Association of Evangelicals, and Rutherford Institute. It was the author's privilege to assist in the drafting of that petition. Unfortunately, the petition was denied on June 4, 1990, with Justices Stevens and O'Connor dissenting.

A situation similar to *Smith* is likely to develop in the Court's establishment clause jurisprudence. At least four justices have sharply criticized the Court's prevailing doctrine,[10] and a shift seems inevitable in light of Justices William Brennan's and Thurgood Marshall's recent retirements and the fact that separationist Harry Blackmun is now in his eighties.

The fountainhead of this anti-separationist sentiment is none other than Chief Justice William Rehnquist. Dissenting in the 1985 Alabama "moment of silence" case, Rehnquist described the wall of separation between church and state as "a metaphor based on bad history, a metaphor which has proved useless as a guide to judging. It should be frankly and explicitly abandoned."[11] Rehnquist went on to suggest that the sole purpose of the establishment clause was to prohibit aid that discriminated among religions or the designation of a single national church. Nonpreferential aid, such as silent prayer, tuition tax credits, or vouchers, would not in the view of the Chief Justice offend the establishment clause.

Justice Scalia likewise has made no secret of his disdain for the separationist position. He and Chief Justice Rehnquist were the sole dissenters in the 1987 case striking down a statute that mandated "balanced treatment" for "creation science" alongside the teaching of evolution in Louisiana public schools. Scalia's dissent came in the face of overwhelming evidence that the purpose of the legislation was to advance a religious viewpoint.

Finally, Justices White and Kennedy have also advocated relaxing existing standards to allow more government support for religion. Kennedy, one of the younger members of the Court, has written extensively on the subject. Most notable was his opinion voting to uphold the display of a free-standing nativity scene located at the heart of the Allegheny County, Pennsylvania, courthouse. Included in the display was a prominent banner proclaiming glory to God for the birth of Jesus Christ.[12] Equally significant was Justice Kennedy's concurring opinion in *Bowen* v. *Kendrick* in which he argued that the "pervasively sectarian" nature of an institution should not disqualify it from receiving federal funds to teach sex education—even sex education that discouraged abortion.[13]

Any change in the Court's jurisprudence is almost certain to result in more deference being paid to the legislative branches of government. This is of critical importance to public education as such issues as school prayer, creationism, vouchers, and tuition tax credits would be put to majority vote. And, whatever decisions the majority makes—whether through its elected representatives or by a referendum—are almost certain to be upheld if challenged in federal court. If, for example, a state legislature approves a program of aid to parochial schools, the prospects of having the program overturned are slim. Similarly, if present trends continue, the Court will be far less likely to overrule a school board's decision to include prayer at graduation exercises or sporting events.

This shift from the judiciary to the legislature has important implications for friends of religious liberty and public education. First, individuals and organizations can no longer rely on their national affiliates to maintain the wall of separation between church and state. Because education policy is primarily a state and local matter, Congress may be unable to offer much assistance. And, as indicated, federal courts may be unwilling. Conversely, supporters of religious liberty and public education must do a better job of organizing at the grassroots level. While grassroots lobbying takes considerable planning and energy, organizations should be encouraged by the fact that separationist groups generally do very well at state and local levels.

A case in point was the 1990 Oregon tuition tax credit proposal. The refundable credit would have provided up to $2,500 in benefits per student to offset the tuition costs of private and parochial schools. Supporters of the measure had the endorsement of the Bush administration and raised more than half a million dollars to promote their referendum campaign. Operating with an initial budget of only $7,500 contributed by the Oregon Education Association and Americans United for Separation of Church and State, Oregonians for Public Education and Religious Liberty (OPEARL) ran an opposition campaign that relied primarily on individual contacts (by letter, telephone, or personal visit) augumented by radio ads and appearances on local talk shows.[14] The results were remarkable. Oregonians defeated the measure by a better than two-to-one margin. The defeat was the seventeenth time since 1967 that voters had rejected a parochiaid proposal at the polls. It was the second time such a plan had failed in Oregon.[15] Supporters of public education have little time to rest on their laurels, however, as more than a dozen other states face similar battles.[16]

Local PEARL affiliates should be established in every state where parochiaid proposals are likely. Telephone chains should be organized, speakers' bureaus assembled, and op ed pieces and letters to the editor written to keep the compelling constitutional and policy arguments against any form of aid to parochial schools constantly before the public. Such grassroots organizing is likely to become even more important as nonseparationist Reagan-Bush appointees begin to make their views felt in the federal judiciary.

Finally, supporters of public education must become more adept at consensus building. This will require a willingness to accommodate the concerns of the religious community when it can be done without compromising the establishment clause or the integrity of public education. Religious leaders wield great influence in most communities, and typically they are strong supporters of public education.[17] That support is eroded when schools appear callous or indifferent to religious concerns. For example, a school's refusal to accommodate a student's need to be absent for the observance of religious holidays, or a school's use of textbooks that ignore the role religion has played in history and contemporary society, can galvanize hostilities toward the public schools and generate support for funding educational alternatives. Even worse is the occasional teacher or administrator who denigrates religion or forces students into a faith versus science dilemma.

The nation's expanding pluralism underscores the need for accommodating religious concerns when reasonably feasible and consistent with the principle of nonestablishment. Obviously, schools would not wish to allow a student to opt out of an entire course in the core curriculum or to be absent for an excessive number of religious holidays, but if public education is to be maintained as we know it, schools must be sensitive to students' religious needs.

The recent guidelines on religion and the public school curriculum, and religious holidays—jointly sponsored by the National Education Association (NEA) and other leading educational groups as well as the Christian Legal Society, National Council of Churches, American Jewish Congress, Baptist Joint Committee, and National Association of Evangelicals—serve as a model for consensus building and reasonable accommodation of religion. Such joint efforts with the religious community will go a long way toward defusing the arguments heard in some religious circles that public education is hostile toward religion.

In addition to grassroots organizing and consensus building, separationist groups may find that an effective litigation strategy may be pursued on the basis of state constitutions. Most state constitutions have provisions similar to the establishment clause, some of which have been interpreted as requiring a stricter separation of church and state.[18] The increasing willingness of state supreme courts to provide greater protection for civil liberties on the basis of state constitutions offers groups an alternative strategy if they are unsuccessful in the political process.[19]

In conclusion, the Supreme Court's increasing deference to the legislative branches of government has profound implications for religious liberty and public education. Such controversial issues as school prayer, creationism, vouchers, and tuition tax credits may soon be put to majority vote. While the federal judiciary's abdication of its responsibility to maintain the wall of separation between church and state is cause for concern, separationist groups should not despair. Through less reliance on their national affiliates, better grassroots organizing, consensus building, and a litigation strategy based upon state constitutions, advocates of religious liberty and public education should be able to prevent public funds from being diverted to private and parochial schools and public education from becoming the handmaid of religion.

NOTES

1. *West Virginia State Board of Education* v. *Barnette,* 319 U.S. 624, 638 (1943).

2. In *Webster* v. *Reproductive Health Services,* 494 U.S. 490, 109 S.Ct. 3040 (1990), the Court upheld a Missouri statute regulating performance of abortions that (1) declared life to begin at conception; (2) required physicians, prior to performing an abortion on any woman believed to be twenty or more weeks pregnant, to perform medical tests for the purpose of determining whether or not the fetus was viable; (3) prohibited the use of public employees or facilities to perform or assist in abortions not necessary to save the mother's life; and (4) prohibited the use of public funds, employees, or facilities for the purpose of "encouraging or counseling" a woman to have an abortion not necessary to save her life.

3. The First Amendment's religion clauses read: "Congress shall make no law respecting an establishment of religion, or prohibiting the free exercise thereof. . . ."

4. The Supreme Court, in *Sherbert,* ruled that the state of South Carolina could not withhold unemployment compensation benefits from an Adventist who refused Saturday work. In reaching its decison the Court ruled that government may not burden one's exercise of religion unless it is essential to accomplish a compelling governmental interest.

5. 494 U.S. 872, 110 S.Ct. 1595, 1606 (1990).

6. See the *New York Times,* Friday, May 11, 1990, A-16.

7. "Faith, Tribe, Nation: Top Story of 1990," *The Christian Century* 107 (1990): 1187–88.

8. Ibid.

9. *Harvard Law Review* 103 (1990): 1409.

10. The prevailing doctrine, as set forth in *Lemon* v. *Kurtzman,* 403 U.S. 602

(1971), provides that in order to pass muster under the establishment clause a law must (1) have a bona fide secular purpose, (2) have a primary effect that neither advances nor inhibits religion, and (3) not result in excessive governmental entanglement with religion.

11. *Wallace* v. *Jaffree,* 472 U.S. 38, 91 (1985) (Rehnquist, J., dissenting).

12. *County of Allegheny* v. *American Civil Liberties Union,* 494 U.S. 573, 109 S.Ct. 3086 (1989) (Kennedy, J., dissenting).

13. *Bowen* v. *Kendrick,* 487 U.S. 573, 108 S.Ct. 2562, 2582 (1988).

14. R. Boston, "Misbegotten Measure," *Church and State* 43 (1990): 244–45.

15. Ibid.

16. R. Boston, "Parochiad Crusade," *Church and State* 43 (1990): 7.

17. The support of Seventh-Day Adventists, for example, was a key factor in the Oregon parochiaid battle. In the words of Richard Fenn, of the Northwest headquarters of Seventh-Day Adventists, "This department finds Measure Eleven to be a bad proposal. It would make the taxes we pay government available for the support of religious schools whose beliefs we cannot espouse. It would make the taxes others pay government available for the support of religious schools whose beliefs they cannot espouse. Oregon Seventh-Day Adventists do well to resist the temptation to grab government dollars to pay tuition at our own schools." Boston, "Parochiaid Crusade," p. 244 n. 12.

18. See, e.g., *Witters* v. *State Commission for the Blind,* 771 P. 2d 1119 (Wash. 1989).

19. See *The Wall Street Journal,* December 31, 1990, A-10.

12

Theocracy versus Democracy in the Empire State: Three Decades of Church-State Entanglement in the Schools of New York

Florence Flast

It is widely recognized that the foundation of American democracy rests on fundamental principles embodied in the Bill of Rights and the principle of free, universal public education. Of all the civil rights protected against government tampering, preeminent in the First Amendment to the United States Constitution is that of religious liberty, a guarantee of the separation of church and state, as defined by Thomas Jefferson.

Jefferson was also a strong advocate of universal education, stating, "If the condition of man is to be progressively ameliorated, as we fondly hope and believe, education is to be the chief instrument in effecting it."

The responsibility for providing education was left to the states, and following the Civil War, every state admitted into the union was mandated by Congress to include in its constitution a provision for establishing and maintaining a statewide public school system.

New York State's constitution makes such a provision for free public schools for all children in Article XI, Section 1. The constitution, as revised

Florence Flast is Chair of the Committee for Public Education and Religious Liberty (PEARL), and was a plaintiff in *Flast* v. *Cohen*.

in 1894, also embodies the principle of separation of church and state in education in Article XI, Section 3, although the prohibition against the use of public funds for any school—public or private—in which religious doctrine or tenets were "taught, inculcated, or practiced" had been a part of the laws of New York State since 1844.

Just three years prior to the passage of that statute—in 1841—a religious group, the "Catholic Party," appeared on the ballot in New York State. Its candidates pledged to support the position of the Church in its efforts to obtain public funds for parochial schools. Although the Catholic Party disappeared as a separate entity after receiving only a few votes, the Church remained a political force in the state. This essay will provide an historical survey of public aid to sectarian education in New York State, and how state government has increasingly bowed to Church pressures to provide monetary and other assistance to religiously oriented schools.

NEW YORK'S CONSTITUTIONAL PROVISION FOR SEPARATION OF CHURCH AND STATE

Article XI, Section 3 in the State Constitution was sponsored by State Senator Elihu Root, later the nation's Secretary of State, and Nobel Peace Prize recipient. It reads:

> Neither the state nor any subdivision thereof shall use its property or credit or any public money, or authorize or permit either to be used, directly or indirectly, in aid or maintenance, other than for examination or inspection, of any school or institution of learning wholly or in part under the control or direction of any religious denomination, or in which any denominational tenet or doctrine is taught.

With one amendment, which was passed many years later, permitting transportation of students to and from school, this provision has remained part of the basic law of New York State for almost a century, despite many attempts to repeal it.

The detailed language of Article XI, Section 3, while embodying the principles of the First Amendment's religion clauses barring government from any "establishment of religion or prohibiting the free exercise thereof," contrasts, in its length and specificity, with the brevity and general applicability of the latter.

Nevertheless, despite such a clearly stated prohibition, the power of the church and the nature of politics in New York State have been such that laws and regulations have been adopted, particularly in the past thirty years, that do violence to these principles.

THE REGENTS' PRAYER

In 1962, the United States Supreme Court handed down a landmark decision against a government-sponsored prayer in the public schools of New York. Justice Hugo L. Black, who delivered the opinion of the Court in *Engel* v. *Vitale*, cited the prayer that had been composed by the Board of Regents and was required to be recited by each class at the beginning of the school day: "Almighty God, we acknowledge our dependence upon Thee, and we beg Thy blessings upon us, our parents, our teachers, and our country." Justice Black stated, "We think that by using its public school system to encourage recitation of the Regents' Prayer, the State of New York has adopted a practice wholly inconsistent with the Establishment Clause." He pointed out that even though the prayer was voluntary and might be considered "denominationally neutral," it was still impermissible, adding that the Establishment Clause did not depend upon any showing of direct government compulsion. The ruling noted, "When the power, prestige, and financial support of government is placed behind a particular religious belief, the indirect coercive pressure upon religious minorities to conform to the prevailing officially approved religion is plain." Justice Black also stated that the underlying purpose of the Establishment Clause "rested on the belief that a union of government and religion tends to destroy government and to degrade religion."

Supreme Court decisions, however, do not serve to inhibit religious groups from continuing to bring tremendous pressure upon public officials for governmental support of their beliefs. The support they seek falls into two categories: (1) ideological, as in promoting school prayer, influencing curriculum content to reflect religious tenets, religious observances in public schools, and censorship of textbooks and library books on religious grounds; and (2) financial, seeking tax dollars to support sectarian schools.

TEXTBOOK AID

New York State has been most responsive to such pressures. In the mid-sixties, New York enacted a law that required local public school authorities to lend secular textbooks free of charge to all students in grades seven through twelve, including those attending parochial schools. Though technically considered a loan to the students, the textbooks were not required to be returned to the public school authorities but were permitted to be stored by the parochial schools. Challenged by a school board in upstate New York, the State was upheld by the U.S. Supreme Court in 1968 in *Board of Education* v. *Allen*. Absent proof that the books were being used to enhance religious teaching (although a later study reported in the *Yale Law Review* demonstrated that they were), and finding that sectarian schools provide secular as well as religious teachings, Justice Byron R. White, delivering the majority opinion, held that the state law did not violate the Establishment Clause. Since that time this program has been expanded to include elementary school pupils and the allocations have been increased substantially.

Though this and subsequent laws were in clear violation of the New York State Constitution, the challenges were brought in federal, not state, courts, because the courts of New York did not permit suits by taxpayers except in a limited category of cases. Limitations on taxpayer suits in federal courts challenging violations of First Amendment protections of religious liberty were lifted by a Supreme Court decision in a suit in which this writer was a plaintiff (*Flast* v. *Cohen*, handed down in the same year as the *Allen* decision).

CHURCH-STATE BATTLE AT A CONSTITUTIONAL CONVENTION

In 1967, a Constitutional Convention was called to revise the Constitution of the State of New York. One of its main purposes was to revise or repeal Article XI, Section 3, so that religious schools could be subsidized by the state.

The campaign for repeal of this constitutional provision was led by the Roman Catholic Archdiocese of New York and by Citizens for Educational Freedom, formed to organize public support for religious schools. The goal of both, as described in their literature, was "parity"; that is, that government should finance private and parochial schools to the same extent that it finances public education. The State Constitution was an impediment to such a goal.

The majority of those who held political office in New York State jumped on the repeal bandwagon, and although many aspects of the State Constitution were in need of revision and reform, this one issue dominated the public discourse.

To counter this threat both to church-state separation and the public schools, the Committee for Public Education and Religious Liberty (PEARL), a coalition of twenty-two New York civic, religious, and educational organizations, was formed. (It now has forty member organizations.) PEARL distributed literature explaining the issue, supplied speakers for public meetings and talk shows, and mounted a statewide effort to mobilize public opinion in support of the retention of Article XI, Section 3.

A tactical decision was made by the leadership in the Constitutional Convention to draw up a new constitution, rather than amend the existing document. In that way, a vote would be taken on the entire text rather than on individual sections, thus limiting the debate. The proposed new constitution, having no specific prohibition against aid to religious schools, was adopted by the Constitutional Convention delegates. The leadership anticipated that when it went to a referendum, the voters would be so supportive of the many reforms in the new constitution that they would approve it even without the parochiaid prohibition. However, it was a gamble that backfired as the proposed constitution was defeated in the referendum by a vote of three to one. The church-state issue was the major factor in its defeat, with religious divisiveness one of the by-products of this battle.

However, though the prohibition remained the law of the State, legislators and governors of the State of New York chose to ignore it or to reinterpret its meaning. Governor Nelson A. Rockefeller proposed and encouraged passage of parochiaid measures. He never vetoed one.

THE 1970S: A RASH OF PAROCHIAID LAWS

Thus, in 1970 the "Mandated Services Act" was enacted, providing $28 million a year to private and parochial schools for record-keeping, testing, and other services, at the rate of $27 per elementary school pupil and $45 per secondary school pupil. PEARL brought suit, and the United States Supreme Court ruled the Act unconstitutional in June of 1973. Chief Justice Warren E. Burger delivered the opinion of the Court in *Levitt* v. *Committee for Public Education and Religious Liberty*. He noted, as was pointed out by PEARL counsel Leo Pfeffer, that the most expensive service to be reimbursed to the religious schools by the state was the administration and grading of tests and the reporting of test results. These tests included state-prepared examinations, such as Regents examinations, but the great majority were tests prepared by teachers within the nonpublic schools. Chief Justice Burger wrote that "despite the obviously integral role of testing in the total teaching process, no attempt is made under the statute, and no means are available, to assure that internally prepared tests are free of religious instruction." The statute was struck down as "an impermissible aid to religion."

In 1971, the "Secular Educational Services Act" was passed. Governor Rockefeller signed it into law even though the Supreme Court had ruled a similar law in Pennsylvania unconstitutional. The New York law allocated $33 million per year to pay for a portion of teachers' salaries and other "secular" services in parochial schools. PEARL brought suit again. The law was invalidated by the United States District Court, Southern District of New York, on January 11, 1972. The State did not appeal.

The following year, in *Committee for Public Education and Religious Liberty* v. *Court of Claims*, PEARL challenged a statute, "Court of Claims of 1972," which was intended to enable the parochial schools to sue in the State's Court of Claims to obtain the funds they would have received under the Mandated Services Act if it had not been declared unconstitutional by

the U.S. District Court. PEARL challenged this as a blatant attempt to negate the Federal court decision. The state agreed not to implement this law
until the U.S. Supreme Court ruled on the appeal in *Levitt.*

However, 1,700 parochial schools filed suits, claiming $15 million. The
New York State Court of Appeals ruled in their favor in July 1976. PEARL
held its suit in abeyance pending the decision of the Attorney General as
to whether the State would appeal to the U.S. Supreme Court. The State
did so in *New York* v. *Cathedral Academy.* On December 6, 1977, the United
States Supreme Court reversed the Court of Appeals, declaring that the State
law was effectively modifying a federal court's injunction.

A subsequent "mandated services" law was then enacted, excluding teacher-
prepared tests and requiring an accounting of the expenditure of the state
funds. The Supreme Court upheld it.

In 1972, New York State passed the "Omnibus Education Act," which
would subsidize parochial schools in three ways: (1) direct grants to the schools
for maintenance of buildings, grounds, and equipment, termed "health and
welfare" grants, at an estimated cost of $4–5 million per year; (2) tuition
reimbursements to low-income families with children in parochial schools,
estimated to cost between $5 and $25 million per year; and (3) $10–15 million
for tuition tax credits for families with gross incomes up to $25,000, who
paid at least $50 per year for tuition at parochial schools.

On June 25, 1973, the United States Supreme Court ruled these three
forms of aid to parochial schools unconstitutional in *Committee for Public
Education and Religious Liberty* v. *Nyquist.* Justice Lewis F. Powell, Jr.,
delivered the opinion of the Court. In it he noted that almost all the nonpublic schools benefiting from the act were Roman Catholic and that the
maintenance grants, tuition grants, and tuition tax credits all would have the
effect of placing the State of New York in the business of advancing religion.
The Court ruled that giving tuition grants or tuition tax credits to the parents was just as invalid as giving the funds directly to the sectarian schools,
as with the maintenance grants. It stated, "By reimbursing parents for a portion of their tuition bill, the State seeks to relieve their financial burdens
sufficiently to assure that they continue to have the option to send their children to religion-oriented schools. . . . The effect of the aid is unmistakably
to provide desired financial support for nonpublic, sectarian institutions." Justice Powell warned of the grave potential for "continuing political strife over
aid to religion" and the tendency for aid programs to "become entrenched,
to escalate in cost, and to generate their own aggressive constituencies."

Much of New York's legislative activity in the 1970s proceeded on the
assumption that a 1965 federal aid to education law, the Elementary and
Secondary Education Act (ESEA), was constitutional even though it provided for the remedial education of parochial school pupils. (The term "paro-

chial" or any other reference to religious schools did not appear in the law, only the euphemism "nonpublic schools.") ESEA was predicated on the "child benefit theory," that "aid to the child" as opposed to "aid to a religious school" would survive a constitutional test; but ESEA excluded a provision for judicial review which had been proposed as a means of getting an early decision in the courts.

PUBLIC SCHOOL TEACHERS ASSIGNED TO RELIGIOUS SCHOOLS

New York State's education authorities chose to implement ESEA in a manner that served the interests of the religious schools. Instead of providing the remedial and guidance services to public and parochial school children together in special classes in public school buildings, which would have given an opportunity for the intermingling and "shoulder-rubbing" referred to in the congressional debate, the authorities bowed to the threat that religious school children would boycott such classes and funding for the public schools would be affected. So public school remedial teachers and guidance counselors were assigned to serve religious school students in the schools they attended.

PEARL filed suit in federal court in August 1977. It took six years before an unfavorable decision was handed down by the District Court in October 1983. PEARL appealed to the Court of Appeals for the Second Circuit where a three-judge panel unanimously ruled the program unconstitutional on July 9, 1984. Noting that 84 percent of the nonpublic school students attended Roman Catholic schools and 8 percent attended Hebrew day schools, the Court rejected the government's arguments that the schools were "not predominantly religious"; that this was a benefit to the child, not the school; that state surveillance assured religious neutrality by the public employees; and that the government was not advancing religion by only providing "indirect aid." It held that the Establishment Clause was an "insurmountable barrier to the use of federal funds" for this program.

Parochial school parents, together with the U.S. Secretary of Education and the New York City Schools Chancellor, appealed that decision to the U.S. Supreme Court. On July 1, 1985, in *Aguilar* v. *Felton* (Felton was one of the PEARL plaintiffs), the high court affirmed the decision of the Court of Appeals, and ruled the program to be an unconstitutional violation of the First Amendment's Establishment Clause in that it would "inevitably result in the excessive entanglement of church and state."

Justice William J. Brennan, Jr., writing for the majority, noted that the aid was provided within a "pervasively sectarian environment." He also identified as other "critical elements" of entanglement the ongoing inspection needed to ensure that religious messages were not included in instruction and the close coordination required between public and parochial school teachers and administrators.

Justice Powell, in a concurring opinion, added that "the type of aid provided in New York by the Title I program amounts to a state subsidy of the parochial schools by relieving those schools of the duty to provide the remedial and supplemental education their children require."

In a companion case decided on the same day (*Grand Rapids School District* v. *Ball*) the Court also put to rest the "child benefit theory." Justice Brennan observed that all parochiaid eventually benefited students but that "no meaningful distinction can be made between aid to the student and aid to the school," and that the aid in question constituted an impermissible "symbolic union of government and religion in one sectarian enterprise."

Despite the ruling of the Court, the New York City Board of Education, encouraged also by then Mayor Ed Koch, began an elaborate maneuver to circumvent and delay implementing the decision it had so long opposed. In the summer of 1985, Board President James Regan wrote to the then U.S. Secretary of Education, William Bennett, that it was "obviously" impossible to provide equitable services while developing a plan and that it would be "necessary to start the 1985–1986 school year with Chapter 1* services provided in the same manner as they were last school year." As though there had been no Supreme Court decision! The Board of Education and the City of New York then submitted affidavits to the District Court requesting a year-long delay to consider alternative methods of providing the services to religious school pupils. The same judge who had ruled the program constitutional in the first instance granted the delay.

New York received encouragement from Washington. Secretary Bennett, in a speech to the Knights of Columbus, bemoaned the "misguided Court decisions," which have "thrust religion . . . out of the public schools; and made it far more difficult to give aid to parents of children in private, church-related schools." He said, "We, at the Department of Education, will do our best to nullify the damage done by the *Felton* decision. . . . We are about to introduce legislation allowing local school authorities to convert Chapter 1 funds into a voucher program."

TUITION TAX CREDITS AND THE RELIGIOUS RIGHT'S AGENDA

The major proposal for financing parochial schools in the late 1970s and the beginning of the 1980s was tuition tax credits. Although the Supreme Court had ruled against New York's program of tax credits for parochial

---

*Chapter 1 provides remedial services to children from low-income families.

school tuition in the *Nyquist* decision, the Chancellor of the New York State Board of Regents appointed a Regents Task Force to again study the question of tuition tax credits for New York; and U.S. Senator Patrick Moynihan of New York co-sponsored a national tuition tax credit bill in 1981. It was estimated that the bill would cost America's taxpayers seven billion dollars. It failed to pass.

Tuition tax credits also became an issue in the campaign for Governor of the State of New York in the 1982 election. In the primary, Mayor Ed Koch reiterated his support for tuition tax credits while Mario Cuomo announced his opposition. Koch lost; Cuomo gained the support of organized teachers and administrators in New York's public schools as well as the backing of the AFL-CIO, which also opposed the tax credits. Cuomo won the Democratic primary. He also stated his opposition to organized prayer in public schools.

Both of these stated positions were contrary to those of the Catholic Church. Not only did the Church support tuition tax credits, but the U.S. Catholic Conference had also come out in favor of President Reagan's proposal for a constitutional amendment to permit "group prayer" in public schools. The U.S. Catholic bishops similarly pressed for "voluntary religious instruction in public schools."

Cuomo's opponent, Republican Lew Lehrman, campaigned in support of tax credits for parochial school tuition and prayer in public schools, both advocated by the Religious Right. It was a close contest on Election Day, but Cuomo won.

STATE AID TO PAROCHIAL SCHOOLS CLIMBS

In addition to its lobbying for tuition tax credits, the Church also continued to press for other forms of government support, and state funds flowed increasingly into parochial schools through a variety of programs.

While several studies have been conducted by various groups to determine the extent of state tax support for religious schools in the 1980s, it has always been difficult to track down all the forms of government aid because they are not generally identified as aid to sectarian schools in any of the state budget documents.

However, the League of Women Voters of New York State issued a report in November 1982, showing that the cost of state subsidized services to nonpublic schools (94 percent of which were religious schools) had risen over 30 percent in two years. Another survey conducted by the National Education Association (NEA) concluded that New York provided $160 million in 1982 in direct aid to nonpublic elementary and secondary schools, and a considerable unspecified sum for indirect aid, such as the use of public school buildings for athletics and other services provided by local tax dollars. NEA's "conservative estimate" of this total cost was a quarter of a billion dollars a year for private K–12 education. It further found that "New York State spends more tax dollars on nonpublic education than all other 49 states combined." The survey results were reported in the November 14, 1983 issue of *Newsday*.

Federal aid to nonpublic school students under ESEA also continued to climb each year. In 1984, for the range of services which local school boards were required to extend to nonpublic schools, the estimated expenditure was $250 million according to the Office of Nonpublic School Services/Division of Educational Finance in the State Education Department. This included aid for transportation, textbooks, computer software, nutrition programs, federal ESEA-ECIA* remedial education programs, programs for handicapped children attending nonpublic schools under contracts for services rendered, and mandated services (testing and reports).

Based on these costs, the State figured that—with the exception of handicapped children—the average expenditure per nonpublic school child was $312, while that per public school child was $1,844. However, these figures ignored categories of expenditures that were not listed in the state's computation, such as those by local school districts from local revenues (including summer school programs, attendance services, dual enrollment in vocational education classes, and use of public school gymnasiums for team practice) and did not include the cost of computer software. Despite these omissions, the figures provided by the State showed an increase of $56.5 million (a 22 percent rise) in aid to nonpublic schools in two years. Increased state and federal aid to nonpublic schools was occurring in an environment and at a time when the disparity and reduction in resources available to less wealthy public school districts was increasing.

Two years later, a report published by the Coalition for Public Education, in Albany, New York, titled "The State of New York and Nonpublic Schools," revealed that in the first three years of Governor Cuomo's term, state aid to nonpublic schools had increased 36.4 percent. As for aid to public schools, the governor, in his budget message, took credit for what he considered a demonstration of his support for public education—a 28 percent increase in state aid to public schools during the same period.

THE CHURCH-STATE PARTNERSHP

In the State Senate, where public schools often got short shrift, catering to the interests of the religious schools was common practice. In December 1983,

---

*ECIA = The Education Consolidation and Improvement Act of 1981

a Senate Task Force on Critical Problems had issued a report titled "Educational Partnership—Nonpublic and Public Elementary and Secondary Education in New York State." It began with the statement that "the promotion and support of two educational sectors, public and nonpublic, has been fundamental state policy for the past 200 years," and that by financially assisting nonpublic schools, New York has helped maintain "a healthy nonpublic educational sector" which offers "diverse educational opportunities to the State's children," provides their parents with "an alternative to public education," is a "vitally important component of the State's educational system," and "represents one of this State's most notable achievements." No such praise was heaped on the other "partner"—the public schools. On the contrary, all the negative judgments about public education were repeated.

The report suggested that nonpublic education was a state responsibility and should be adequately funded from the public purse. It lamented the fact that nonpublic schools did not come close to receiving the same percentage of "either State or federal assistance" that their enrollment warranted, even though they acknowledged that 90 percent of the nonpublic schools were sectarian and that they interspersed religious instruction throughout.

Yet, while the report extolled the virtues of the nonpublic school sector, it admitted that "no mechanism currently exists whereby the state can measure the quality of the nonpublic elementary and secondary school programs"; that "the state appears impotent in its ability to establish and enforce nonpublic school reporting and curricular standards"; that information regarding student performance in these schools was "inadequate and unreliable"; and that many of the schools, particularly the increasing number of Christian fundamentalist schools, refused to provide access to any information about their students.

Getting involved in questions of nonpublic school program accountability was referred to as a "political hot potato."

Another series of problems surfaced in this report regarding textbook aid, with some school districts spending twice as much on nonpublic school textbook aid as on public school textbook aid, a lack of standards for determining "whether or not expensive curricular materials requested by nonpublic schools should be accepted for textbook aid"; and a "lack of any evaluation standard to measure whether or not textbooks requested by nonpublic schools are classified as sectarian or nonsectarian."

In 1984, the New York State legislative session had scarcely begun when the Senate Education Committee proceeded to schedule hearings on a series of proposals for tuition tax credits and other tax benefits for parochial school parents. On five of the seven days scheduled for the hearings, the evening sessions of these "public" hearings were held exclusively in Catholic high schools—in New York City, Syracuse, Albany, Utica, and Tonawanda. Public school parents protested not only the tax subsidy proposals, but the holding of these hastily scheduled meetings on parochial school premises during the only hours when working parents could attend.

However, a year later, in the 1985 legislative session, State Senator John Marchi introduced a bill that would have provided parents of children in parochial schools with tax credits of $650 to $1,000 per child for tuition and other education expenses.

Governor Mario Cuomo, who had opposed tuition tax credits in his 1982 campaign for election, now gave unabashed support to the bill, noting that for thirty years he had been a supporter of church school aid, and that New York State was then currently giving substantial aid to religious schools. The bill, however, encountered fierce opposition from public school advocates, civil rights groups, and local editorial writers, and failed to reach the Senate floor for a vote.

Meanwhile, in letters to the *Jewish Ledger* and the Rochester Catholic Diocese's *Courier Journal* in upstate New York, Governor Cuomo sought appreciation for the financial package he had proposed for nonpublic schools. He stated: "In the budget for fiscal year 1985–86, that I proposed on January 22, support for nonpublic elementary and secondary schools will increase by nearly $54 million, from $156.5 million in 1982–83 to $210.4 million in 1985–86. That increase of 34.4 percent is substantial and well exceeds the rate of inflation."

New York's partnership of religion and government appears in sometimes obscure forms. Thus hidden within the state's 1984–85 budget bill was an amendment to the State Education Law, authorizing up to $2.50 per pupil for computer software programs in both public and nonpublic schools. The law required school boards to "loan" such software programs to pupils attending nonpublic schools, subject to rules and regulations set by the Board of Regents and local school authorities. The proposed rules permitted the nonpublic school officials to make the requests on behalf of their pupils and permitted the software to be stored on the property of the nonpublic schools. It barred, however, the purchase of programs that were "sectarian" in "nature or content." Such parochiaid laws, providing "loans" of "secular" educational materials other than textbooks, had previously been found unconstitutional by the U.S. Supreme Court in cases coming out of Pennsylvania and Ohio.

In New York City, the Board of Education calendars for its public meetings require constant monitoring. As an example, in November 1985, a resolution was submitted by the chancellor to accept $377,573 in federal funds for a "Follow Through" program "designed to maintain and extend the gains of preschool children through the primary grades," with a target population of "approximately 987 public school and 148 nonpublic school children." A PEARL speaker rose to remind the Board members that the Supreme Court decision in *Felton* prohibited on-site services by public school personnel. The Deputy Chancellor responded that they had received advice from the State Education Department that the *Felton* decision applied only to ESEA's Chapter 1 and, therefore, they could continue this other educational program on the premises of the religious school—a glaring distortion of the high court's rulings in *Felton* and *Grand Rapids*.

The project involved four education agencies: the Archdiocese of New York, which provided the classroom teacher; the New York City Board of Education, which, as the agency responsible for administering the program, provided a full-time teacher coordinator and three paraprofessionals; the U.S. Department of Education, which financed the program; and a university which developed a teacher training model. An 85-page descriptive document revealed some startling requirements for the position of the Board of Education's Teacher Coordinator, the person responsible for unifying the entire program, managing its finances, obtaining supplies, and scheduling workshops and staff meetings. The first requirement was "the approval of the Superintendent of Schools of the Archdiocese of New York"; another was "experience within the non-public school setting." A public school professional who might have been the most able administrator and teacher would not have qualified for the position if she or he had only taught in public schools or could not win the approval of the Archdiocese School Superintendent.

In another instance, the Board approved, at a public meeting, what appeared to be a routine contract for supplies and equipment for the city's schools. It was later discovered that several of these contracts were for the installation of computer systems for the Chapter 1 program in forty-four religious schools, at a cost of over $4 million. The item listed in the Board's calendar gave no hint that its purpose was to equip parochial schools. Moreover, the school's Chancellor had assured the Federal District Court judge that PEARL's counsel would be notified when decisions were made to implement alternative plans for providing Chapter 1 services to parochial school students. No such notification had been given.

In 1986, Governor Cuomo again presented a budget proposal with significant increases in aid to parochial schools through the categorical programs. These categorical aids, such as textbooks, computer software, and school library materials apportioned to public and nonpublic schools, provided the vehicle for aiding parochial education. School districts would prefer, and sound educational policy dictate, that local educational authorities determine public schools' needs and have the ability to spend according to local need instead of by category, whose purpose is to circumvent the Constitution and aid religious schools.

The New York State Board of Regents also, in its annual recommendations for legislative action on State aid to schools, almost invariably includes requests for increased aid to nonpublic schools, often in response to requests received from the State Catholic Conference and the State Council of Catholic School Superintendents. In 1986, the Regents included a proposal for transportation to nonpublic pre-kindergarten programs; space rental and acquisition of mobile classrooms for remedial educational services to nonpublic school pupils with special needs; inclusion of fire safety inspection as a "mandated service" for reimbursement; and increases in library aid, textbooks, and so on.

Not surprisingly, church and state also mix at the level of local school boards. In April 1986, *Newsday* ran a series of articles on the political and religious motivations of members of the Community School Boards in New York City, and the influence and impact these have on the public schools. Programs, jobs, and promotions are all affected. Notably, one Community School Board President in the Borough of Queens, whose daughter attended a parochial school, reportedly admitted that he ran for his post "to get as much aid as possible to parochial school students," and "to instill church views on controversial issues like sex education in the public school system." Another school board member said religion was a critical factor in deciding whom the Board appointed to school positions.

CIRCUMVENTING THE *FELTON* DECISION

When the school year ended in June 1986, the New York City Board of Education reported to the Federal District Court on how it planned to deliver federal Chapter 1 remedial services to religious school children during the next school year. Of the sectarian schools that had received on-site services in the prior year, 80 percent would be offered remedial instruction in nearby public schools. The balance would receive instruction in mobile instructional units (MIUs)—vans outfitted as classrooms—at a cost of over $7 million a year for seventy such vehicles, which would be parked in front of the parochial schools. The cost of these would come "off the top" of the federal Chapter 1 allotment for New York City schools, creating an inequality of expenditure for public and nonpublic school pupils, with the latter being favored. For the religious school pupils receiving instruction in the vans, the per capita cost would be triple the amount spent for Chapter 1 services per public school pupil. The cost of the van alone was more than double the instructional cost per pupil. The Board attributed its choice of this alternative to the overcrowding of public schools in some districts. PEARL's suggestion, that in those districts the public schools could be used after regular school hours, when there was no problem of space shortages and where the cost could be contained, had been rejected out-of-hand.

The Board's report to the court indicated that other plans were being formulated because almost all of the religious school principals had stated that neither they nor the parents of the parochial school students wanted the children to attend a Chapter 1 program in a public school.

In late June, the New York State Legislature passed enabling legislation sought by Governor Cuomo in his executive budget, allocating $10 million to provide, in his words, "remedial education services for nonpublic school pupils consistent with the U.S. Supreme Court decision in the *Aguilar* v. *Felton* case." Such a statement implied that the Supreme Court had ruled that some specific form of state aid for remedial services would be constitutional. It had not done so; it had referred the case to the lower court.

What the Supreme Court had said in regard to *Felton* and *Grand Rapids*, in striking down the government-funded remedial programs in parochial schools, was: "In both cases, publicly funded instructors teach classes composed exclusively of private school students in private school buildings. In both cases, an overwhelming number of the participating private schools are religiously affiliated. In both cases, the publicly funded programs provide not only professional personnel but also all materials and supplies necessary for the operation of the programs."

If, in fact, the parochial school children came to the public schools for these services and were grouped in classes with public school children, and there was no interaction between the teachers and administrators of the religious and public schools, the program might stand the constitutional test. If that was what the governor had in mind, then the $10 million should have been designated for the expansion of the public schools' remedial program to include religious school pupils.

The governor's bill required that the state monies, to be apportioned to school districts, be "expended only for direct noninstructional costs attributable to the provision of instruction at a site other than a sectarian school for eligible students enrolled in nonpublic schools," and that these funds be spent before any federal Chapter 1 funds were used for such a purpose. It also provided that if the monies were not needed to pay for such noninstructional costs, then they "shall be expended solely for the instruction of eligible students who are enrolled in nonpublic schools and who are receiving remedial instructional services pursuant to Chapter 1." Subsequent rules established by the Regents stated that the funds "may be used for buying, leasing, and installing mobile classroom units, for transporting pupils from a nonpublic school to the site where instruction actually takes place or for instructional technology."

The Secretary to the Governor, responding to objections raised by PEARL, defended the State's action as constitutional and added, "This administration will continue to develop its education proposals to direct funds to meet the needs of our State's pupils in both our public and nonpublic schools."

At another level, correspondence between the office of the Department of Education of the Archdiocese of New York and the City's Corporation Counsel (with copies to Mayor Ed Koch) revealed that they had held a joint meeting with a representative of the U.S. Department of Education regarding the proposed implementation of *Felton*. The Archdiocese had proposed a third-party contractor system for the provision of Chapter 1 services on the premises of religious schools, exclusive of those to be served by the mobile classrooms. This would apply to all parochial schools where the Boards's plan called for their pupils to obtain their Chapter 1 services in public schools. In June, the Corporation Counsel, while turning down such a system-wide program of independent contracting, did indicate that he had requested permission from the U.S. Department of Education to mount a pilot program using independent contractors for the purpose of testing its constitutionality. To his credit, however, the Corporation Counsel did urge that the parochial school administrators encourage participation by their pupils in Chapter 1 programs offered at the public schools, which he described as "the most practical and equitable means of delivering those services to the majority of eligible nonpublic school students."

In August 1986, a resolution appeared on the Board of Education's calendar, to lease space in fourteen church properties for the Chapter 1 program for parochial school pupils. They included Immaculate Conception, St. Mark the Evangelist, Transfiguration School, St. Clement Pope, St. Agnes, Holy Name of Jesus, Our Lady of Peace, Our Lady of Loretto, St. Brigid, Most Precious Blood, Our Lady of Mount Carmel, Our Lady of Lourdes, Our Lady of Bedford Stuyvesant, and St. Luke. These locations were religious schools, rectories and parish centers. Each of these churches had schools that had received Chapter 1 services in 1985–1986. All their pupils had been assigned to local public elementary schools in September to obtain Chapter 1 instruction during part of the school day.

The resolution called for the Board to undertake the cost of making physical changes in the leased buildings for the "health, safety, and comfort of its occupants and for the proper maintenance and operation of the physical plant." In its report to the District Court, the Board described these as "neutral sites."

PEARL Counsel Stanley Geller, who had argued the *Felton* case in the courts, said the sites were substantially indistinguishable from those the Supreme Court had ruled against. The Board of Education President, Robert F. Wagner, Jr., was reported in the *New York Times* to have said that the facilities had been carefully reviewed and been found to be "neutral" sites. A Board spokesman was quoted in the August 13, 1986 *New York Daily News* as saying that "neutral" status would be achieved by removing or covering religious symbols while the city was using church buildings. According to the Chancellor's office, the Board's lawyers had advised that the spaces would comply with the Supreme Court ruling and that the parochial school principals had been consulted about the choices.

Sadly, of the 194 schools for which appropriate and nearby public school space had been found, only twenty-two had agreed to that alternative.

The leasing of the so-called "neutral sites" was approved at the Board's meeting of September 17, 1986. Only one Board member, Gwendolyn C. Baker, had the courage and integrity to vote against the resolution. Another member publicly declared that he was opposed on a personal level, but was following the advice of the City's Corporation Counsel.

In one situation where a public school's space was accepted, the preparation for its use led to an angry confrontation and a court suit. In its zeal to segregate and insulate religious school pupils from public school pupils, a local school board in the Williamsburg section of Brooklyn accommodated the wishes of the principal of Beth Israel School for Girls, an Orthodox Jewish day school, and blocked off a section of Public School 16 for their use. The physical barrier separated a wing of nine classrooms, corridors and stairwells from the rest of the school, to meet the requirements of the sectarian school whose four hundred Hasidic girls were to come there for remedial instruction in English and math. They would displace a group of seventy handicapped public school students and pre-kindergarten pupils who ordinarily used that space. The handicapped students were to be bused to another public school.

The public school parents, most of whom were Hispanic or black, went to court, claiming that the plan violated civil rights laws protecting the handicapped and prohibiting segregation in public schools. The school district, however, claimed the "wall" was necessary to meet the Hasidic sect's requirement of separation of the sexes in school and because of racial tensions in the community.

The public school parents were represented in their court challenge by Brooklyn Legal Services and the Puerto Rican Legal Defense Fund. PEARL filed an *amicus* brief in their behalf. The Federal District Court Judge ruled against them on September 15, stating that the Constitution "does not require a complete separation" of church and state, "but firmly mandates accommodation . . . of all religions." He found no violation of the constitutional rights of the public school parents. He had reached these conclusions without a trial.

The public school parents appealed. Two weeks later, a three-judge panel of the U.S. Court of Appeals for the Second Circuit held a hearing on the appeal. The attorney for the parents of P.S. 16 opened his remarks by noting the irony of the situation—that two hundred years after the signing of the U.S. Constitution, the Board of Education had given a new meaning to the "wall of separation" between church and state. Within two days the Appeals

Court, reversing the decision of the lower court, ordered that a preliminary injunction be issued and that a trial be held on the merits of the case. A month later it issued a written opinion, in which it disagreed with the district court's view that what was being asked would "in effect force the Hasidic children to give up sincere religious beliefs." It pointed out that the Free Exercise Clause of the First Amendment "does not prohibit a government from forcing a choice between receipt of a public benefit and pursuit of a religious belief if it can show a compelling reason for doing so," and added, "Avoiding a violation of the Establishment Clause that would otherwise result from an apparent endorsement of the tenets of a particular faith is ample reason for compelling that choice."

The "wall" came down and other space was found for the religious school pupils.

The Regents were also receiving requests for parochiaid for Jewish day schools. The September 26, 1986 *Jewish Week* reported the recommendations for legislation which were made to the Regents by Agudath Israel of America to aid two hundred yeshivas and day schools in New York State. They called for tuition tax credits, higher textbook and computer funding, transportation for preschoolers, a voucher system providing for alternative transportation arrangements for yeshiva students whose school hours did not coincide with state-provided transportation, reimbursement to yeshivas for general improvement programs to help students score higher on standardized tests, and summer teacher training for nonpublic school teachers. The Regents were favorably responsive in their recommendations for increased aid for textbooks, computer software, pre-K transportation, and teacher training.

Each year, near the end of the state budget negotiations, members of the Legislature divide up millions of dollars of state funds for pet projects in their districts. In 1987, these "member items" totaled $80 million, a huge pork barrel that slips through without any public debate or input. While some legislators allocate funds for causes which serve the public, such as libraries, special public school programs, and programs for the needy, several use this back door financing to aid religious institutions. Through this device, the Franciscan Academy, a parochial school in Syracuse, received a New York State grant of $100,000, thanks to two legislators, Senator Tarley Lombardi and Assemblyman Melvin Zimmer, who had daughters enrolled there and who had inserted the item in the state budget. Other religious schools and institutions received grants through this process for school remodeling, after-school programs, preschool, weekend and summer school programs, computer equipment, and other uses.

PEARL CHALLENGES ASSIGNMENT OF PUBLIC SCHOOL TEACHERS TO MOBILE CLASSROOMS AND TO SPACE LEASED FROM CHURCHES

In 1987, PEARL filed suit again in Federal District Court, challenging the alternative methods adopted by the New York City Board of Education to provide remedial education to religious school pupils in the aftermath of the *Felton* decision barring such services on the premises of the religious schools. The pending action, *Committee for Public Education and Religious Liberty et al* v. *Secretary, United States Department of Education, Commissioner of Education of the State of New York, and Chancellor and Board of Education of the City of New York,* charges that "the use of public tax-derived funds" (federal, state, and city) "to provide teachers, guidance counselors and educational equipment, material and supplies" for the benefit of religious schools or their students violates both Federal and New York State Constitutions.

In particular, the lawsuit challenges: (1) "mobile instructional units" (MIUs) parked so close to the parochial schools whose students they serve that they function as annexes to those schools; (2) use of so-called neutral sites located in buildings owned by religious organizations or denominations, serving only the children of the same religious group, for which the city pays for leases, renovation, and maintenance, thus providing additional income to the religious groups; and (3) the provision of Chapter 1 instruction and counseling conducted in classes in public schools where the classes "are composed exclusively of students from the same religious school," being "escorted to and from such schools as a group," and "segregated in virtually all respects from the public school students regularly enrolled" there.

One of the ironies in the "neutral site" arrangements was that prior to the *Felton* decision, the religious denominations made classroom space available for the program at no cost; now the Board was enabling them to receive a financial windfall from the state. For example, students from the Immaculate Conception School in the Bronx were now receiving Chapter 1 instruction from public school teachers at a building owned by Immaculate Conception located only a few doors away, for which the Board was paying $14,250 per year. A church in Brooklyn received over $50,000 a year in rent paid by the Board of Education for classroom space for its parochial school pupils in the Chapter 1 program. In addition, Chapter 1 funds were being used to improve church property at the expense of the taxpayer. With limited funding for Chapter 1, these federal monies diverted to such use were coming out of the appropriation for the remedial education of public school pupils.

PEARL's complaint also challenges the New York State statute providing $10 million for this program for nonpublic schools, and the use of Federal Chapter 2 funds to "furnish computers, computer software, audio-visual equipment, library materials and supplies and similar equipment, materials and supplies for use on the premises of religious schools," all of which are "capable of being used for instruction in religious subjects" and which relieve the religious institution of the financial burden of procuring them.

In December 1987, in a case that was brought in a New York State court by another school district, a three-judge panel of the Appellate Division of the Supreme Court of the State of New York, Second Department, in a unanimous decision, ruled unconstitutional the provision of special education services by public school personnel to religious school pupils in mobile vans or other "facilities and under conditions that constitute a religious setting."

The case, *Monroe-Woodbury Central School District* v. *Abraham Wieder et al.*, arose when Hasidic parents of handicapped children who were enrolled in Jewish parochial schools in upstate New York requested that the school district's Board of Education provide special education for their children. The Board complied, evaluating the needs of the children and then offering them placement in appropriate public school programs. The parents refused to allow their children to attend school outside their religious community or to mix with public school children. In proceedings in State Supreme Court, the court ordered the Board of Education to provide secular educational, remedial, and therapeutic services to these children "in a mobile or other appropriate site not physically or educationally identified with but reasonably accessible to the parochial school children." The Board of Education appealed, contending that the requirement violated the Establishment Clause of the First Amendment. The Appellate Division agreed. It found that the remedy imposed by the lower court had been "fashioned" by its concern for the religious and social practices of the Hasidim and "might well be viewed as a special governmental accommodation occasioned by, and thus an endorsement of, the Hasidic customs and lifestyle," a result that was "constitutionally impermissible."

The court also ruled "the creation of a facility for the obvious purpose of accommodating the Hasidic community without regard to secular factors will effectively render it inaccessible to other handicapped children. As such, it cannot be considered a truly neutral site." Finding that the "mobile units" constituted "a religious setting," the judges ruled the program unconstitutional under both the First Amendment and under Article XI, Section 3 of the State Constitution.

When the decision was appealed, the State's highest court, the Court of Appeals, chose not to rule on the constitutional issue. Instead it ruled narrowly that the State Education Law did not require the school district to provide the special education services in the mobile vans or other nonpublic sites.

SEPARATE SCHOOL DISTRICT CREATED
FOR RELIGIOUS GROUP

The Hasidim won their battle on a different battleground two years later, however. Having failed in the courts to force the public school district to set up special education programs in mobile vans or "neutral sites," they turned to the politicians. The legislature and the governor accommodated them. In July 1989, Governor Cuomo signed into law a measure that gave Kiryas Joel, an all Hasidic village in the town of Monroe, its own public school district, enabling this religious sect to receive state funds to educate their children without sending them to public schools in the school district serving their area. Although it is hard to believe that a separate school district for the Hasidic community could be any less unconstitutional than a separate mobile van, this consideration did not deter the lawmakers in New York State.

The law is being challenged by the New York State School Boards Association. Under the provisions of the statute, the separate district, known as the Kiryas Joel Village School District, is to "have and enjoy all the powers and duties of a union free school district." It is under the control of a board of education elected by voters of the village of Kiryas Joel, a village in which all the residents are Hasidic Jews. They receive state aid for the education of the handicapped children in their village. (Nonhandicapped children all attend private religious schools maintained by the sect, which presumably would not qualify for state aid except for transportation and other categorical aids.)

NEW YORK CITY DEFENDS ITS USE OF MIUS

New York City's Board of Education, unlike that of Monroe, New York, wholeheartedly embraced the idea of mobile instructional units for the parochial schools receiving Chapter 1 services, and defended their use against all criticism, even that of the Comptroller of the City of New York. His office had conducted an audit on the award of the contract for leasing the MIUs and found the cost excessively high, much higher than that of other cities. In its response the Board stated that only in New York was the vehicle designed for a dual purpose—having a classroom for remedial instruction of a small group of ten and a separate section outfitted for individual counseling and guidance services. An oversized vehicle to accommodate the latter, it said, was needed to meet the requirements of the nonpublic school administrators who "have exercised the option of spending a portion of their allocation on these support services." *Their* allocation? The Board obviously viewed these public monies as rightfully belonging to the religious schools. Justifying its expenditure, the Board also stated that the area in the van which had been set aside for guidance services was also used for classes in "English as a Second Language" to kindergarten and first grade children, and for staff conferences with parochial school parents and nonpublic school personnel.

In addition to the MIUs, the Board of Education had also considered stationary instructional units (SIUs) as an option for providing Chapter 1 services to parochial school students. Such a plan envisioned leasing property from the parochial schools and placing the SIUs on that property. Since there had been no discussion of this plan for three years, it was assumed that the idea had been abandoned. However, in mid-August 1988, a resolution appeared on the Board's calendar for its public meeting. It indicated that the Board was to lease space in the schoolyards of three Roman Catholic schools in Brooklyn "to erect structures for providing Chapter 1 instruction to nonpublic school students or for whatever purposes the Board of Education deems appropriate." No mention was made of what it would cost to build the SIUs or to make the "alterations, installations, decorations, and improvements on and to the demised land" which it planned to do at public expense, or of the expense of ongoing repair and maintenance of the property.

The Board sent specifications for the SIU buildings to potential contractors, requesting bids by November. The buildings were to be 47 feet long and 23 feet wide, have four classrooms, be fully furnished and equipped, and have planters at their entrances. In the blueprint drawings they looked like pretty suburban homes. The only thing to distinguish this facility from the main parochial school building would be a Board of Education emblem affixed to the outside. Only two contractors submitted bids, both incomplete and very expensive. Both were rejected.

The grandiose plans for the SIUs were in sharp contrast to newspaper headlines that fall about the deteriorating public school buildings in New York City and the horrendous conditions in which public school pupils and teachers were expected to function.

By 1991, the number of religious schools receiving Chapter 1 remedial services from the City's Board of Education reached 278. Only seventeen of these accepted services for their children in nearby public schools, although 82 percent of the religious schools were within one to six blocks of a public school. The number of mobile vans providing services at the curbside of parochial schools had grown to 106 at an estimated cost of about $120,000 each per year. The pupils in thirty religious schools were provided with take-home computers, a unique privilege not afforded public school pupils.

According to an estimate by a State Education Department official, federal and state aid to nonpublic schools in New York State had now reached half a billion dollars; according to another estimate by a State Senator it was closer to $700–800 million. Yet while public schools faced drastic cuts due to budget deficits in the State and City of New York, no corresponding cuts were being made in the appropriations for religious schools.

THE STATE REQUIRES RELIGIOUS INPUT
ON AIDS EDUCATION IN PUBLIC SCHOOLS

In the fall of 1987, the Board of Regents adopted emergency regulations requiring AIDS education for all students in New York State schools, both public and private. One of the regulations required that the board of education of every public school district "establish an advisory council responsible for making recommendations concerning the content, implementation, and evaluation of an AIDS instruction program." The regulations required that "representatives from religious organizations" be included in these advisory councils. The Executive Director of the State School Boards Association, Louis Grumet, in a letter to State Commissioner of Education Thomas Sobol, strenuously objected to this mandate, stating that the First Amendment's establishment clause "not only stands for the proposition that government shall not establish a religion, but that government shall abstain from fusing the functions of government and religion." This and other opposition were to no avail. The New York State School Boards Association filed suit in 1989 in State Supreme Court. That court and the Appellate Division both upheld the regulation. In the fall of 1991, the New York Court of Appeals, the State's highest court, agreed to hear a further appeal and PEARL filed an *amicus* brief challenging the regulation. Unfortunately, on March 31, 1992, the Court of Appeals upheld the decision of the lower court in a 5–2 decision.

The close ties between the Regents and the Church in New York State was evident in a news item that appeared in the February 2, 1989, edition of the publication *Catholic New York* reporting on the formation of the "New York State Coalition for Nonpublic Education," which, it stated, included Catholic, Jewish, Christian, Lutheran, and Independent private school groups. Its chairman was quoted as saying that its purpose was "to protect the independence of nonpublic schools and to ensure freedom of choice in education." ("Choice" is often the code word for state support for tuition in a sectarian school.) Brother James Kearney, Superintendent of Schools for the Archdiocese, indicated that the coalition was "a powerful influence in lobbying." It was reported that the groups involved in the coalition were "all part of the advisory council for the Commissioner of Education."

A STATE VOUCHER PROPOSED

State Education Commissioner Thomas Sobol, in a memo to the Board of Regents in May 1990, proposed that parents of children in public schools that had been "de-registered" for poor performance be given vouchers to pay for tuition in private, parochial, and other public schools. It was one of several proposals for "improving" elementary and secondary education in the 1990s.

At hearings throughout the fall, the proposal generated such intense public opposition that Sobol withdrew it. At a March 1991 meeting of the Board of Regents, they limited the use of public funds for any such transfers, or "choice," to public schools. They were also reportedly advised by the State Education Department lawyers that the proposal to include religious schools would violate the State Constitution. However, when the Vice Chancellor of the Regents was not satisfied, a subcommittee on "choice" to study the matter further was approved, with him as chairman.

Its recommendation to extend "choice" to nonpublic schools was presented to the Regents in July 1991. It would have involved up to 5,000 pupils —10 percent of the enrollment in fifty-nine public schools—each of whom would receive a $2,500 voucher for tuition at a nonpublic school. The proposal itself was a slight modification of one suggested by the New York State Catholic Conference, and the sample enabling legislation made clear that vouchers would subsidize the religious mission of participating sectarian schools by assuring that the law, if passed, would not abridge "the right of a participating nonpublic school to control its policies and programs."

The Regents defeated the proposal by a narrow margin of eight to six. Chancellor Martin Barell was reported to have said, "I do not believe we have been chosen as Regents to aid and abet the liquidation of the public school system." Both Governor Cuomo and New York City Schools Chancellor Joseph Fernandez had publicly stated their opposition to diverting public funds from public schools to nonpublic schools.

Nevertheless, the powerful influence of religious leaders on the political leaders in New York State has remained such that the state government and its administrative arms, such as the State Education Department, are zealous about aiding religious schools and have no compunction about using the State's taxing powers to tax all its citizens to support the religious teaching of some, in violation of the conscience of those who would choose not to do so voluntarily, a right guaranteed by the Constitution.

Religious liberty is not alive and well in New York.

Part Two

The Need for Public Schools

Introduction

William J. Jefferson
United States Congressman

The late Supreme Court justice Felix Frankfurter wrote that "the public school is at once the symbol of our democracy and the most pervasive means for promoting our common destiny." While the federal government has never had the primary responsibility for the education of our people in this country, it has an overriding interest in ensuring that all Americans not only have access to education but receive equity in educational offerings. The public school is both the vehicle by which we have sought to provide equal educational opportunity in this country and the engine that empowers individuals of all races and classes to achieve their potential. It is the fundamental means by which individuals and the nation as a whole attain social harmony and economic prosperity.

A central issue in the ongoing congressional debates over federal policy toward public education is the question of whether federal funding should be provided for parents to choose among private, parochial, and public schools. It is difficult to see how public schools could be improved by fostering private school choice. It is more likely, some in Congress have argued, that choice would lead to the ruination rather than the revitalization of public schools, and that vouchers would provide encouragement and a publicly funded mechanism for abandoning public schools.

The fundamental problem with education today is not that people lack the option to choose a good school; rather, the problem is that all schools are not equally as good. Choice does nothing to solve or even to address the problem of inequity that is the real source of its appeal. Choice leads parents to believe that it is finally possible for them to give their children the kind of quality education they believe other children are getting somewhere else. But if all schools were roughly equal in resources, teacher preparation, per-pupil spending, library collections, sports facilities, academic curriculum, and the like, choice would lost its appeal and its rationale. Without a strong commitment to ensuring that all schools are institutions where quality learning can take place, choice is a game of chance. As in all games there are winners and losers. The losers under choice are the same people who are losing today— urban and rural school children born into poverty. What parents are longing for is not the opportunity to give their children an education purchased in this or that private school, it is the opportunity to give their children a quality education.

Rather than look to unproven and simplistic so-called solutions like choice, Congress should encourage introspection on the part of states and school districts that will lead to a determination of the factors that contribute to quality teaching and pupil achievement in public schools. Herein lies the real challenge for the Congress and for the nation.

13

What If Government Subsidies for Private Schooling Are Legislated?

Donald E. Frey

After a period of relative quiet, the movement to maintain government subsidies for private schooling is active again. With the defeat in 1983 of the
Reagan administration's push for a tuition tax credit, followed by years of
escalating federal deficits, the timing had been bad for federal private school
subsidy proposals—all of which would have increased the federal deficit. But
for fiscal year 1992, President George Bush proposed a $200 million fund
for federal incentive payments to states and local school districts to initiate
parental-choice programs; this included the choice of private enrollment. States
and local school districts would have to provide most of the funding, since
the funds proposed by the president would be inadequate to cover more than
a fraction of the potential costs. This proposal came one year after the publication of a study by a mainstream think tank advocating a universal choice
plan,[1] Milwaukee's subsidization of some 260 lower-income students enrolling
in private schools, a ballot by Oregon voters on a tax credit plan (defeated
by a wide margin), and a New Hampshire town's decision to subsidize private
tuition payments.[2] In addition, a former governor of Delaware recently began
lobbying for a tuition voucher plan for that state.[3] This activity represents
the fourth peaking of the subsidy movement since the late 1960s. After a

Donald E. Frey is a professor of Economics at Wake Forest University, and author
of *Tax Credits for Private Education: An Economic Analysis* and other works.

short history of the subsidy movement, this essay will consider the likely economic consequences of subsidies for private schooling.

HISTORY OF THE SUBSIDY MOVEMENT

A continuous movement for subsidy of private schooling dates to the late 1960s when early congressional efforts to extend federal subsidies to private education failed. In 1972, President Nixon endorsed subsidies when his Commission on School Finance recommended government aid to private and parochial schools. At a time when Roman Catholic schools were losing enrollment, the proposed subsidies were supposed to arrest this trend. According to this argument, slowing parochial losses would reduce the need for public schools to pick up educational costs of the students leaving parochial schools. This logic was convincing neither to public school authorities nor to Congress, and in 1972 some one hundred tax-subsidy bills for private schooling failed to be enacted.

Proponents of subsidies, however, were also busy in states that had high concentrations of private schools. In 1973, the Supreme Court in *PEARL* v. *Nyquist* ruled against a New York State tax-subsidy plan for private education and set the legal climate for approximately the next decade. Courts were to apply three rules to decide whether an aid plan for private schools was constitutional. Such a plan had to have at least a nominally secular purpose; it would neither actively advance nor hinder religion; and it had to avoid excessive entanglement of church and state. In the years that followed, most state subsidies for private education failed to satisfy one or another of these three criteria when challenged in court.

The next peak in the subsidy movement occurred in 1977–1978. By then a popular "tax revolt" was underway across the nation, and the congressional proponents of tax subsidies for private schooling tied their bills to the notion of "tax relief." The opening shot was a 1977 effort to provide tax credits for college tuition. In 1978, the tax credit was reintroduced with the inclusion of elementary and secondary tuition—again in the name of tax relief. Despite strong opposition by the Carter administration, which countered with large increases in conventional aid for college students, Congress failed to pass the tuition tax credit by only a slim margin.

Following passage in 1981 of a major income tax cut, the Reagan administration could hardly argue the need for tax relief. Nevertheless, in 1982 and 1983, it supported plans for tuition tax credits, perhaps out of a belief that the private sector is almost always superior to the public sector in providing services. In an economy where federal deficits were growing at an alarming rate, a new open-ended tax loophole proved hard to sell and the tax-credit bill was defeated.[4] During the remainder of the decade, with a large deficit looming over tax-policy debates, proposals for private school tax subsidies failed to receive major support in Congress.

After the 1983 defeat, the hope for private school subsidies was sustained in two ways. First, in 1983 the Supreme Court loosened the application of its previous strictures by finding constitutional a Minnesota tax deduction for educational expenses (*Mueller* v. *Allen*). Second, the U.S. Department of Education supported research on choice in education, thus promoting yet another rationale for government subsidies of private schools. Even though not explicitly stated, the conclusion clearly was that the private alternative ought to be tried to see if it worked better than public education—whose weaknesses the Department of Education let no one forget.

Some in the Department of Education even implied that religious schools are a legitimate part of a choice strategy. For example, in the foreword to *Choice of Schools in Six Nations* an assistant secretary of education informed the reader that ". . . parental choices motivated by religious conviction are routinely accommodated in other Western democracies."[5] With the subsidy movement having thus been sustained during its passive period, the Bush administration has now adopted a more aggressive posture.

From this brief history of public subsidies for private education we may draw some conclusions and inferences for the future. First, the stated reasons for private school subsidization vary over time, depending on what popular notion of the moment may sell the concept. Whether the reason given is tax relief, parental choice, the supposed superiority of the private sector, or sparing public schools the cost of educating dislocated parochial school students, the outcome will be public funding for private schooling. Second, so long as the federal deficit remains large, subsidization efforts may emerge at the local and state levels with the national government reduced to playing an instigating role. Finally, the current case for private subsidies is that private schools will solve the ills of public education. This strategy will inevitably lead to an exaggeration of the ills of public schools.

THE DESIGN OF SUBSIDIES FOR PRIVATE SCHOOLING

A common element unites education vouchers, tuition tax credits, tuition tax deductions, or property tax reductions for tuition payments. Each is a governmental subsidy for private tuition that is given nominally to the parent instead of directly to the school. Subsidies that pass through the hands of parents before reaching the schools have been preferred for constitutional reasons since the Supreme Court's *Mueller* decision. (As extra legal window dressing, subsidies must be available for some public school fees too, even though the largest subsidy is for private tuition.) The subsidy amounts to a discount of private tuition, and thereby stimulates demand for nonpublic education. Let us consider each of the major kinds of tuition subsidies in more detail.

Tuition Tax Credits

A tuition tax credit allows a taxpayer to reduce taxes owed by some portion of tuition paid to private schools. Usually the credit would be applied against income taxes at the state or federal level. It might be possible to design a property tax credit; but since not everyone owns property, and since local jurisdictions are not uniform in levying the property tax, such a credit would be unevenly applied. A tuition tax credit would usually be subject to restrictions, e.g., the percentage of tuition that can be credited against taxes. Second, the credit usually would be capped at a maximum dollar figure. Third, income eligibility requirements may prevent those with income above a certain level from receiving the credit. Last, the credit may be restricted to the amount that a person owes in taxes; that is, it would be nonrefundable. For example, a low income person owing only $300 in taxes could receive a credit for only up to $300. Conversely, a refundable tax credit would be paid by the government to a person even if the credit exceeded the tax owed.

Consider a hypothetical tuition tax credit with restrictions. The credit might be for 50 percent of tuition paid, up to a maximum credit of $1,500. Further, the credit might be reduced $100 for every $1,000 of taxable income above some limit, say $80,000. The credit might also be made refundable.

Restrictions help to limit the government's revenue loss, and this is a necessary consdideration. After all, the tuition tax credit is an open-ended commitment to providing a tax reduction for all eligible taxpayers, no matter how many apply. And more than just private school parents may apply because of the Supreme Court's ruling that any tax break for private schooling would have to be available also for the miscellaneous fees and expenses of public school pupils. Public school districts might well increase a host of fees so as to shift more expenses to the federal government if a federal credit is enacted. (This, in itself, may be viewed as a retreat from the concept of free public schooling for all.) If public schools invented such fees, it would soon be apparent what a revenue loser for the federal or state government the tax credit loophole could be.

Restrictions on the tuition tax credit, however, do more than limit federal revenue losses. They also serve to target the credit on certain categories of beneficiaries. For example, with the 50 percent credit capped at the $1,500 maximum, parents of a child in a Protestant fundamentalist elementary school charging $2,500 would receive 50 percent ($1,250) from the credit, while parents of a student at a parochial high school charging $4,000 would receive

37.5 percent (the maximum $1,500), and parents of a student in an independent school charging $8,000 would receive only 18.8 percent (the maximum $1,500). If the parents of the independent school student earned taxable income of $90,000, their credit would be phased down to only $500, or about 6 percent of tuition. Thus, our hypothetical credit would give relatively greater benefits to parents whose children attend low tuition schools. And low tuition schools tend to be church-related rather than independent.

Tuition Tax Deductions

Tuition tax credits have been preferred to tuition tax deductions for several reasons. A tuition tax deduction is applicable only if one itemizes deductions, whereas a credit can be taken even if one does not itemize. Because mostly higher income taxpayers itemize deductions and because higher income people are also in higher tax brackets, the tuition tax deduction would tend to favor higher income parents. Of course, tuition tax deductions may be made subject to some of the same kinds of restrictions that apply to tax credits.

Tax subsidies have been the workhorse of the private schooling subsidy movement in the past; and since the *Mueller* decision, they would also seem to be a legally preferred method for the future. A tax subsidy permits a quick start-up because existing tax authorities can administer a tax subsidy, although new auditors may be needed to verify claims of tuition payment. The tax system puts the subsidy nominally into the hands of the parents, not directly into the coffers of the private schools, which the Supreme Court regarded as a significant distinction in its 1983 decision. Although the funds benefit the schools ultimately, the initial payment of the subsidy to the parent is useful for political reasons as well. The electorate may be more favorable to the claim that students are being aided than to the idea that the private schools are collecting funds from the government directly. (However, when private school subsidy plans are put directly to the voter, they are usually defeated—as happened with the Oregon tax credit plan in 1990 or the Washington, D.C., tax credit plan in 1981.)

Vouchers

Despite the advantages of tax subsidies, vouchers sometimes are proposed. Although the voucher is given to parents, the parent pays tuition with the voucher, which is then presented by the private school for payment by the government. As with tax credits, the voucher usually would be subject to a maximum limit. An open-ended commitment to pay the full tuition for any private school student could be exceptionally costly to the government. Also, unlimited vouchers would be politically unpopular, since in some instances they could exceed what is spent per pupil in public schools, thus creating an obvious and glaring inequity. As with tax credits, vouchers that were limited to a relatively modest maximum size would tend to favor less expensive elementary and parochial schools.

Like tax credits, vouchers might be limited to only some percentage of tuition. Also, vouchers might be targeted on only some segments of the student population by establishing income-eligibility standards. With these restrictions, vouchers and tuition tax credits can be designed so they are equivalent in terms of the financial benefit to the parents.

A voucher subsidy might be chosen over a tax subsidy if an "up front" payment by the government is desired. Tax subsidies are returned to the parent after taxes are filed, which may be some months after tuition has been paid; a voucher gives an immediate subsidy, and so may stimulate greater response among those parents who would have trouble waiting until tax time for a refund. Since vouchers must be presented by the private schools to the government for payment, they clearly present the payer with some leverage over those seeking payment. This might be useful, say, in enforcing a rule that private schools meet accreditation standards. However, this arrangement also increases the possibility of entanglement of church-run schools with government authorities and the possibility of the voucher being ruled unconstitutional even by the attenuated *Mueller* standard.

THE ECONOMIC CONSEQUENCES OF SUBSIDIES

Standard economic analysis can provide significant insights into the behavior of private schools and their clients when a tuition subsidy is introduced. Demand and supply equations for private enrollment have been estimated statistically, so it is possible to project how a tuition subsidy would disturb the equilibrium of tuition and enrollment.

A tax or voucher subsidy acts as a discount on tuition. The greater the discount, the more parents will seek to enroll their children in private schools. According to conventional economics, this increase in demand for places in private schools has two effects. First, the private schools may increase their tuition and so capture part of the subsidy for themselves. Second, with the larger revenues, the private schools can expand their capacity and so accommodate some of the additional enrollment demands. Some private schools might react to higher demand in other ways; they may, for example, become more selective in admitting students. However, the available evidence suggests that in the aggregate, the private sector would react by increasing both enrollment and tuition. These effects are shown in the following example.

The DuPont Plan

Recently former Governor Pierre DuPont of Delaware proposed that his state provide a tuition voucher to all parents, capping the value at $2,150 because that is the average tuition at private schools in his state. Although it would be best to use supply and demand equations specifically for Delaware, it is possible to use available national supply and demand equations to project the effects of the voucher.[6] If Delaware followed national patterns, private enrollment demand would increase about one-half a percent for every one percent discount of private tuition, and private enrollment supply would increase about one percent for every one percent increase in tuition. Under these assumptions, the DuPont voucher would increase private enrollment by about 33 percent, while driving up the long-run equilibrium value of tuition from $2,150 to about $2,866. Parents, of course, would not personally pay the $2,866; rather, they would pay $2,866 minus the voucher, or about $716. This net payment of about $716 would be sufficient to deter many low-income parents from utilizing the private sector, which is why enrollment increases do not exceed an estimated 33 percent. Parents who had already been using private schools would find this net reduction (from $2,150 to the net payment of about $716) to be a windfall. The schools, too, would gain, for they would now collect $2,866 for every student who used to pay only $2,150—in effect an apportionment of part of the government subsidy directly to the schools.

These projections, of course, should not be taken literally. The Delaware supply and demand equations might differ somewhat from the national equations. Further, an ideal estimate would project elementary and secondary results separately. However, these projections clarify the tendencies inherent in the private school sector.

If the DuPont plan were to be applied nationally, most of the extra revenue would go to religious schools. Suppose that religious schools capture subsidy dollars in proportion to their enrollment shares. In 1986, about 85 percent of private enrollment nationally was in religious schools.[7] More specifically, about 60 percent of the total was in Roman Catholic schools. If Catholic schools stem their relative decline while other religious schools continue to expand, an even higher proportion of private schools may have religious affiliations in the future.

GOVERNMENT SUBSIDIES FOR CHARITABLE DONATIONS

While most attention centers on tuition subsidy plans, government has long subsidized nonprofit schools in other ways. Charitable donations to nonprofit schools, or to the churches that sponsor the schools, are normally deductible from federal and state income taxes.

Among some private schools a significant portion of expenses is covered by non-tuition revenue, mostly through subsidies from sponsoring churches or direct fund raising.[8] Thus, charitable donations are given to the school directly or to the church sponsoring the school. The heavy use of tax deductible donations to churches (passed on to schools) or directly to schools means that tuition rates are kept artificially low because tuition needs to cover only a portion of expenses.

Because tuition at many private schools is already lower than per-pupil expenses, implementation of a governmental tuition subsidy may have surprising results. As soon as a tuition subsidy was introduced, private school tuitions would jump from the artificially low level underwritten by charitable donations toward the real level needed to cover expenses. How could a school, or its sponsoring church, make a case to donors for gifts to keep tuition low once a tuition subsidy existed? Once parents could collect a tuition voucher or tax credit, schools could no longer plausibly claim that parents needed all the help donors could provide. Why should a donor give $100 to keep tuition low and receive a charitable deduction worth, say, 28 percent when a parent could pay the $100 as tuition and receive a credit or voucher worth, say, 50 percent—or even 100 percent under some voucher proposals? In short, every incentive would exist to raise tuition to levels that would cover average expenditures and to stop depressing tuition artificially through charitable donations.

In such a world, the government that implements a tuition subsidy should beware twice. Tuition will rise, first, because higher demand for private schooling will drive it up, as shown in the calculations for the DuPont voucher plan. But, second, tuition rates that previously have been depressed artificially by donations will rise. As tuition rises, government funds diverted to credit or voucher payments will rise as well. In view of this, legislators passing a tuition-subsidy law will almost certainly underestimate the burden on the governments' finances that they are creating.

What is the legitimacy of donations to nonprofit private schools or the churches that sponsor them? As long as donations are not disguised tuition payments, they are legitimately tax-deductible. At one end of the spectrum, an individual without children may donate to the schools, expecting no tangible benefit in return, and legally deduct the gift. At the opposite extreme, a parent may make "donations" in return for tuition concessions; such donations would not be legitimate tax deductions because they were really disguised payment for educational services received. In between, there would be charitable behaviors representing various shades of legal gray, some of which would probably not stand scrutiny. Scholars are beginning to deduce, by their own reasoning and from circumstantial evidence, that a portion of donations given in support of some private schools probably does not meet the strictest standards for deductions.[9] How, then, can proponents be sure that additional tuition subsidies are "needed" when the extent of subsidization already occurring through charitable donations (both legitimate and "gray") is not even well known.

CHOICE AT WHAT PRICE?

To be equitable, a voucher or tax credit plan must not discriminate between parents already using private schools and new users who are induced to switch by the subsidy. After all, if it is right to pay Jack's parents $1,000 to enroll him for the first time in private school, then one may not deny the same $1,000 to Susie's parents just because they enrolled her a year ago.

Available evidence suggests that there are several children already in private schools for every Jack (who would enroll for the first time due to the voucher or tax credit). So, in order to enhance the "freedom of choice" for the parents of each Jack, the government would have to make payments to the parents of several Susies. For the DuPont voucher it would appear that about three dollars of windfall subsidy payments to the parents of Susies would be made for every dollar to the parents of a Jack. Tuition tax credits of the type proposed in the early 1980s would have cost an estimated $8 in government expenditure just to get $1 into the hands of someone who actually changed schools. The tuition subsidy is therefore an enormously inefficient device for "enhancing choice" of the Jacks of the world.

There is an alternative scenario. Suppose the voucher is limited to very low income students. Therefore, the children already in private school are there by virtue of scholarships. Their parents won't receive a windfall when the voucher is implemented. Instead, the school itself will receive the windfall as it substitutes the voucher payment for scholarships.

REAL CHOICE?

When 85 percent of private enrollment is in religious schools, any tuition subsidy enhances the choices only of those who are members of the churches that run the private schools. In some locations, the only private schools may be run by churches that insist on teaching creationism instead of biology. All the parents who prefer that real science be taught have no meaningful option to utilize such schools. (Note also how religion is not limited to what is taught in a course called "religion," or to devotional activities, but may permeate all parts of the curriculum—even science.) When such educational "choices" are provided by government subsidy—that is, options that are out of the question—no increase in choice has occurred at all, except for those who share narrow confessional views.

A rejoinder of choice theorists would be that even if significant choices do not now exist among private schools, new schools will fill whatever demands are stimulated by tuition subsidies. However, almost no nonsectarian school can be started from scratch at a per-pupil cost low enough for modest government subsidies to make the difference. Even the DuPont voucher plan, which is unusually large, proposed a subsidy of less than $2,200 per year. Such a plan would provide a significant subsidy for parochial schools; but most potential new nonsectarian schools, unable to rely on the support of donations from parishioners, would find even the DuPont voucher too little support. While special circumstances may permit some additional nonsectarian schools to open around the margins, the advent of government subsidies would mainly increase the enrollment of existing denominational schools.

Stated differently, the private education sector is not the hotbed of competition that subsidy advocates seem to believe it is. The notion of new schools springing up to meet the varied demands of all types of parents is simply uninformed. Schools not affiliated with churches typically have expenses about 100 percent higher at the elementary level, and up to about 250 percent higher at the secondary level, than Catholic schools.[10] A fixed government subsidy equivalent to 30 percent of Catholic secondary expense would be worth as little as 8.5 percent of nonsectarian secondary expense. An eight percent subsidy is unlikely to stimulate the creation of very many nonsectarian secondary schools.

Would subsidized parents choose private schools for academic reasons? In Minnesota, which has had a tuition tax deduction for several years, parents make choices for private schools for reasons other than the strictly academic. According to a RAND study, reasons given for private enrollment included educational quality slightly less than forty percent of the time. Moral and religious factors, when added to discipline, were cited more often as criteria prompting private enrollment.[11] The available evidence suggests, then, that in a majority of cases, a subsidy would not stimulate choices in which academic exellence was the dominating consideration.

Finally, are proponents of subsidies correct in concluding from survey results that parents want government subsidies for private tuition? Based on hypothetical choices, some surveys have reported that fairly large numbers of parents would switch to private schools if given government subsidies. The available evidence, however, shows that when the question ceases to be hypothetical, and an actual choice is to be made, parents do not choose to switch to private schools. In Minnesota, a large number of parents claimed that a subsidy like the state's actual tuition deduction would cause them to enroll a child in private school; yet they had not actually made the switch at the time of the survey. That is, they were ignoring the actual subsidy even while answering the survey that such a subsidy would cause them to choose private schools.[12] If this result can be generalized, it suggests that opinion surveys probably greatly overestimate the desire of parents for choices that involve private schools. The other problem with opinion research is that it is out of line with available statistical analysis of naturally occurring differences in private-sector tuition. Naturally occurring differences in private-sector tuitions imply that reductions in tuition stimulate only relatively small increases in private enrollment. In short, the desire of parents for the kinds of choices represented by the present private school sector is not great.

ACADEMIC QUALITY IN PRIVATE SCHOOLS

Some tuition-subsidy advocates suggest that private schools would produce better academic results than public schools. Some no doubt believe this because their theory of competition or free market dictates that private schools ought to do better than public schools—even in the absence of any evidence. But if one would judge such claims by the evidence, one discovers that evidence favoring private schools is tenuous. In fact, even some rather simple statistics suggest that public schools can at least hold their own. On the math portion of the Scholastic Aptitude Test public students outscored students from religious private schools in both 1987 and 1988.[13] Furthermore, this result occurs without any adjustments for different student characteristics between public and private schools that would probably enhance the advantage of the public schools.

Parents themselves apparently do not believe that private schools are better than public schools. Between 1974 and 1977, Gallup surveys showed a collapse of confidence in public education. However, private schools failed to convert this opinion shift into convincing enrollment increases. Apparently parents did not see private schools as superior enough—even after an erosion of confidence in public schools—to justify making enrollment changes.

Undoubtedly the two most publicized studies to find that private schools are best at educating were by James Coleman, Thomas Hoffer, and Sally Kilgore in 1982,[14] and by John Chubb and Terry Moe in 1990.[15] Although these two studies are nearly a decade apart, significantly, both draw on portions of the same data base—the High School and Beyond survey of 1980–1982. Thus the latter study is not a truly independent replication of the results of the earlier because it fails to use an entirely independent data base.

Consider two subsequent analyses of the Coleman study. Richard J.

Murnane[16] asked what would happen in private schools if their students were replaced completely by the student populations of the public schools—thereby capturing peer-group effects. His statistical techniques allowed him to conclude that non-Catholic private schools would actually produce students with worse test results than public schools. Catholic schools would produce slightly better results, but their advantage would be far smaller than estimated by Coleman and his colleagues.

J. Douglas Willms[17] attempted to explain why Coleman's results differed from the findings of the 1980 National Assessment of Educational Progress. It had reported, after adjusting for differences in student characteristics between public and private sectors, that no statistically significant differences existed in reading or math results. When Willms eliminated an additional apples-and-oranges problem by comparing only students in the public and private academic tracks (and compensating for differences in family circumstances), no statistically significant difference between public and Catholic student performance remained.

The approach used by Chubb and Moe does not involve comparing the achievement of public and private students head-to-head. Rather, they seek to show the effects on achievement of effective school organization. Then, in a second step, they try to show that private schools are more effectively organized than public schools.

The fatal problem with the Chubb and Moe approach is that effective school organization, as they define it, is likely to be reflective of the achievement level of the student population. For example, Chubb and Moe believe a school has an effective organization where, among other things, the principal thinks highly of the teachers. But if students are high achievers in the first place, this will surely enhance the principal's rating of the teachers— the teachers are bound to be suffused by the halo effect of their high-achieving students. Thus, in their correlations, Chubb and Moe may be measuring how student achievement shapes the organization of the school rather than how school organization contributes to student achievement. Chubb and Moe are caught in a statistical loop: school organization affects achievement but achievement affects organization. They fail to utilize methods to disentangle these simultaneous effects and so fail to establish their main point. It then becomes irrelevant that private schools are rated high on their school organization index.

Another problem with both the Coleman and the Chubb and Moe studies is that even if they were correct, their data base was only for students in the last two years of high school. Research that uses senior high students as a data base simply cannot be used to justify policy recommendations for any other age group. Unfortunately, Chubb and Moe are not careful about this and make broad policy recommendations that are not warranted by their data.

CAN PRIVATE EDUCATION SURVIVE A SUBSIDY?

A government subsidy for private education would, clearly, expand the size of the private sector. One possibility is that this very expansion would undermine the distinctive features that have characterized private education in the past. For example, a major influx of students in the Roman Catholic system might well increase school size and the layers of bureaucracy of the overall system. If, as Chubb and Moe claim, a small bureaucracy has been a hallmark of private education *as it existed in the past,* then a subsidy might strike at this very hallmark. In the case of Roman Catholic schools, the need to hire more and more lay teachers to meet the enrollment demand would further dilute the religious atmosphere of the schools—an attraction to their clients in the past. Is it possible to subsidize the growth of the private sector without making it into something its clients won't like?

Research from Canada seems to suggest that the nature of private schools begins to change substantially when a major subsidy program is enacted. Donald E. Erickson[18] reports that after long periods of subsidization in three Canadian provinces, the Catholic schools there had substantially different characteristics from those in provinces where subsidies did not exist. And for the patrons who wanted a religious education the difference was not viewed in a favorable light. Although private schools are not for everyone, those who have traditionally utilized private schools might well sense a loss of identity and meaning after implementation of a governmental subsidy plan. The private sector would be inundated with students and new faculty who did not share all the values of the former students and faculty, and those who valued the old ways would be the losers.

CONCLUSION

The choice philosophy is only the newest reason in a long line to be given by the movement that seeks subsidization of private schooling. Such subsidies have been sought, for a variety of reasons, for more than a generation. Should the movement succeed, the result would be a stimulus to the private sector that would show up as enrollment and tuition increases. Because tuition would rise as a result of government subsidies, the private schools would share in the subsidy with the parents. Thus, government would be channeling funds—via the parents—to religious schools, which account for about 85 percent of private enrollment. If such a subsidy program were enacted, it would provide windfall payments mostly for students already in private schools. For the money spent, choices of a relative few would be enhanced: those who found the subsidy a significant inducement and who also could accept the particular views of religious schools. Would academic achievement improve as students switched to private schools? Not likely, for most don't enroll for reasons of academic quality in the first place. Nor is there strong evidence that private school students perform better than pubilc school students.

In sum, a costly program of private school subsidies, which raises serious First Amendment issues, would achieve little that the proponents claim. And the private sector itself may pay dearly for the "gains" bestowed by government subsidy. Church schools might well lose their distinctiveness, which is what their clients have traditionally desired. In a sense, they would lose their souls for a subsidy.

NOTES

1. John E. Chubb and Terry M. Moe, *Politics, Markets, and America's Schools* (Washington, D.C.: Brookings Institute, 1990).

2. For a review see the February 20, 1991 issue of *Education Week*.

3. See the *New York Times*, February 27, 1991.

4. See the Senate debate in *Congressional Record* of November 16, 1983.

5. Charles L. Glenn, *Choice of Schools in Six Nations* (Washington, D.C.: U.S. Department of Education, 1989), p. x.

6. The projections that follow are based on the methods described in Donald E. Frey, *Tuition Tax Credits for Private Education: An Economic Analysis* (Ames: Iowa State University Press, 1983), chapter 3.

7. These data are derived from *Statistical Abstracts of the United States* (Washington, D.C.: Department of Commerce, 1990), Table 242.

8. Frey, *Tuition Tax Credits for Private Education,* Table 1.4.

9. See Robert A. Blewett, "Hidden Tax Preferences for the Real Costs of Tuition Tax Credits," *Public Finance Quarterly* 16, no. 3 (July 1988): 330–40, and Frey, *Tuition Tax Credits for Private Education,* chapter 2.

10. Frey, *Tuition Tax Credits for Private Education,* Table 1.3.

11. Linda Darling-Hammond and Sheila N. Kirby, *Tuition Tax Deductions and Parent School Choice: A Case Study of Minnesota* (Santa Monica, Calif.: RAND, 1985), Table 4.7.

12. Ibid., p. 75.

13. National Center for Education Statistics, *1989 Education Indicators* (Washington, D.C.: U.S. Department of Education, 1989), p. 29.

14. James S. Coleman, Thomas Hoffer, and Sally Kilgore, *High School Achievement: Public, Catholic, and Private Schools Compared* (New York: Basic Books, 1982).

15. Chubb and Moe, *Politics, Markets, and America's Schools.*

16. Richard J. Murnane, "Comparisons of Private and Public Schools: The Critical Role of Regulations," in Daniel C. Levy, ed., *Private Education: Studies in Choice and Public Policy* (New York: Oxford University Press, 1986).

17. J. Douglas Willms, "Do Private Schools Produce Higher Levels of Academic

Achievement? New Evidence for the Tuition Tax Credit Debate," in Thomas James and Henry M. Levins, eds., *Public Dollars for Private Schools* (Philadelphia: Temple University Press, 1983).

18. Donald E. Erickson, "Choice and Private Schools: Dynamics of Supply and Demand," in Levy, *Private Education: Studies in Choice and Public Policy.*

14

The People Say No!
The Parochiaid Referenda, 1966–1990*

Edd Doerr and Albert J. Menendez

INTRODUCTION

One of the perplexing features of the long struggles and debates over tax aid or support for nonpublic, predominantly sectarian schools—known as parochiaid—is the scant attention paid to the eighteen referendum elections on the subject that have been held over the past quarter century. While opinion polls often show a degree of popular confusion over the issue of tax support for nonpublic schools—due generally to pollsters' use of confusing or misleading questions—and court decisions have upheld the church-state separation principle with less than strict consistency, the decisions of voters in a dozen states from coast to coast show a consistent pattern: overwhelming support for the principle of separation as it applies to the financing of education.

Since 1966, eighteen referendum elections in twelve states and the District of Columbia have resulted in seventeen wins and only one loss for church-

Edd Doerr and Albert J. Menendez are Executive Director and Research Director, respectively, of Americans for Religious Liberty. Both are former secondary school social studies teachers.

*This essay originally appeared in Edd Doerr and Albert J. Menendez, *Church Schools and Public Money: The Politics of Parochiaid* (Buffalo, N.Y.: Prometheus Books, 1991), pp. 69–85.

state separation in education. Time after time in state after state, voters have rejected schemes to divert public funds to religious schools or to weaken state constitutional prohibitions on state aid to sectarian institutions. The pattern is so clear and decisive that political observers and politicians should take note.

A HISTORY OF CHURCH-STATE REFERENDA

1966: Nebraska

A proposed amendment to the state constitution to allow tax funds to be used to provide bus service for parochial schools was rejected by the state's voters 57 percent to 43 percent.

1967: New York

When New Yorkers voted in 1965 to approve the calling of a state constitutional convention, a predominantly Catholic parochiaid lobby group called Citizens for Educational Freedom (CEF) saw its chance. In a quiet but intense campaign, CEF won a majority of the delegate seats at the convention by concentrating votes on the minority of candidates favoring removal of the anti-parochiaid section of the state constitution. The "stacked deck" convention did what CEF wanted. But then their luck ran out.

Religious, educational, parent, labor, and other groups formed the Committee for Public Education and Religious Liberty (PEARL) to counter the threat to church-state separation. In the November 1967 constitutional ratification election, New Yorkers voted down the whole proposed new state constitution 72.5 percent to 27.5 percent. Since the rest of the proposed constitution was generally unobjectionable, its defeat may fairly be ascribed to the single overriding issue—parochiaid.

The New York vote was also significant because the parochiaiders spent a reported $2 million to win the referendum, compared to only about $50 thousand by the defenders of church-state separation.

Every county rejected the constitution. Protestant rural areas were four to one against it, as were Jewish strongholds. But even Catholic voters were opposed, despite Cardinal Francis Spellman's very visible campaigning in the measure's favor.

1970: Michigan

Michigan's legislature proved increasingly compliant to the demands of parochiaiders in the late 1960s. So a coalition of defenders of church-state separation initiated by petition a proposed amendment to the state constitution to make even more explicit the already existing prohibition of parochiaid. When the November votes were counted, the church-state separation amendment had won 57 percent to 43 percent. The outcome caught pollsters, editorialists, and local politicians by surprise. Expenditures favored the parochiaid side, and polls failed to capture voter sentiment accurately.

Parochiaid carried in only thirteen of Michigan's 83 counties. An examination of these thirteen counties indicates that eight are predominantly Roman Catholic, while four of the other five counties have substantial Catholic minorities. However, of the five heaviest counties for parochiaid, only two are predominantly Catholic. One county is half Catholic, half Lutheran. The other two are heavily Christian (Dutch) Reformed, a church that operates many parochial schools. Another significant point is that other predominantly Catholic counties voted against parochiaid. The nineteen most heavily Catholic counties, taken as a whole, cast only 51 percent of their votes for parochiaid, only 8 percent higher than the statewide average.

Of the 70 counties that opposed parochiaid, eleven of them voted over 70 percent against it. Several of these counties are referred to as "Yankee-Protestant counties" because their original inhabitants came from the New England states whose leading churches are Methodist, United Church of Christ, Baptist, and Disciples of Christ. University counties voted two to one against parochiaid.

1970: Nebraska

In Nebraska, CEF and the Catholic hierarchy got the legislature to initiate a proposed state constitutional amendment to authorize a tuition reimbursement plan. On election day the amendment was defeated 57 percent to 43 percent. Parochiaid carried in only eleven of the state's 93 counties. Seven of these are predominantly Roman Catholic, while three are predominantly Lutheran but with large Catholic minorities. Of Nebraska's eight predominantly Catholic counties, seven voted for parochiaid with an aggregate support of 56 percent. Of the 82 counties that voted against parochiaid, ten cast majorities of better than 70 percent. These counties are either Lutheran or Methodist. In none of these counties is there any significant Catholic population.

1972: Idaho

Idaho voters rejected a proposed constitutional amendment to allow transportation aid for parochial schools by 57 percent to 43 percent.

Only three of Idaho's 44 counties voted for parochiaid. Two of them are predominantly Catholic, while the third has a majority of Mormons. Of the state's five Roman Catholic counties, only two voted for parochiaid with only 48 percent of the aggregate vote favoring it. Most of the state's counties are predominantly Mormon. The six completely Mormon counties voted two to one against parochiaid.

Even the political right wing failed to support the Idaho measure. In four of the state's counties—Fremont, Jefferson, Lemhi, and Madison—the American party's presidential candidate, John Schmitz, actually ran ahead of Democrat George McGovern in 1972! Schmitz received 28 percent of the vote cast in Jefferson County and 17 percent in Madison County. These counties voted better than 70 percent against parochiaid.

1972: Maryland

In 1971, the Maryland legislature, after several years of defeat for parochiaiders, passed a bill to provide $12 million per year to parochial schools under a complex voucher plan. Opposing groups gathered enough voters' signatures to put the bill to a referendum in November 1972. Marylanders then voted the bill down 55 percent to 45 percent.

Outside of Baltimore City, only two of the 23 counties—predominantly Catholic Charles and St. Mary's Counties in southern Maryland—favored the voucher and auxiliary services proposal. The Catholic stronghold of Emmitsburg in Frederick County supported the measure 70 percent to 30 percent. Maryland has a number of solidly Methodist counties, all of which opposed parochiaid. The seven strongest Methodist counties on the Eastern Shore opposed parochiaid by margins ranging from 63 percent to 79 percent. The Methodist opposition to parochiaid was a major factor in the state's rejection of the proposal.

In western Maryland, three counties are historically German-American, and a majority of church members are either Lutheran, Reformed, or Brethren. These counties voted 62 percent–67 percent against the measure. Garrett, the state's banner Republican county, which has never gone Democratic for president, voted two to one against.

Precinct data from Montgomery County and Baltimore City are quite revealing. In Montgomery County almost every precinct opposed parochiaid, but in two particular areas the vote was better than two to one in opposition. The Jewish vote in Rosemary Hills and south Silver Spring, that went heavily for McGovern for president, went strongly against parochiaid. The conservative Protestant vote in some of the county's rural areas, such as Clarksburg and Poolesville, the heaviest precincts in the county for Nixon, also went heavily against parochiaid.

In Baltimore City, Jewish and liberal pro-McGovern areas voted most heavily against parochiaid, as did the majority of blacks. The Jewish precincts opposed parochiaid by about 65 percent–35 percent. Black precincts cast 58 percent of their votes against parochiaid but were quite erratic. A number of black ghetto precincts voted for parochiaid, but those in more middle-class areas voted against it. The black turnout was also erratic: only 36.8 percent who voted in the presidential race cast votes on the parochiaid referendum.

The Catholic vote in East Baltimore's Polish enclaves voted 69 percent for parochiaid, some precincts as much as 77 percent in favor. An Italian precinct voted 68 percent in favor. A Catholic middle-class suburb voted about 65 percent for the measure. The Catholic voter turnout on the referendum exceeded that of all other groups, perhaps because they felt most directly affected by the measure. (One interesting result came in blue-collar Catholic Dundalk, where voters narrowly rejected the proposal.)

1972: Oregon

Oregon voters were presented by the legislature with a proposed amendment to replace a strong anti-parochiaid state constitutional provision with a weaker, vaguer one, patterned after the provision voted down in New York just five years earlier. Oregonians defeated the measure 61 percent to 39 percent, a fact which the state's junior senator, Robert Packwood, seemed to have forgotten during the 1977–1978 congressional battles over tuition tax credit parochiaid.

All 36 of Oregon's counties voted against parochiaid and in only one county was it even close. In most other counties the margin was quite heavy. Parochiaid ran slightly better in Portland and its suburbs than elsewhere. Oregon has a low percentage of church members and this secular orientation undoubtedly contributed to the defeat of the parochiaid measure. Oregon is also very much a WASP state; it does not have large numbers of minorities or ethnic groups.

1974: Maryland

Less than two years after their 1972 electoral defeat, Maryland parochiaiders got the legislature to enact another bill, this time for $9.7 million per year for books, equipment, supplies, and transportation for parochial schools. Once again groups concerned with defending church-state separation and public education petitioned the bill to a referendum. After an acrimonious campaign Maryland voters defeated the new parochiaid bill by almost 57 percent to 43 percent.

Pro-parochiaid forces were dealt a heavier defeat than in 1972. Parochiaid was defeated by greater margins than before in seventeen of the state's

24 jurisdictions while receiving a slightly higher vote in seven of them. The Greater Baltimore area alone gave parochiaid a slightly higher vote than in 1972, while the Washington, D.C., suburbs voted against parochiaid by a 4 percent greater margin.

The state's heavily Methodist Eastern Shore counties turned in even heftier majorities than in 1972, with margins ranging from 75 percent to 83 percent against the proposal. Some of the more stunning swings against parochiaid came in several western Maryland counties, which historically are mixed religiously but have a predominance of Lutherans. In Washington County, for example, parochiaid was defeated by 78 percent compared to 67 percent two years before. In Allegany, Carroll, and Garrett Counties, the defeat was 4 percent to 6 percent greater than before. The polarization between Catholics and non-Catholics on this issue seems to have increased.

Jewish voters turned in strong majorities against the measure, although the pattern was mixed. The Jewish precincts in Silver Spring increased from 70 percent to 73 percent opposed, while the Jewish ward in Baltimore City declined from 65 percent to 60 percent. The more rural Protestant precincts in several counties tended to be heavily against. University students in two precincts also voted against parochiaid; the same majority of 57 percent was recorded in the Johns Hopkins University precinct in Baltimore, while the University of Maryland precinct increased from 56 percent to 62 percent against.

The state's black voters showed the biggest swing against the parochiaid measure. In two precincts in Prince Georges County (suburban Washington), opposition increased almost 11 percent, as 65 percent of the voters rejected parochiaid. In nine key black precincts in Baltimore City, opposition increased from 65 percent to 72 percent.

Other than Roman Catholic areas, the only precincts that showed greater support for parochiaid were several blue-collar Protestant precincts in Baltimore City, where opposition to public school busing had been running high. These precincts, in fact, turned in a much larger increase in parochiaid support than the Catholic areas.

1975: Washington State

The next state to face a referendum on parochiaid was Washington. The legislature, responding to pressure from both parochial schools and denominational colleges, proposed a state constitutional amendment to allow unlimited tax aid to denominational private education. The state's voters defeated the amendment 60.5 percent to 39.5 percent.

The parochiaid measure was defeated in all of the state's 39 counties, in seven counties by more than 70 percent of the voters. In only five counties did the margin of victory drop to between 55 percent and 60 percent.

The state's four urban-suburban counties voted against parochiaid 58 percent to 42 percent. The small-town and rural counties voted no by a 65 percent margin. The three most heavily Republican counties voted 65 percent against the measure, while the three heaviest Democratic counties voted 63 percent against. It appears that voter turnout affected the size of the defeat for the measure. Washington has always had a remarkably vigorous electorate: fifty-five percent of the state's registered voters turned out for this off-year election, which also included other important referendum questions. The three counties that had the highest turnout voted 64 percent against the measure, while the three counties having the lowest turnout voted 59 percent against parochiaid.

Religious influences on the election were minimal. Washington, like Oregon and California, has a low percentage of residents who are church members. About one third of the state's church members are Roman Catholic, but only about one in nine of the state's total population is Roman Catholic. An analysis of the vote shows a modest correlation between Catholic population and the vote in this referendum. Spokane, the state's most heavily Catholic county, gave a higher than average vote in favor of the measure. On the other hand, two of the six counties that voted most heavily against parochiaid also have large Catholic populations.

1976: Alaska

In November, Alaska voters turned down a proposed amendment to allow unlimited state aid to private denominational schools and colleges. The vote was 54 percent to 46 percent.

1976: Missouri

Parochiaid advocates in Missouri, long a battleground on the issue, initiated by petition a proposed state constitutional amendment to authorize $10 million in state aid in the form of transportation, textbooks, and auxiliary services. The parochiaiders induced Governor Christopher Bond to schedule the ratification referendum on August 3, in the hope that public school teachers and parents would be unable to organize during the summer to defeat the measure. The strategy failed. On August 3, Missourians defeated the amendment 60 percent to 40 percent.

Missouri's referendum produced the tenth straight defeat in as many years for the advocates of government aid to nonpublic schools. Missouri, which probably has the strictest constitutional prohibition on government assistance to religion, faced a referendum after Roman Catholic and Missouri Synod Lutheran school patrons gathered enough petition signatures to force the issue to a vote.

From the outset, observers worried about a Baptist-Catholic clash in a state where religious antagonisms are an established political fact. Both proponents and opponents of Constitutional Amendment Number 7 denied that sectarianism would determine the level of debate or the ultimate outcome. Instinctively, though, Baptists and Catholics, the state's dominant religions, lined up on opposite sides of the fence. The pro-parochiaid campaign was quiet; Catholic newspapers did little more than urge a yes vote. The statewide Baptist paper *Word and Way* gave the issue tremendous prominence, calling it "the most crucial issue of the decade." Baptists and many other Protestants saw the election as a showdown on religious liberty and plunged into the fray with great élan.

The results were decisive. By a 60 percent to 40 percent margin, voters rejected the constitutional change. The vote was much heavier than anticipated. Jerome R. Porath, the pro-parochiaid Fairness in Education executive director, accurately forecast 450,000 yes votes but admitted that his group underestimated the volume of opposition feeling.[1]

Once again religious affiliation shaped the voters' response to this issue. More than in any other state, the Missouri electorate divided along religious lines. The two most heavily Catholic counties voted yes 79 percent and 72 percent. The four overwhelmingly Baptist counties said no, with margins ranging from 74 percent to 82 percent. The Catholic character of Greater St. Louis and Kansas City resulted in a 50,000-vote majority for the proposition there, but in the solidly Protestant rural and small-town areas the measure lost by 275,000 votes. The county containing the University of Missouri voted no 64 percent. A "Yankee Protestant" and Republican county voted no four to one. A German Protestant Republican stronghold voted no 68 percent, while a banner Democratic county in "Mark Twain country," the only county outside of St. Louis to back George McGovern, voted no 64 percent.

A survey conducted on election day among 900 voters in Boone County revealed the tremendous religious cleavage. Almost 80 percent of the Catholics voted yes, while 75 percent of the Baptists voted no.[2] The survey also found that 14 percent of the voters were confused by the ballot wording. Apparently 11 percent who opposed parochiaid voted for the amendment, while 3 percent who favored it voted no.

Baptist leaders hailed the vote as a reaffirmation of religious liberty. Catholics were disappointed, even angry, at the outcome. The *St. Louis Review* (August 6, 1976) claimed that "ignorance and bigotry" were accountable for the defeat of this proposal. It accused opponents of carrying on a "vicious campaign stirring up anti-Catholic bias." Protestant clergymen, it said, "were leaders in fanning the flames of prejudice." The paper ended with a warning for the future: "Victims of prejudice often band together for redress of grievances. Those who made this election into a religious controversy may have sparked such a reaction." Yet the fact is that the controversy was precipitated by the efforts of Catholic and Missouri Synod Lutheran school patrons to impose some of the costs of denominational schools on all taxpayers.

1978: Michigan

The next referendum on parochiaid took place in Michigan. Parochial school interests went all out, initiating by petition a proposed constitutional amendment to provide parochial, private, and public schools with equal support under an unspecified voucher plan. The parochiaid amendment also included a sweetener, a clause abolishing property taxes for education! But Michigan voters were not buying, and on November 7 voters buried the amendment in a 74 percent to 26 percent landslide.

1981: District of Columbia

Washington, D.C., voters went to the polls in record numbers on November 7 and dealt the tuition tax credit parochiaid plan a crushing defeat. The final vote count on Initiative 7 was 73,829 to 8,904, an 89 percent–11 percent drubbing that had profound effects on the campaign to get Congress to enact a national tuition tax credit plan.

Over 30 percent of the District of Columbia's registered voters turned out to vote, more than double the percentage in off-year elections. The 8,904 votes for the plan amounted to only a third of the number of voters who signed petitions the previous summer to put the controversial measure on the ballot.

The Initiative 7 parochiaid plan was petitioned onto the ballot by the D.C. Committee for Improved Education, an affiliate of the National Taxpayers Union (NTU), which put up 99 percent of the estimated $135,000 spent putting the measure on the ballot and campaigning for its passage. (The NTU has also been the main force behind a campaign to have state legislatures force Congress to call a national constitutional convention, the first since 1787. Although the ostensible purpose of the convention would be to amend the Constitution to require a balanced federal budget, constitutional authorities generally agree that, as in 1787, a new convention could not be limited to a single amendment, but could very well consider amendments that would conceivably gut the Bill of Rights.)

Under the Initiative 7 plan, each D.C. resident taxpayer, including businesses, could have gotten a 100 percent credit of up to $1,200 against the D.C. income tax for paying for each child for such "qualified education expenses" as tuition, fees, transportation, uniforms, books, materials, and incidentals. The tax credit would have applied to school expenses for D.C.

children attending parochial or private schools in the District of Columbia, in neighboring Maryland or Virginia, or anywhere else in the world.

Moreover, the language of the defeated bill would not have limited the tax credit to $1,200 per student, but would have allowed more than one taxpayer to receive up to $1,200 each in education tax credits for a single student. Thus, an employed couple could each have gotten a $1,200 credit for a single child's parochial or private school expenses, and their employers could each have received a $1,200 credit against D.C. taxes for contributing to the couple's child's schools expenses, for a total D.C. tax expenditure of $4,800.*

Estimates of the costs to D.C. taxpayers of the Initiative 7 parochiaid plan ranged from $25 million to $75 million annually, depending upon how many taxpayers would have been able to take advantage of it. The full $1,200 per taxpayer credit would have gone only to taxpayers earning over $21,500 per year, thus benefiting to the maximum only a minority of D.C. residents.

Most of the opposition to Initiative 7 was coordinated by two separate but cooperating coalitions, the D.C. Coalition Against Tuition Tax Credits and the D.C. Coalition for Public Education.

Working in and parallel to the two anti-parochiaid coalitions were teacher and parent organizations, labor unions, the Council of Churches and the Jewish Community Council of Greater Washington, the D.C. Baptist Convention, the National Conference of Christians and Jews, the League of Women Voters, the ACLU, the National Urban League and the NAACP, the D.C. Federation of Civic Associations, the D.C. City Council and Board of Education, Mayor Marion Barry, the D.C. Chamber of Commerce and the Board of Trade, and other groups.

While Catholic archdiocesan school board president Terence Scanlon and some Catholic priests and laymen worked to pass the measure, Archbishop James A. Hickey publicly took a neutral stance and ordered Catholic parish and school officials likewise to remain neutral. Hickey noted that more than half of the Catholic children in Washington attend public schools. "I am concerned for the children in all our schools," Hickey said.

Other parochial and private school officials in the District either remained neutral or opposed the plan. Many of them said that Initiative 7 would harm the public schools and have adverse effects on the city's already strained budget.

1982: California

By a 61 percent to 39 percent margin, California residents turned down Proposition 9, an amendment that would have allowed a publicly financed program

---

*The NTU had tried unsuccessfully to get a similar proposal, a state constitutional amendment, onto the ballot in California in 1979.

of textbook aid to parochial and other private schools. The $5 million program was in operation until 1981, when the state supreme court held that it violated the state constitution's prohibition of aid to church education.

At least ten of the state's twelve Roman Catholic dioceses "lent" large sums of money to the committee pushing Proposition 9. The Catholic parochial school system would have been by far the largest beneficiary of the textbook aid program.

The *National Catholic Reporter* revealed that diocesan spending included $100,000 from Los Angeles; $45,410 from San Francisco; $38,110 from Oakland, $29,405 from San Jose; $28,000 from Sacramento; $25,000 from San Diego; $20,000 from San Bernardino; $12,670 from Stockton; $10,500 from Santa Rosa; and $10,000 from Monterey. Dr. Joseph McElligott, director of education for the California Catholic Conference, told the *Reporter* that the loans were to be repaid "to some extent."

The large sums of money paid for various campaign activities, including sophisticated statewide television advertising. The ads featured veteran actress Helen Hayes, a New York resident, urging Californians to "vote for books for children." The campaign was also supported by a full page ad in the *Los Angeles Times* by the local Catholic archdiocese urging a yes vote on the proposition.

Both candidates for governor and both candidates for state superintendent of public instruction also endorsed the ballot measure. Several state newspapers, including both San Francisco dailies, endorsed the proposition. The *Los Angeles Times* and the *Herald-Examiner* both came out against the measure, however.

The opposition to Proposition 9, including the public school community, civil liberties groups, and many Jewish and Protestant religious organizations, fought the measure with only volunteer efforts. The "No on Nine" committee spent less than $10,000, according to local estimates.

A Mervin Field poll on election day said voters opposed the parochiaid plan because they thought that private schools' books should not be purchased by the taxpayers.

1982: Massachusetts

The citizens of Massachusetts voted 62 percent to 38 percent against Question 1, which would have allowed "aid, materials, or services" to pupils in private schools. The proposed state constitutional amendment was intended to replace the existing strong anti-parochiaid section and allow the legislature to start programs of textbook aid and other forms of assistance to nonpublic schools by funneling the money through students.

Question 1 appeared likely to pass. The state's Catholic bishops issued a pastoral letter to be read in all parishes urging Catholics to vote for the measure (Massachusetts is 52 percent Catholic, the second most Catholic state in the union). In addition, public schools in Boston and some other areas of the state had been beset with problems.

A coalition of public school, civil liberties, and Jewish and Protestant religious groups, similar to the one in California, managed to get the No-on-One message out to the voters. A combination of factors further prompted the measure's defeat, including concern that funds would be diverted from the already underfunded public schools to private schools, the possibility of a tax increase to pay for new private school programs, and support for the principle of church-state separation.

Voters of all faiths rejected the proposal.

1986: Massachusetts

Parochiaid advocates once again tried to weaken the Bay State's strict constitutional prohibition against church-state entanglement. They hoped to open the door to such "indirect" programs as vouchers, tax credits, textbook loans, and auxiliary services. Question 2 on the ballot was designed to accomplish their purposes, and a Committee for Educational Equality was set up to shepherd the campaign.

Cardinal Bernard Law of Boston pulled out all the stops to promote this referendum, as well as an anti-abortion question also on the ballot. Pastoral statements from the state's bishops and sermons in parish churches attempted to get the message to the half of Massachusetts voters who are Catholic.

Meanwhile, the measure's chief sponsor, State Senate President William Bulger of South Boston, raised the issue of anti-Catholicism, accusing opponents of Question 2 of bigotry.

The voters turned down the proposal by a 70 percent to 30 percent margin. Every county and almost every voting precinct opposed it. Only in three Boston wards (including Bulger's South Boston district) and in the town of Webster did parochiaid triumph. Elsewhere, it was a disaster. Question 2 lost heavily in college towns like Amherst (86 percent against) and Cambridge (77 percent against) and upper-income Protestant Beacon Hill (80 percent against).

But parochiaid also failed in working-class Catholic towns like Gloucester (76 percent against), New Bedford (60 percent against), and Chelsea (63 percent against). In other such Catholic strongholds as Holyoke, Springfield, Lawrence, and Lowell, a majority of voters rejected the parochiaid lobby.

1986: South Dakota

The parochiaiders won their only victory in the past quarter century when voters approved a textbook loan proposal by 54 percent to 46 percent. Sponsored by Republican Governor William Janklow, a conservative Lutheran, the proposal, Amendment C, was apparently considered a relatively harmless indirect form of aid in this predominantly Lutheran state. Public educators and civil libertarians estimated the proposal would cost the state about $2 million yearly.

1990: Oregon

Despite being outspent at least two to one, Oregon's defenders of church-state separation and public education won a solid 67 percent to 33 percent victory at the polls on November 6. At issue in the referendum was a proposed tuition tax credit of $2,500 per child for students who attend parochial and private schools or who are educated at home. The proposal would have cost taxpayers between $60 and $100 million per year.

This costly and unconstitutional parochiaid scheme attracted considerable out-of-state money. The last report showed $260,000 in expenditures for the scheme's front group, Oregonians for Educational Choice. An astounding 93 percent of the funds came from out of state, including a $60,000 donation from the Washington, D.C.-based Citizens for a Sound Economy (CSE), a group that supports "free market economic policies and supply side economics," according to its media relations director, Sedef Onder. CSE, founded in 1984, claims 250,000 members nationwide. Ms. Onder said that the group had used Oregon as an "experiment" in grassroots advocacy.

Other supporters of the proposal included Vice-President J. Danforth Quayle; voucher advocate John Chubb of the Brookings Institution; conservative economist Milton Friedman; conservative writer William F. Buckley, Jr.; and former Secretary of Education William Bennett. The far right advocates included Paul Weyrich's Free Congress Foundation, Phyllis Schlafly's Eagle Forum, and Beverly LaHaye's Concerned Women for America.

Supporters of church-state separation and public education raised $130,000, almost all of it from in-state. Oregon teachers' organizations and the National Education Association spearheaded these efforts.

LESSONS OF THE REFERENDA

Advocates of tax aid or support for sectarian and other nonpublic schools often claim wide support for their point of view. Their claims, however, are usually based on poorly designed poll questions. While permitting families greater choice among public schools is at least a superficially popular idea, mixing together public school choice and tax support for nonpublic schools in a single poll question to be answered "yes" or "no" is sure to produce ambiguous if not meaningless results.

However, when the issue is placed concretely before a large group of voters, with advocates and opponents of the proposed constitutional amendment or law slugging it out in the public arena and the media, then a meaningful test of public opinion is possible. As we have seen, electorates educated about the parochiaid issue in a rough-and-tumble election campaign almost invariably (94 percent of the time in the last quarter century) vote no on diverting public funds to nonpublic schools, even though the opponents are almost always outspent by a considerable margin.

Other valid tests of public opinion occurred in the 1970s when the Nixon and Ford administrations put considerable effort and money into trying to get individual school districts to experiment with federally funded voucher schemes. Despite all that effort, only one district in the nation, the Alum Rock district in San Jose, California, agreed to participate in a three-year experiment, and only after stipulating that no religious schools whatever be involved. The experiment was not considered a success. Efforts by the Ford administration to sell a federally funded voucher plan to communities in New Hampshire and Connecticut came to naught when local opinion polls, sponsored by the voucher promoters, consistently rejected the plans.

Promoting parochiaid, then, would seem to be the wrong horse for a politician to hitch a wagon to, though some politicians in some areas might gain from it. Parochiaid supporters are more likely to be single-issue voters than parochiaid opponents.

Unfortunately, the parochiaiders' horrendous losing streak is not widely known. For obscure reasons, about which we can only speculate, the media have largely ignored this quarter century of electoral defeats for parochiaid. They rarely rate a mention outside the states in which they occur, and generally receive far less coverage than referenda on far less significant matters.

Finally, despite the deficiencies of our public schools, which educators acknowledge and would largely be able to correct if they had the necessary funds and political support, a larger percentage of American families send their children to public schools now (89.3 percent) than did so twenty years ago (88.9 percent), and annual Gallup surveys show that serious discontent with public education is confined mainly to underfunded, troubled inner-city areas.

The American people, it is safe to conclude, support public education and do not want to be taxed to aid or support nonpublic, mainly sectarian schools.

NOTES

1. James E. Adams, "Warns of Catholic Backlash on Schools," *St. Louis Post-Dispatch,* August 8, 1976.
2. Allison Finn, "Wording Confused Some Voters," *Columbia Missourian,* August 6, 1976.

APPENDIX

State Referenda on Parochiaid, 1966–1990

Year	State	% Against	% For
1966	Nebraska	57%	43%
1967	New York	72%	27%
1970	Nebraska	57%	43%
1970	Michigan	57%	43%
1972	Oregon	61%	39%
1972	Idaho	57%	43%
1972	Maryland	55%	45%
1974	Maryland	56%	43%
1975	Washington	60%	39%
1976	Alaska	54%	46%
1976	Missouri	60%	40%
1978	Michigan	74%	26%
1981	District of Columbia	89%	11%
1982	California	61%	39%
1982	Massachusetts	62%	38%
1986	Massachusetts	70%	30%
1986	South Dakota	46%	54%
1990	Oregon	67%	33%

15

Private School Vouchers: Separate and Unequal

Arnold F. Fege

BACKGROUND

The chances are that your school district or your state will be debating the merits of parental choice soon, if they have not done so already. Sparked by the various parental choice plans, and the push for national educational reform, the concept of vouchers to be used in private schools is being marketed as the panacea for public school improvement. Exploiting the current fervor for more parental choices in public schools, voucher proponents are taking advantage of the "moment" to pursue what they have not been able to accomplish during the past years: direct public financial aid to private and parochial elementary and secondary schools, and the creation of an exclusionary school system subsidized through public money.

On its face, providing vouchers to parents to select whatever schools they wish for their children seems to be a simple proposition. However, each plan needs to be examined on the basis of a number of fundamental premises that are critical to assuring an excellent and equitable public education for all children. Voucher plans must be examined on the basis of whether transportation is provided to children who cannot afford their way to the school they select; whether children with vouchers will have equal access to the school

---

Arnold F. Fege is Director of Governmental Relations for the National PTA.

of their choice; whether due process procedures will be created for parents who believe that a school's admission practices are discriminatory; whether all schools that receive vouchers will be required to adhere to the same policies regarding school access, accountability, safety standards, and curriculum; and whether vouchers will promote the unconstitutional advancement of religion through the direct public funding of parochial schools.

In reality, vouchers will provide a benefit to some and play a cruel hoax on others. Given that the "some" and the "others" are children, teachers, and public education, it is the responsibility of those of us on the front line to ask the tough questions about programs that may threaten a free, universal, and equally accessible public education for *all* children no matter what their religion, disability, income, academic level, or language. It is an important public policy to assure that all children are winners, and that decisions about private school vouchers are made on the basis of solid educational benefits rather than on the political whims of the policy makers.

WHAT IS AN EDUCATIONAL VOUCHER?

A unit of government, whether local, state, or federal, provides parents with a voucher or chit to pay for their child's education at the school of their choice. The parents then give the voucher to the school officials when the child is enrolled. The school returns the voucher to the government, which in turn sends the school a predetermined amount of publicly raised tax dollars. In most plans, the dollars follow the child; therefore, the school receiving the child gains the voucher dollars, while the school losing the child also loses money.

WHICH SCHOOLS ARE ELIGIBLE TO RECEIVE VOUCHERS?

According to the concept, voucher schools could be public and nonpublic, public only within or outside of the attendance boundaries in which the child resides, contiguous school districts, or within an entire state or interstate; or else vouchers could pertain to special circumstances. For instance, in Milwaukee, one percent of the most economically disadvantaged public school students are eligible to "choose" among a number of predetermined private, nonreligious schools. It is possible that vouchers could be extended to home schooling, trade and proprietary schools, and to private and public post-secondary institutions, similar to the Minnesota Postsecondary Enrollment Options Program, which allows for eleventh and twelfth grade students qualifying to attend college.

In another twist, a New Hampshire town has authorized tax abatements for property owners who sponsor a high school student's private education. Under the plan, property owners in Epsom, New Hampshire, can have their property taxes cut by as much as $1,000 if they pay at least a portion of a high school student's tuition at a private school—secular or religious. The student need not be the property owner's child. Businesses, neighbors, or even strangers can earn the abatement as long as they produce a "voucher" from the school verifying payment.

Proponents contend that this arrangement can save the town money. Epsom sends approximately 180 secondary students to a public high school in a neighboring community at a cost of $4,600 per student, most of the tuition coming from the Epsom tax rolls. With the abatement, every public secondary student who transfers to a private school could, it is reasoned, save the town approximately $3,600; but, at the same time, this transfer from public to private school reduces public school resources by $4,600 for every student who does so. For the most part, however, there are few other voucher programs in actual operation.

ARE VOUCHERS A NEW IDEA?

No. Vouchers are based on economic theories of the marketplace and the laws of supply and demand. Milton Friedman, an economist and the modern architect of vouchers, first proposed an unregulated voucher model in 1955. Under his plan, all parents would receive vouchers equal to the cost of educating a child in the public school system; but schools, public or private, could charge whatever tuition the market would bear. Parents who desired more expensive schools could choose them by supplementing the value of the voucher with their own income. Under this plan, education became a consumer item to be purchased, similar to a car, a can of soup, or the latest sneakers. Since Friedman, a variety of voucher plans have been proposed with certain "add-ons" to the standard voucher, such as student transportation, compensatory weights for the poor, and nondiscrimination provisions.

With each attempt to refine voucher plans and make them more politically palatable, new tiers of complex and often confusing provisions have been added. Instead of clarifying the issue, each succeeding model poses more questions than answers—questions such as these:

- What if a school is oversubscribed? What provisions will be made for students who are shut out of school because there is no more space?

- Who certifies employees and oversees contract negotiations?

- Who assures equal access to educational opportunities, nondiscrimination, desegregation, due process for student expulsions, and employee dismissals?

- How often can students move and still retain a voucher? How much is the voucher worth after each move?

- What detailed record keeping will be necessary to handle financing, student mobility, auditing of school records and certification of voucher schools?

- Who provides transportation?

- What happens in the case where a school falsely or deceptively advertises in an effort to entice students and parents? Who regulates such a practice?

- What about the quality of education for the children of those parents who do not "choose"?

HOW WILL VOUCHERS BE FUNDED?

Currently, our public schools are supported through a combination of tax revenues at the local and state levels, with approximately 6.3 percent coming from the federal government. These monies are administered by departments of education and school boards, and then channeled to individual schools. A voucher program would radically alter this system. Although tax dollars would continue to be collected and regulated centrally, these funds would be dispersed in a decentralized manner, not through school boards or publicly controlled agencies, but rather to parents or "sponsors" through the voucher certificates. The parents' decision as "consumers" would determine which schools are funded, while the value of the voucher would determine the extent of funding.

CLAIMS AND RESPONSES

There are fundamental flaws in private and religious school voucher proposals. By diverting attention and resources away from the public schools, the controversial voucher movement may have the effect of dismantling public education rather then strengthening it. There is also the possibility that private schools will lose the freedoms they have due to encroaching government regulations as a trade-off for receiving public dollars. The following scenario offers a series of responses that may be voiced in objection to the typical claims made by proponents of private school vouchers.

Claim: Parents need more school choices.

Response: Parents already have a considerable amount of choice within the public schools. Many districts have open enrollment plans; magnet schools; and schools that provide various curricular options such as basic education, individualized education, special education, and summer programs. In addition, many American high schools have adopted just about every fad, fancy, or option that has been marketed over the past fifteen years. In school districts where parents wish more choices, working through the school administrators, teachers, school boards, city councils, parent advisory councils, or school site management councils is an effective means of producing change—all within the public sector.

Claim: Since public schools are not doing a good job, we should promote private education.

Response: Whatever the shortcomings of public schools, the way to improve them is not to abandon them and run to private schools. The more people abandon public schools for private choice, the less incentive there is to improve the public schools.

Claim: Private school vouchers will improve public education by creating competition.

Response: The "healthy rivalry" between the public and private schools envisioned with the introduction of a voucher program is really an unfair match in which one competitor—the private school—does not have to play by the same rules as the public schools. Many public schools and those receiving federal monies must adhere to:

- Title VI of the Civil Rights Act of 1964, which protects students against discrimination on the basis of race, color, or national origin

- Title IX of the Education Amendments of 1972, which protects the rights of women and girls in educational programs or activities

- Section 504 of the Rehabilitation Act of 1971, which prohibits schools from discriminating against disabled persons

- the Age Discrimination Act of 1975, which prohibits discrimination on the basis of age.

In addition, many states and local communities have created public policies related to safety, curriculum, teacher certification, and environmental protections for public schools. With the exception of race, nonpublic schools receiving vouchers do not have to abide by these regulations, especially if they do not receive federal dollars. Vouchers then become a vehicle that allows circumvention of laws and regulations designed to meet the common needs of children, parents, the community, and the nation. Private schools are then able to pick and choose those regulations and policies that they wish to follow. For instance, if a private school does not wish to educate handicapped children because the cost is too great, they do not have to admit them. If a religious school wishes to admit students only of their own faith, they may. If a private school wishes to exclude women from their sports program, they may. This unfair framework of "competition" would have the effect of creating a dual school system: a public one that would be required to meet the common needs of a community and nation, and a private one that would be exempt from many of the regulations in order to accommodate the special requirements of its children and their parents.

Claim: A private school voucher program would promote quality in all schools.

Response: It is difficult to understand the logic of this conclusion. First, upon the inception of a private school voucher program, the children already in private schools would receive vouchers. This would have no affect in improving any schools because the parents have already made their selection *without* the incentive of a voucher.

Second, the cost of each voucher would be skimmed off the top of the respective public education budget, local and/or state, and funneled to the private schools. This financial drain would be at the expense of the public schools, many of which are already experiencing funding shortages and a "no new taxes" environment. For instance, the average per-student expenditure for each elementary and secondary school student in the United States in 1990 was approximately $4,200. In a state that had 50,000 nonpublic school students and that provided a voucher to each of those students at, shall we say, $2,100, or half of the per-student average, it would reduce public school funds by approximately $105 million unless the taxpayers decided to increase revenues. It is inconceivable how such a program would enable the public schools to improve. In fact, vouchers would have the effect of giving private schools a distinct advantage by redistributing existing education dollars in favor of nonpublic schools without any assurances that education will improve for *all* children.

Third, a 1991 report released by the Committee for Economic Development, an independent research and educational organization comprising over

250 business and education leaders, concluded that "new research into student achievement demonstrates that, by itself, choice does not guarantee educational quality. . . . We believe that where choice systems are put into place, they should involve the public schools only."

Claim: Research suggests that parents who are able to "choose" the kind of education they want for their children are more satisfied, and thereby more supportive of the school.

Response: Certainly, parents who are able to send their children to a private school subsidized by public monies should be satisfied. But the research seldom concentrates on the obvious dissatisfaction of parents whose children are denied admission to a private school. In addition, what about the parents who are not active "choosers" and are left behind? In his book *Choice in Public Education,* Richard Elmore points out that the test of whether choices work is the extent to which the children who do not choose receive an excellent education, or the extent to which the losing school actually improves. Let us say that a child moves from public school A to private school B. State and local aid follows the child to the private school, which may or may not have a better program than the public school, but will probably benefit from the added resources. In addition, private school B can select or deny entrance to any students it wishes. Public school A, meanwhile, loses both a student and resources that may already have been budgeted. If enough students move from public school A, programs must be reduced and the remaining students' ability to compete thereby diminished. The students left behind may be relegated to low-quality public schools, or else they may be students who were denied access to the private school for lack of space or because they are cursed with poor grades or the wrong religion; if they are disabled or non-native English speakers, they may be considered too difficult or expensive to educate. The "winners" in this case are certainly the nonpublic schools, and conceivably the few former public schol students who have been accepted for admission at the private school. The "losers" will be those remaining children who cannot choose and whose schools lose the ability to compete as a result of student and financial loss. These children would include the sons and daughters of the lowest income families, handicapped children, or simply those whom the private school chooses not to enroll.

Claim: When a child transfers from a public to a private school and the public funds follow the child, the resulting loss of money does not reduce the public school's effectiveness, because it no longer bears the cost of educating that child.

Response: The loss of students does not occur in neat patterns. For instance, an entire class usually does not leave at once, thereby allowing the district to eliminate a full-time teacher and the cost of maintaining a classroom. The school still has to maintain the building, support a principal, keep up the grounds, operate a library, offer breakfast and a hot lunch, and administer a program. A school may or may not be losing students as a result of a poor program, but one thing is certain: the program will not improve as a result of lost resources. When Lee Iacocca wanted to restore Chrysler Motors to competitive health, he didn't do it with two billion *fewer* dollars; instead, he asked the federal government to provide an infusion of resources in order to catch up with the Japanese and Western Europeans. In the Epsom, New Hampshire, case, a loss of $4,600 per student incurred by the public school is sure to weaken the existing program or increase the student-cost ratio.

Claim: The market will weed out bad schools and reward good ones, much as the marketplace drives out bad businesses.

Response: It is one thing to close the local hardware store and liquidate the leftover inventory at half-price; it is quite another to liquidate our children in the same manner. Voucher proponents often have a romantic view of the marketplace: that badly performing businesses are squeezed out of the market while only the sound enterprises remain. That, unfortunately, is not how the marketplace works. Thousands of establishments went out of business in 1990, but many closed despite good performance. Variables such as the recession, a regional economic downturn, a loss of interest in the product, the ineptitude of the savings and loans industry, and/or inability to compete with the "giants" were all determining factors in many bankruptcies. We also know of inefficient and badly performing businesses that stay alive despite atrocious practices. It is in the public interest to improve public schools that are not performing well rather than flee to the private schools or resort to the marketplace "remedy" of closing the schools down.

Claim: Competition leads to quality; therefore, the privatization of schools will lead to excellence.

Response: Voucher proponents assume a cause-effect relationship between competition and quality in the marketplace and that a similar dynamic would work with schools. In business, however, the relationship between competition and quality is a function of profit. If a company can show greater profit by providing a cheaper, lower-quality product or no-frills service, it will. If a service—e.g., hospitalization for the poor or airline service to smaller communities—is not profitable, it won't be provided. A company is not in business to give the consumer the best product or service at the lowest price but to improve its profit margin by any method that will work. Competition, then, impacts pricing far more than it does product quality.

Claim: Parents of modest economic means deserve the same options the rich have in regard to where their children should attend school.

Response: Within the public arena, this issue should be debated and means found to eliminate any discrimination that exists between classes of children. However, private schools, because they are private, retain the prerogative of choosing what students they wish. According to Albert Shanker, president of the American Federation of Teachers, it is a mistake to think that using private school vouchers is equivalent to shopping at Macy's with a "big fat gift certificate." Using private school vouchers, says Shanker, is more analogous to applying for membership in an exclusive club. He contends that "private country clubs don't accept you merely because you have filled out an application form and you can pay the fees. A club that needs more warm bodies might be happy to get money on the barrel. But in an exclusive country club, the membership committee might ask itself how you fit in with the crowd that already belongs. And if they have any doubts, they'll probably decide that it's not worth the risk of losing a bunch of old members to get one new member. You can choose a country club, but the real choice is the club's."

Claim: Private school choice must be a major component in school reform, academic achievement, and parental control.

Response: This is an argument advanced in a book published in 1990 by John E. Chubb and Terry M. Moe titled *Politics, Markets, and America's Schools*. As we have discovered, however, control of admission to private schools is not exercised by parents, but by the schools themselves. Furthermore, many parents who send their children to private schools do not usually participate in the policies of that school. The mere choice of a school does not guarantee meaningful involvement. Finally, choice, as an end in itself, does not reform a school or improve its performance. In a RAND Corporation study by Paul T. Hill, Gail E. Foster, and Tamar Gendler called *High Schools with Character*, the authors contend that "choice does not guarantee that demand will elicit a supply of good schools, especially in the inner cities." In a study of thirteen high schools, the report concludes that it is possible for public school systems to make the key features of private and special public schools available to all students. Such quality elements as teacher empowerment, parental involvement, deregulation, a clear educational mission, and accountability to the people who depend on their performance can be replicated for students in the public schools.

Claim: Private school vouchers will provide increased educational opportunities, especially for minority and disadvantaged children.

Response: Not so, says a study conducted by the Chicago-based Designs for Change in its report titled *Questioning the New Improved Sorting Machine*. In a study of open-enrollment programs in New York, Philadelphia, Chicago, and Boston, Designs for Change discovered that the public schools sorted and selected students by income, color, and achievement. The most selective schools—vocational selective, magnet, and exam high schools for the highest achievers—had more white students, fewer students with attendance problems, fewer low achievers, and fewer handicapped students or at-risk children. There is little evidence that choice produces higher levels of achievement, particularly among at-risk students. If a public school open-enrollment plan can create such inequities, how much greater will they be within a private school voucher program where exclusivity, rather than inclusivity, will be the overriding admissions criteria?

In his article "Is Choice-Alone the Best Solution for Public Education?" David Seeley warns that unlimited free market choice could lead to:

> segregation not only by race but by socioeconomic class, religion and clique; the further ghettoization of American society that is already too ghettoized; the risk that the amount of government subsidy for choice we might get through our political system would be enough to facilitate further middle-class flight from public schools but not enough to enable poor people to pay for adequate education; and the risk of increased government control of private education once it became dependent on a government subsidy.

Claim: Religious schools perform a public service by educating children and, therefore, should receive public assistance.

Response: This is a position advocated by John E. Coons in his article "Choice Plans Should Include Private School Options." But whom does Mr. Coons suggest as an appropriate regulatory body to see that the "public" responsibilities are being carried out by religious schools? How does a state monitor such an objective without either violating the free exercise clause or the establishment clause of the First Amendment? Would religious schools be regulated by boards of education? state legislatures? accrediting associations? If not, how would unsuspecting parents be protected from unscrupulous schools out for a quick voucher buck? While it is magnanimous of parochial schools to be concerned about disadvantaged children, it is not the responsibility of the public to provide the dollars so that religious schools may accomplish this objective. We are not willing to sell the traditional freedoms of religious schools in exchange for government subsidies. While many religious schools do serve legitimate public educational needs, their primary purpose is to establish special and separate educational services to meet the *private, denominational needs of students and parents.* To subsidize such choices with public money would be contrary to established public policy.

Claim: Vouchers "cashed in" at religious schools would not be a violation of the separation of church and state. Since vouchers would go to parents, rather than the schools themselves, vouchers would not constitute direct aid.

Response: Wrong. Because the monies received from cashing in the vouchers would go into the operating budget of the parochial schools, the public funds could subsidize religious instruction and thereby have the effect of promoting religion. If, on the other hand, the government set up a monitoring system to assure that parochial schools were not using public voucher money to teach religion, they would surely litigate, claiming that such a system would inhibit the free exercise of religion, also a violation of the First Amendment. Therefore, the redemption of the voucher for federal funds by the parochial schools would create a pipeline from the public treasury to the parents to the parochial school—a flow of dollars that is clearly direct aid.

The Supreme Court has provided some guidance related to the unconstitutionality of parochial school vouchers. In *Grand Rapids School District* v. *Ball,* 105 S.Ct. 3216 (1985), the Court ruled unconstitutional a shared time and community education program offered by the Grand Rapids (Michigan) Public School district to nonpublic and parochial schools. Referring to *Sloan* v. *Lemon* and *Nyquist* v. *Committee for Public Education and Religious Liberty,* where parochiaid was given to parents and not directly to the religious schools; and to *Wolman* v. *Walter* and *Meek* v. *Pittenger,* where the aid was in-kind assistance rather than a direct contribution of public funds, the Court said, "Nonetheless, these differences in form were insufficient to save programs whose effect was indistinguishable from that of a direct subsidy to the religious schools." If, in fact, there can be no meaningful distinction made between aid to the student and aid to the school when a loan of instructional material is involved, or when shared time services are provided to religious schools, it would seem to be doubly true that there cannot be a meaningful distinction made between whether the school or the parents benefit when a voucher program requires parents to be a conduit of tax funds to the school for either secular or religious purposes.

Claim: Private school vouchers enhance, increase, and promote parental involvement.

Response: The mere act of "choosing" constitutes only a small part of parental involvement. Proponents of vouchers have generally sought to blur the distinction between parents' involvement and the parental choice of schools, treating each as closely related if not synonymous. In many cases, vouchers have been characterized as the "ultimate" in parental choice and involvement, but studies suggest that parents who choose private schools rarely get involved in the schools' curriculum, policy decisions, or governance. In the market, the consumer seldom gets or needs to get involved in the production of the product; he is primarily interested in the product itself. Judgment about product quality is usually determined by the satisfaction of the customer regarding the end result.

In the education of children, however, parents must become involved in helping to mold, shape, nurture, and develop the resource—in this case, the child. Vouchers would transform parents from citizens into consumers. Seeley maintains that vouchers would "make education a purely private affair . . . and not a community responsibility." He argues that choice alone "has the virtue of being a familiar concept, since we have grown up with it as the way for providing everything from toothpaste and automobiles to giant real estate developments. . . . But none of this means that it is the right policy framework for public education in the United States in the 1990s." Choice alone, says Seeley, won't create the loyalty necessary for cohesion and commitment through the various social and political processes that improve education for all children. Such loyalty is not achieved solely by parents-as-consumers, but by those parents who participate and are involved in supporting better education not only for their own children, but for all children.

Claim: Opponents of private school vouchers discriminate against the parents who send their children to private schools. Private school parents end up having to shoulder a double burden: they pay for the public schools through their tax dollars and for private schools through tuition.

Response: This alleged "double burden" exists only because these parents choose not to send their children to the public school system provided through the tax dollars. It also ignores the basic premise that distinguishes public from private schools. The public education system was founded on certain fundamental beliefs—that there should be equal educational opportunities for all children; that an educated public is in everyone's interest; and that by providing a universal and tuition-free system of education for all children, we will ensure that this public interest is best served.

In a diverse society, the public schools actually provide the only forum where all viewpoints regarding a particular issue receive consideration and scrutiny without the *a priori* biases found in private education. Public schooling is the only educational enterprise dedicated, by design, to offering a program that respects the myriad outlooks and values held by all the children of all the people. Parents who wish to send their children to private schools certainly should have that choice. Just as with the elderly, childless couples, and single adults, however, this does not relieve them of their responsibility as citizens to support a vital public service.

Claim: Private school vouchers will have the effect of reducing burdensome regulations because accountability would rest solely with parents.

Response: Although initially, private school vouchers might result in less regulation, private schools would inevitably become increasingly accountable to the public. They would come under mounting pressure for public regulation in the areas of curriculum, teacher certification, safety, nondiscrimination, and fiscal oversight. In addition, state and local school districts would become responsible for ensuring that vouchers are properly used, recovering misused monies, verifying that private schools have full-time instructional programs, and tracking students and voucher programs from one school to another. If parents believe they have been treated unfairly in a public school, they can appeal to the school board. What agency will receive complaints if parents contend they are treated unfairly at a private school? Will a separate agency be created to hear complaints? Will a Board of Private Education be developed? How will a public agency hold religious schools accountable without running afoul of the First Amendment's separation of church and state principles? The beauty of our current approach to education is that we enjoy both a public and a private system. Private school vouchers would irreparably damage public schools by diverting much-needed funding from the public schools and changing private schools by subjecting them to much greater government control.

Claim: Opposing vouchers shows that one does not want parents involved in educational decision making.

Response: This claim is as preposterous as the argument that if one does not support prayer in the schools, then one is anti-religious. Indeed, evidence abounds of effective parental involvement *without* vouchers.

CONCLUSION

There are many parental choice plans, and many public school districts already provide parents a variety of options. However, private and religious school voucher programs do not allow the parents to make a choice—the nonpublic school makes the choice for them, determining on its own the kind of student who will be admitted. Support should be given to those plans which improve the education of *all* children in a school district, encourage parental involvement, and prohibit the diversion of publicly raised funds into private or parochial schools.

The Committee for Economic Development summed up the issue of choice in their recent study titled "The Unfinished Agenda: a New Vision for Child Development and Education." Their concern about the "losers" whom private school choice would produce moved them to state:

> An even more critical issue (in choice) is how to ensure that all children, especially the most disadvantaged, receive a quality education. These are the children who would most likely remain in the worst-performing schools because their parents are unwilling or unable to act as their advocates. We believe that where choice systems are put into place, they should involve the public schools only.

We should heed these words of wisdom spoken by people who understand the difference between private profits and public interest.

REFERENCES

Chubb, John E., and Terry Moe. *Politics, Markets, and America's Schools.* Washington, D.C.: The Brookings Institution, 1990.

Coons, John E. "Choice Plans Should Include Private School Options."

Elmore, R. F. "Options for Choice in Public Education." In *Choice in Public Education,* edited by Boyd H. Walberg. Berkeley: McCutchan, 1990.

Hill, Paul T.; Gail E. Foster; and Tamar Gendler. *High Schools with Character.* Santa Monica, Calif.: RAND, 1990.

Moore, Donald M., and Suzanne Davenport. *Questioning the New Improved Sorting Machine.* Chicago: Designs for Change, 1988.

Seeley, David S. "Is Choice Alone the Best Solution for Public Education? Chubb and Moe Provide Less than a Final Answer." *Future Choices* (Fall 1990).

Shanker, Albert, and Bella Rosenberg. "Politics, Markets, and America's Schools; A Rejoinder." Washington, D.C.: The American Federation of Teachers, Winter 1990.

The Unfinished Agenda: A New Vision for Child Development and Education. New York: Committee for Economic Development, 1991.

BIBLIOGRAPHY

The American Jewish Committee. "Choice Among Public Schools: Policy Statement and Background Analysis," 1989.

Bamber, Chrissie, with Nancy Berla, Anne Henderson, and William Rioux. *Public School Choice: An Equal Chance for All?* The National Committee for Citizens in Education, 1990.

Catterall, James. "The Supply and Demand for Private Education." *Journal of Education Finance* (Fall 1987).

Cooper, Kenneth J. "Minnesota's School Choice Option Inspires Few Students to Transfer." *The Washington Post,* February 24, 1991.

Diegmueller, Karen. "Town in New Hampshire Grants Property-Tax Breaks As Choice Incentive." *Education Week,* January 9, 1991.

Evans, Dennis L. "The Marketplace Mythology in School Choice." *Education Week,* October 17, 1990.

Hirschman, Albert O. *Exit, Voice and Loyalty: Response to Decline in Firms, Organizations and States.* Cambridge, Mass.: Harvard University Press, 1970.

Mueller, Van D. "Choice: The Parent's Perspective." *Phi Delta Kappa* (March 1987).

Nathan, Joe. *Public Schools by Choice: Expanding Opportunities for Parents, Students and Teachers.* Minneapolis, Minn.: Free Spirit Press, 1989.

The National PTA. *Guidelines on Parental Choice—An Educational Issue,* 1989.

"The National PTA Speaks Out on Private School Vouchers." *What's Happening in Washington* (February/March 1991).

New Jersey State Department of Education. *Public School Choice: National Trends and Initiatives,* December 1988.

Poinsett, Alex. "Reform Activists Say 'No' to Choice." *Catalyst* (November 1990).

"Problems with the Administration's Voucher Proposal for Chapter 1: The Equity and Choice Act." Prepared For The U.S. House of Representatives Subcommittee on Elementary, Secondary, and Vocational Education, February 1986, Committee Print Number 99–M.

Raspberry, William. "Give Choice a Chance." *The Washington Post,* December 31, 1990.

Rosenberg, Bella. "Public School Choice: Can We Find the Right Balance?" *American Educator* (Summer 1990).

"Schools of Choice?" *Educational Leadership* 48, no. 4 (December 1990/January 1991). (Entire issue comprises articles on choice.)

16

The Milwaukee Parental Choice Program

Herbert Grover and Julie K. Underwood

Wisconsin has become the inadvertent test site for the privatization of education. With the enactment of the Milwaukee Parental Choice program in May of 1990, Wisconsin became the first state to have a private school choice program. Public educators have vigorously opposed this program, including challenging its constitutionality.

In spite of the fact that the Wisconsin Supreme Court approved the program in a 4–3 decision on March 3, 1992, the debate clearly will continue over the desirability of choice and vouchers as a solution to the perceived problems of public education. President Bush, Education Secretary Lamar Alexander, and Deputy Secretary David Kearns are pushing strong for unproven concepts like school choice, yet the public education community continues to plead and work for solutions within the public system.

The Milwaukee Parental Choice program originated as a separate legislative bill; but during the final days of the 1989 legislative session, it was added to the budget adjustment bill with little debate. The Choice program permits up to 1,000 low-income Milwaukee students to attend private, nonsectarian schools and pays participating schools about $2,500 for each participating student. Funds for the program are taken from general school

Dr. Herbert Grover is Superintendent of Public Instruction for the State of Wisconsin. Julie K. Underwood is an associate professor at the University of Wisconsin-Madison. She serves as consultant to the Wisconsin Department of Public Instruction on the Milwaukee Parental Choice program.

aid which would otherwise be paid to Milwaukee public schools. The $2,500 is equivalent to the per-pupil state aid the Milwaukee public schools receive, and represents more state aid per pupil than is received by a majority of other public school districts in the state.

The income of families in the choice program cannot be higher than 175 percent of the federal poverty level. Schools must select eligible children for enrollment on a random basis with no more than 49 percent of the participating school's total enrollment being choice students.

The statute places the program under the administration of the Department of Public Instruction (DPI), which must collect student achievement, attendance, dropout, suspension and expulsion, and parental involvement data from choice schools. That information is to be compared with data from the Milwaukee public schools in a report to the legislature.

Within weeks after the governor signed the legislation, several Wisconsin citizens, the Wisconsin Education Association Council, the Wisconsin Association of School District Administrators, and the Milwaukee chapter of the National Association for the Advancement of Colored People filed a lawsuit challenging the constitutionality of the program. On the other side, the Washington, D.C.-based Landmark Legal Foundation, acting on behalf of some parents and the participating choice schools, challenged the DPI's implementation of the program. Both lawsuits were decided at the same time by Dane County judge Susan Steingass, who ruled that the program is "not facially unconstitutional." While she agreed that the state superintendent has rights and duties to guarantee that participating schools meet the requirements both of the parental choice law and of the state and federal provisions, she ruled that "he may not insist on compliance in a manner more onerous or demanding than insisted upon for other participating programs and public schools." Steingass called the Milwaukee Parental Choice program a public program operating in a private school. She said that because parents still had the option to choose the public schools, the private school should not be obligated to match the public schools' programs. On August 20, 1990, Steingass approved DPI implementation procedures that eliminated references to the Education of the Handicapped Act in the Intent to Participate form which the participating schools must complete, and the program began on schedule for the 1990-1991 school year with seven private schools enrolling 341 students. (In January 1992, there were 525 students enrolled in six schools.)

Public school advocates appealed the trial court decision, and in November 1990, the Wisconsin Court of Appeals ruled that the program was unconstitutional based on the legislative procedure. In March 1991, the Wisconsin Supreme Court agreed to review the matter and twelve months later reversed the decision of the Court of Appeals.

The arguments raised during this process deserve further attention since they will be raised in similar situations across the nation. First, there must be a system of accountability to assure that children who participate receive an adequate education. Second, the students' individual rights, both statutory and constitutional, must be assured. Finally, this choice plan does not legally or practically accomplish these goals.

CHOICE LACKS ACCOUNTABILITY

In Wisconsin, regulation of private schools is *de minimis*. A private school need only certify that its program provides at least 875 hours of instruction each school year and that it has a sequentially progressive curriculum of fundamental instruction in reading, language arts, mathematics, social studies, science, and health.[1]

While this "regulation" may provide sufficient assurance that some education is taking place so as to fulfill a parental obligation under the compulsory attendance statute, it does not ensure that participating schools meet state requirements for educational excellence as outlined in Wisconsin's 20 Standards. The question, therefore, is whether the state should expend funds on an educational program that has no guarantee of quality. In contrast, public school districts must meet twenty minimum education standards[2] as well as comply with numerous other state and federal requirements.

The only quality assurances contained in the Milwaukee Parental Choice law are that the participating schools must be currently operating as a private school and meet one of the following standards:

1) At least 70 percent of the pupils in the program advance one grade level each year.

2) The private schools' average attendance rate for the pupils in the program is at least 90 percent.

3) At least 80 percent of the pupils in the program demonstrate significant academic progress.

4) At least 70 percent of the families of pupils in the program meet parent involvement criteria established by the private school.[3]

The first and fourth standards are completely within the control and discretion of the private school itself. The school makes its own decision on promotion and sets its own definition of parental involvement. There is no assurance that students will be promoted justifiably or that their promotion to the next grade level will be based at all on academic achievement. Parental involvement may be as little as attending one parent-teacher conference or signing a student's report card. The measure of "significant progress" also is largely determined by individual private schools, because there is no measure of accountability such as that faced by public schools.

Proponents of choice programs argue that sufficient regulation and control are given through parental control of the private schools. They contend that if students are not receiving an adequate education in a private school, parents will withdraw them. If that argument is accepted, it would follow that any school that has a sufficient number of students enrolled to allow them to operate must be providing an adequate education. This statement simply begs the question. To justify the expenditure of public money, there should be sufficient objective safeguards to assure that the direct public purpose of education will be achieved. This program fails even to require the private schools to spend the $2,500 per child they receive on education. Accreditation with an independent national educational accrediting agency is not required. There are no "public" members on the boards of the schools. The schools need not go through a publicly scrutinized annual budget process, but can continue in the program year to year until the state legislature acts or one of the four weak criteria mentioned above is not met.

Proponents of the Milwaukee Choice program argue that there is no need for educational controls because the purpose of the program is an experiment in providing education to economically disadvantaged youth. But even if it is an experiment, the following questions should be addressed.

- What state purpose is served?

- Who protects the interests of the children if the experiment fails?

- Who and what determines the success or failure of the experiment?

The drafters of the Milwaukee Parental Choice program contend it was narrowly designed to address the problems of disadvantaged youth. However, nowhere in the program are these problems directly addressed. Children in high-poverty urban areas especially need the following types of programs:

- early childhood education

- compensatory education

- supportive services

- exceptional educational needs

- dropout prevention programs

- vocational technical programs.[4]

The choice schools are not required to provide special services. Thus, no assurances are given that the severe problems facing disadvantaged youth will in any way be closer to being solved because of this program.

STUDENTS' RIGHTS MUST BE GUARANTEED

As recipients of public tax monies, the participating private school should be required to provide the same guarantees students would have in public schools. As stated by the United States Supreme Court, students should not be forced to "shed their rights at the school house gate."[5] Public schools are subject to all of the restrictions and restraints placed on the state through the United States and Wisconsin constitutions. Students have the right to free exercise of religion, freedom of expression, freedom of association, freedom against unreasonable search and seizure, equal protection, and due process.

As recipients of federal funds, both the State of Wisconsin and the Department of Public Instruction also have obligations under federal statutes. The U.S. Department of Education's regulations require each state's compliance with Title VI of the Civil Rights Act of 1964,[6] Title IX of the Education Amendments of 1972,[7] the Age Discrimination Act,[8] and Section 504 of the Rehabilitation Act of 1973.[9]

Section 504 of the Rehabilitation Act of 1973 states: "No otherwise qualified handicapped individual . . . shall, solely by reason of his handicap, be excluded from the participation in, be denied the benefits of, or be subjected to, discrimination under any program or activity."[10] Under this statute, the State of Wisconsin, the Department of Public Instruction, and programs administered by the state or the DPI are prohibited from discriminating against handicapped persons. The state has two obligations under Section 504: first, not to exclude a person from participating in, or benefiting from, a program it implements;[11] and, second, the State of Wisconsin and the Department of Public Instruction must ensure that all handicapped students who are in publicly funded placements be provided an opportunity to have a free appropriate education[12] as defined in the Individuals with Disabilities Education Act (IDEA).

This statute would be violated by denial of access into one of its programs to "otherwise qualified" handicapped persons. According to the Milwaukee Parental Choice program, a student is qualified for participation in the program if he/she is a Milwaukee resident, meets the family income requirement, and has been enrolled in the Milwaukee public school or not enrolled in school during the 1989–1990 school year.[13] Thus, in order for the Milwaukee Parental Choice program to be implemented in compliance with Section 504, a handicapped child who is otherwise qualified must be allowed to participate in the Choice program. Once enrolled, the child must be offered a free appropriate public education pursuant to all of the federal and state statutes and regulations regarding the education of handicapped children.

If Choice students have no Section 504 and IDEA rights in the program, then the following scenario would be played out. A learning disabled student in the Milwaukee public schools receives assistance from a resource teacher, who provides services and translates information from written to oral form. The teacher also helps the student learn to decode written work. For all other purposes the student participates in the regular curriculum. This arrangement has been determined to be the appropriate education for this student. Before diagnosis of the learning disability, the student was failing classes; the student now is passing in the regular classes. The parents want their child to attend a participating private Choice school, but the private school administrator explains that the school has no resource teacher available, nor is it willing to provide one. The student's parents know that without the appropriate educational services their child will again fail in school; therefore, they must decide if they want to participate in the Choice program this school provides but without the special services available, or remain in the Milwaukee public school and receive the needed services.

If Choice students have no Section 504 and IDEA rights in the program, the dilemma is there, and the discrimination is blatant. Parents should not be forced to choose between two public benefits: participation in a Choice program or receipt of the educational services their children need to succeed educationally. A program which truly offers choices broadens alternatives; it does not limit educational opportunities.

IS CHOICE THE ANSWER?

The arguments discussed above point out that choice is not the simple and easy solution to education's problems as suggested by some of its proponents. If Choice is meant to provide for open competition and thus improve education, as its promoters say, then the playing fields should be equal. Under the Choice law, public money is given to the private schools without regard for the educational level of staff, the availability of counseling and nursing services, the scope of the curriculum, or whether the school's doors are open to handicapped children. From the standpoint of the public trust and standards of public accountability, this is unacceptable.

A private school voucher program encourages the abandonment of the social institution best able and most likely to preserve our commitment to equal opportunity, pluralism, and cultural diversity. Without a societal commitment to the institution of public education, the tendency would be for people to flee one another in search of their own isolated educational repose, returning to pre-1954 when separate passed for equal.

As John Goodlad has argued, there is no freedom without sustained attention to the personal and collective efforts required to maintain it. "This requires, as Jefferson and others forging the Republic argued, a well-educated citizenry, not merely a well-educated elite. Maintaining our freedom requires not merely educated leadership but an educated polity, capable of judging whether this leadership deserves our trust and continued support. There must not be, then, two kinds of education for our citizens."[14]

This nation has seen the benefit of a tax-supported common public school system which, in the 1950s, became the greatest educational engine for progress in the world. It was the foundation from which this nation responded to the challenge of Sputnik in the 1960s. It was the impetus which led to the conclusion that separate could not be equal. Now some people, under the guise of competition, are advocating a new and regressive separatism—a return to racial, economic, and political isolation. As an example, Wisconsin will spend $69 million in 1992 to encourage voluntary integration but up to $2.5 million under the Choice program to support what ends up as being racially isolated private schools.

What effect will vouchers have upon the *real* problems confronting education in America? What impact will choice have on improving the conditions that surround the children? Will such a program improve the United States' nineteenth-place ranking among the nations of the world in infant mortality rates and twenty-ninth in low birthweight babies? Will it address the reality that children are the poorest segment of our society, and that this country ranks eighth among industrialized nations in childhood poverty? Will it reduce the daily ritual in America in which 1,100 teenagers have abortions; six teenagers commit suicide; and 3,000 children see their parents divorced? How does it resolve the Milwaukee condition in which 60 percent of the pupils come from low-income families; 28 percent within the minority community are unemployed; 7,700 child abuse cases are reported; 2,500 children are homeless; the teen pregnancy rate is twice the national average; and 35 percent of the pupils change schools each year because of family housing or employment situations?

How can children learn when their lives are in such turmoil? It takes hard work, dedication, prudent investment, and the ability to resist glitzy, quick fixes. How is it that, between 1982 and 1989, 2.1 million children fell into poverty while the number of American billionaires quintupled? How was this nation able to invest $1.9 trillion in national defense while cutting $10 billion from programs to defend poor children and families? And why does this society spend $27,000 a year to keep a juvenile in custody but only $2,500 a year to support a child in Head Start?

Public education has served us all well. It is in need of improvement—in some cases, desperately in need. But first, a major investment is needed in the infrastructure that supports our children and families. Also needed are the active support and involvement of the public in their schools to provide a solution that will reflect the values of hard work, equal opportunity, public accountability, the willingness to tackle tough issues, and an irrevocable commitment to pluralism and democratic ideals.

CONCLUSION

The Milwaukee Parental Choice program creates a new form of public instruction. The legislature, which has an obligation to provide public elementary and secondary education, traditionally has funded public education through the creation and funding of the "common school." The notion of the "common school" as presented by Horace Mann was to be common, not in the traditional European sense of a school for common people. It is "common" in terms of common to all people. It is available and equal to all, part of the birthright of every American child, for rich and poor alike. Its doors are open to all, no matter how easy or difficult their educational tasks might be. Not only are these schools free of charge, but they provide a predetermined substantive level of education. That educational level is necessary for the common school to fulfill its central purpose: the development of informed and productive citizens, who can actively participate in a democratic society. The common school has educated its citizens for active roles in society through instruction and interaction with others. In this common school, children of all creeds, classes, and backgrounds come together.

The founding fathers and others postulated that through education individual rights and the public good would be secured. Moreover, it is through the common school that a diverse, pluralistic society makes the many into one. Public education and public schools hold a special place in our republic, and as such, the institution of public education must be approached deliberately and solemnly.

This is not to say that all education must be conducted within legislatively created school districts. But, when the legislature supports education with public funds, that education should at least meet the standards established for the "common school." It should be subjected to assurances and standards to ensure that public funds are well spent.

When the legislature undertakes to create a new type of publicly funded elementary and secondary education, that predetermined level of instructional quality should not be sacrificed. The children and parents involved in this program should be able to have confidence that if the state is endorsing the education through payment, the education they receive will meet certain quality standards and will provide them the constitutional and statutory rights guaranteed in any public program.

NOTES

1. Sec. 118.165, Wis. Stat.
2. Sec. 121.02, Wis. Stats.
3. Sec. 119.293 (7), Wis. Stats.
4. *Kukor v. Grover*, 436 N.W.2d at 590–591 (Bablitch, J., dissenting).
5. *Tinker* v. *Des Moines,* 393 U.S. 503, 89 S.Ct. 73 (1969).
6. 20 U.S.C. 2000d.
7. 29 U.S.C. 1671–1682.
8. 42 U.S.C. 6101 et seq.
9. 29 U.S.C. 794. 34 C.F.R. 76.500.
10. 29 U.S.C. 794 (a).
11. 34 C.F.R. 76.500.
12. 34 C.F.R. 104.33.
13. Section 119.23 (2)(a), Wis. Stat.
14. John Goodlad, *Access to Knowledge* (New York: The College Board Press, 1990), p. 5.

17

Why Privatizing Public Education Is a Bad Idea

Bill Honig

John Chubb and Terry Moe[1] propose to transform our public schools from democratically regulated institutions to market-driven ones. They contend that while the past decade has seen the most ambitious period of school reform in the nation's history, gains in test scores or graduation rates have not been achieved. They explain that government, with its politics and bureaucracy, so hampers schools' ability to focus on academic achievement that improvement efforts are doomed.

Using data from the early eighties, Chubb and Moe suggest that freeing schools from democratic control boosts performance a full grade level. Thus, they would give students scholarships for any public, private, or newly formed school; prohibit states or school districts from establishing organizational or effective curricular standards or assessing school performance; and allow schools to restrict student entry. They assert that parent choice alone will assure quality.

Chubb and Moe's proposal to combine vouchers with radical deregulation is completely flawed. They misread the evidence on choice and claim that it is the only answer.

I believe that we should give public school parents more choice, either through magnet schools or open-enrollment plans. Choice builds commitment

---

Bill Honig is California's Superintendent of Public Instruction.

of parents and students and keeps the system honest. But limits are necessary to prevent skimming of the academic or athletically talented or furthering racial segregation. More important, where choice has been successful, such as in East Harlem, it has been one component of a broader investment in quality.

SCHOOLS POST IMPRESSIVE GAINS

Chubb and Moe's basic charge that current reform efforts have not succeeded is dead wrong and, consequently, the need for risky and radical change unjustified. While their data say something useful about the dangers of rigid bureaucracy and overpoliticization of education, their findings cannot be used to judge the reform effort, since the students in their study were tested before reforms began. More recent evidence points to substantial gains.

Consider our experience in California: In 1990, in combined reading and math scores, seniors tested *one year* ahead of seniors in 1984, the exact magnitude of growth which Chubb and Moe say their proposal would achieve and just what they argue couldn't be accomplished within the existing system.

Also, in 1990, eighth graders performed an equivalent of about half a grade level higher than eighth grade students in 1986.

In addition, the number of seniors who scored above 450 on the verbal portion of the Scholastic Aptitude Test grew almost 17 percent and those who scored above 500 on the math portion grew almost 23 percent from 1984 to 1991. Academic course enrollments increased substantially—for example, 53 percent more students are taking chemistry and 63 percent more are taking physics; and students who meet University of California course requirements rose 23 percent between 1985 and 1990. Further, between 1984 and 1991 the rate of public school seniors passing rigorous Advanced Placement exams has increased 179 percent—to over 49,000 exams passed. And between 1986 and 1991, the number of high school students dropping out has declined 19.6 percent.

Our gains are especially impressive since they were made even though our student population is growing dramatically, and both the number of limited-English-proficient students and students living in poverty has doubled during the last decade. Currently, about one out of five California students does not speak fluent English.

Nor are successes in our schools limited to California. Nationwide, the percentage of high school dropouts has shrunk by one-third since 1979. Better yet, almost one-half of the dropouts eventually returned to graduate or received a graduation equivalent.

Nationally, during the past seven years the talent pool of college-bound students who scored above 450 on the verbal portion of the SAT grew 21.6 percent. Over 31 percent more scored above 500 on the math portion of the SAT. Scores above 600 have grown 25 percent in verbal and 36 percent in math.

Some commentators argue that even though there has been some improvement in the past seven years, combined verbal and math SAT scores are still 84 points below what they were in 1963. Actually, one can make a good argument that schools are performing a little better than they did in 1963. In that year only 16 percent of the graduating class took the test; in 1991, 42 percent did—a less elite group. According to recent research on adjusting SAT scores for the percentage of students taking the test, a one percent increase in test takers will lower combined scores two points. Thus, two-thirds of the 84-point gap is a result of a significantly greater percentage of test takers. The remainder is more than accounted for by demographic changes in the test takers.

Further evidence of improvement among college-bound students nationwide is that Advanced Placement courses taken have doubled since 1982. The nationwide college-going rates have increased to an all-time high of 59 percent, up from 51 percent in 1982. The number of youngsters taking the more demanding curriculum, suggested by *A Nation at Risk*, of four years of English; three years of social studies, science, and math; and two years of foreign languages has more than doubled between 1982 and 1987, from 13 percent to 29 percent of high school graduates. In science, the number of graduates taking chemistry grew 45 percent to nearly one out of every two students, and the number taking physics expanded 45 percent to one out of every five students.

Certainly, these gains are not sufficient to prepare our youngsters for the changing job market, to reach their potential, to participate in our democracy, or to keep up with international competition. We still have a long way to go. But that is not the issue. Educators are being challenged on whether we have a strategy that can produce results. We do, and by working with our national leadership, we should be able to galvanize this country towards meeting our national goals.

CALIFORNIA'S COMPREHENSIVE STRATEGY

Of course, the crucial question should be *What caused these gains?* California's experience may shed some light on what it takes for a successful reform strategy.

First, a reform strategy must be comprehensive and spring from what needs to be learned and how best to teach it. We worked hard in California to lay the groundwork for a more demanding curriculum for our youth. We recognized that the ability to abstract, conceptualize, and problem-solve is becoming increasingly important—even for traditional blue-collar jobs.

Realizing that production line work now demands statistical analysis and high-level team work and communication skills, we first agreed that the disciplines of math, science, writing, history, literature, health, and fine arts are the best vehicles to teach these higher level skills and applied academics (problem solving); and cooperative learning becomes crucial in reinforcing these abilities. The same instructional strategies apply to preparing thinking citizens who understand democracy and its ways, and possess the wisdom and character to capitalize on the freedom given them.

Second, using experts in each field, we defined the kind of curriculum and instruction necessary to reach these higher goals—in reading, literature, writing, language skills, science, math, history, foreign languages, vocational education, health, and physical education. We obtained consensus by involving large numbers of teachers and educators without compromising our essential goals.

These agreements were embodied in our state framework and curricular guides, which are widely available and used. These guidelines are sufficiently precise to have a definite point of view (e.g., reading instruction should include serious works of literature), but open enough for teachers to figure out for themselves how best to organize instruction.

Third, we changed our state tests to reflect this more demanding curriculum, and the revision of our testing program continues. We also instituted an accountability system which set specific targets for the state and gave each school and district information on how it was doing in reaching those targets.

Fourth, we developed specific implementational strategies in each curricular area to get the word out on what the changes were and why we were making them. For example, in shifting to a more literature-based English curriculum, we developed comprehensive training through the UCLA Literature Project and numerous documents to support our efforts.

Fifth, a tremendous effort was made to get local school superintendents and board members to participate in the vision and strategies of reform and, most important, to devote substantial dollars during tight fiscal times to staff development. Many in the corporate world are now saying that investment in their employees is the most critical factor in meeting worldwide competition and continuing productivity growth. What technology introduction was to the 1970s and 1980s, staff development will be to the 1990s. Can you imagine IBM or Apple attempting to sell a new product without training its salespeople? The concept seems absurd. Yet, in many political circles the obvious reform strategy of heavy investment in teachers to acquaint them with the improvements in each discipline smacks of a boondoggle. Nevertheless, without that investment, large-scale improvements will not occur.

Currently, schools devote pathetically few resources to staff development, and education remains one of the lowest capitalized enterprises in the country. In California we designed math, history, writing, literature, science, and fine arts training consistent with our revamped curriculum. The training, which includes specific courses and follow-through back to the school level, has had a powerful effect. Unfortunately, because of low levels of funding only a small fraction of teachers have been able to participate.

Sixth, California spends nearly $340 million a year for site planning and implementation through our School Improvement Program. This effort provides resources for the school community to take the general reform ideas and devise specific strategies for curricular and instructional improvement.

Seventh, we designed and implemented specific strategies aimed at improving the quality of instructional materials, enhancing leadership of principals and superintendents, and involving parents. We formed a strong working relationship with the business community, higher education, and law enforcement; and we have initiated hundreds of partnership programs. Finally, we are revamping each special program, such as vocational education, bilingual education, and programs for the children at risk of failing, to assure that these programs will help accomplish the overall reform objectives. We also embarked on a multi-million dollar program of technology introduction.

CHUBB AND MOE'S PLAN JEOPARDIZES STUDENTS

Compared to this comprehensive approach, Chubb and Moe's proposal jeopardizes our youngsters and this democracy. Any one of the following objections should be enough to sink their plan:

1) The proposal risks creating elite academies for the few and second-rate schools for the many. It allows schools to exclude students who do not meet their standards—almost guaranteeing exacerbation of income and racial stratification. We had such a two-tiered system in the nineteenth century before mass education helped make this country prosperous and free. We shouldn't go back a hundred years in search of the future.

2) Cult schools will result. Nearly 90 percent of American youngsters attend public schools, which are the major institutions involved in transmitting our democratic values. By prohibiting common standards, Chubb and Moe enshrine the rights of parents over the needs of children and society. Is it good public policy to use public funds to support schools which teach astrology or creationism instead of science, inculcate anti-minority or anti-white attitudes, or prevent students from reading *The Diary of Anne Frank*

or *The Adventures of Huckleberry Finn*? Absent democratic controls, such schools will multiply.

3) Their plan violates the constitutional prohibition against aiding religious schools.

4) The lack of accountability and the naiveté of relying on the market to protect children is alarming. In the nineteenth century, when the best consumer slogan was "Let the buyer beware," meat packers sold tainted meat to customers. In the twentieth century, deregulation produced the savings and loan crisis. Nobody seriously proposes rescinding all environmental safeguards; why should our children not be similarly protected? In fact, if we look at private trade schools, where regulation is weak and scholarships are available, we find widespread fraud and misrepresentation. Similar problems occurred when New York decentralized its school system. Corruption and patronage surfaced in its local boards of education. All across the nation there are calls for *more* accountability from our schools, not less.

5) The plan would be tremendously chaotic. Vast numbers of new schools would have to be created for this plan to succeed; yet most new enterprises fail. Many youngsters will suffer during the transition period, and with no accountability we will not even know if the experiment was successful.

6) Taxpayers will have to pay more. Chubb and Moe maintain that competition will produce savings, but they offer no proof. A potent counterexample is furnished by the fact that although colleges compete, costs are skyrocketing. Furthermore, if this plan is adopted nationwide, a substantial portion of the cost of private school students—about $18.5 billion—currently being paid by their parents will be picked up by taxpayers (unless public school expenditures are reduced ten percent, which would make the plan doubly disastrous).

In addition, the proposal includes expensive transportation components and the creation of a new level of bureaucracy—Choice Offices. These offices will include Parent Information Centers, where liaisons will meet with parents to advise them on what schools to choose. But how many employees will be necessary for this process if parents are to receive the information they actually need in a timely manner?

NATIONAL POLICY IMPLICATIONS

This country has an incredible opportunity to build a world-class school system. Many educators are not only prepared to improve schools but have already begun to do so. So what are the national policy implications?

President Bush has taken some important steps to define a comprehensive education strategy for this nation. We need to invest selectively in those strategies with a high potential for leveraging the whole system. These strategies are much better investments than the fanciful ideas of Chubb and Moe and their disciples. The issue should be: What can the nation buy with additional investments, and how much return can we expect from those expenditures?

The highest-payoff targets of opportunity include:

1) *Setting goals and strengthening assessment.* Performance targets should be established that include increasing the number of seniors who can read at the "adept" level, use numbers to solve moderately complex problems, and compose an adequate piece of persuasive writing.

We need to reform our mathematics education through concerted actions. New materials and equipment for instruction and assessment must come from the national level because of the intensive research and development that are required. We should also aim at improving students' proficiency in science and history, increasing the number who attend college, and lowering the dropout rate to 10 percent. And standards should be developed for the fifth and eighth grades.

In addition, assessments must be changed from mainly multiple-choice, factual-recall questions to performance-based tasks such as writing and problem-solving. Though more expensive than current methods, performance assessment drives instruction in the right direction.

2) *Investing sufficient capital in staff development.* We must train teachers already in the classroom to teach a more sophisticated curriculum. The strategy outlined in *America 2000* needs to place more emphasis on staff development. Business already recognizes that training its personnel is vital for success. And we need to improve our recruiting, preparing, and certifying of teachers; provide leadership training for principals; and improve technical assistance to districts.

3) *Developing and incorporating technology.* The technology will soon exist to give teachers state-of-the-art curricular support. We need a massive software-development and training effort that would draw on the nation's best minds. This project would require an initial investment of funds, but it could pay huge dividends.

4) *Restructuring schools.* The president's proposal for a new generation of American schools is a critically important one. We should unleash educators' talents to tackle important issues and improve student performance. Once we agree on standards and ways of measuring them, we must move out of the schools' way to allow teachers and principals to do their jobs. We should

study communities that are restructuring, encourage districts to replicate successful projects, and provide developmental grants that foster team building.

5) *Encouraging parent and business partnerships.* If parents read to their children, assure that they do their homework, and stay on top of their performance, students' achievement will soar dramatically.

We need to develop much stronger transitions between school and work. Of the thousands of business-school partnerships, the most promising attempt to change the incentive structure within high schools. Before hiring, businesses should ask for students' grades, or give additional pay or faster employment tracks for good academic performance.

6) *Completing the equity agenda.* We should fully fund programs for at-risk children and expand programs that prevent later failure, such as prenatal and neonatal health care, preschool, and coordinated family services.

Public schools have turned the corner: educators have developed an effective game plan for the nineties, and promising ideas to encourage further flexibility within a context of vision and accountability continue to be implemented. If our leaders support that game plan instead of chasing will-o'-the-wisp panaceas, come the year 2000, our children will enjoy the schools they deserve.

NOTE

1. John E. Chubb and Terry M. Moe, *Politics, Markets, and America's Schools* (Washington, D.C.: The Brookings Institute, 1990).

18

Endangered Species: Children, Democracy, and Public Schools

J. William Rioux

Children are our most important national resource. Yet in the ecology of our democracy, they are surely as threatened as any endangered species. The continued decline in their well-being in and out of school is becoming so critical that it threatens the entire democratic system.

Consider the ground children in this country have lost over the last decade:

- The number of children living in poverty has increased 26 percent.

- The juvenile incarceration rate has increased 41 percent.

- Out-of-wedlock births among teenagers have increased 10 percent.

- Violent deaths among teenagers have increased 12 percent.[1]

During the 1980s, when educational reform rhetoric made daily headlines, one million students per year were dropping out of school. In major cities and among Hispanics, as many as half of high school children fail to graduate with their class. After leaving school, most drift into a job market that has no place for them, and are destined to long-term unemployment or underemployment. Inner city youth who do graduate may nevertheless

J. William Rioux is Executive Director of the National Committee for Citizens in Education (NCCE), headquartered in Washington, D.C.

find themselves no better off than their peers who drop out. For those who can find jobs, employers spend millions annually on training in basic English and mathematics skills.

Clearly, our pompous rhetoric about the importance of children in our society collides forcefully with the limited resources we actually provide for them. Why? One reason may be the low political mileage our leaders receive from children's issues. Space explorations and foreign wars are issues that excite, energize, and unite the national spirit. Serious domestic problems, on the other hand, discourage and frustrate us; their solutions seem complex and beyond reach. Applying military force to schools will not improve them, any more than shooting children into space will teach them life-coping skills. But we *can* learn a lot from the speed with which our government mobilizes for war, the long-term commitment our leaders have made to space travel, and the way legislators consistently appropriate funds for these highly visible activities.

While we say children come first, our national priorities are revealed by our actions, not our words. At the same time the United States was committing one billion dollars a day to war in the Persian Gulf, nearly half the children eligible for Chapter 1 remained unserved because of lack of funding. On the same day American troops were handing rations to war refugees in the Middle East, American children were going hungry because of cutbacks in the federally funded school breakfast program. Until we realize the importance of helping children both for their sake and for our own, and until we develop a national strategy to improve public schools for every child, things will not change appreciably. Until then, children, schools, and our democracy itself will remain in jeopardy.

Will the great awakening occur soon? Not likely. Militating against an all-out improvement is the changing composition of our student population. While the number of children attending public schools has remained constant at 88 percent of the total student population, the number of poor and non-English speaking children has increased and the percentage of all families who have school-age children has declined. Only 25 percent of households now have children in the public schools, a minority by any measure. Delayed child-bearing among working women and an aging population are responsible for the changing demographics. The result is a smaller block of parent voters—the adults most likely to place public schools at the top of their list for funding and services. Among the parents who have children in school, many are themselves poorly educated, lacking the English skills and the self-confidence to speak up effectively for children and schools.

PERSUADING 75 PERCENT TO HELP THE 25 PERCENT

Parents are by no means the only logical advocates for children and public schools. But it remains for the 25 percent of households with children in school to persuade the other 75 percent that good public schools are essential to maintaining a strong democracy and the American way of life.

What is likely to move citizens to support public schools? Setting aside for a moment the moral responsibility a society has to educate its children for their own self-fulfillment, several compelling arguments remain, each sufficient to motivate the self-interest of the business person, yuppie, or senior citizen.

The Economic Argument

Each dropout class of one million students costs an estimated $200 billion in lost tax revenues and increased social welfare expenditures over their lifetime. Those who have the education and earning power must pay for the increasing number who do not. The more well-educated, employable citizens we have, the lower these costs will be and the more the remaining burden will be spread evenly among taxpayers. Industry benefits, too, in lower training costs and higher productivity.

The Public Safety Argument

When a good public education is unavailable to all, a two-tiered society results, which may be expressed in four different ways:

- the educated and the uneducated

- the employed and the unemployed

- the empowered and the disenfranchised

- the upwardly mobile and the permanent underclass.

Those in the top tier fear and resent those at the bottom, while those in the bottom tier feel angry and helpless. In the long term, these divisions undermine and seriously weaken a democratic society. In the short term, they are apparent in far more tangible ways: the defacing of public and private property, street muggings, burglary and armed robbery, the murder of shopkeepers—all the violent and antisocial behavior that has both caused the middle class to flee from our cities and forced suburban homeowners to install expensive security systems.

The Civic Argument

In order to survive as a democracy, this country must train each succeeding generation to fill the roles required of good citizens. Today's students will become tomorrow's informed voters, willing jurors, and dedicated volunteers. Without a majority of citizens who embrace common democratic values and act to preserve them, American rights and freedoms will go unprotected, threatening our way of life.

The millions of Americans who do not have school-age children may believe that they can pursue other interests in their lives, while remaining insulated from the consequences of poor public schools. But they are wrong. The accumulating consequences of poor and deteriorating public schools has and will have a growing national impact.

WHY PUBLIC SCHOOLS?

Some may ask, Are *public* schools the only route to achieving an educated citizenry? If public schools have failed, why not discard them and try something new? If poor children are not well served by public schools (and by and large they are not), why not pay their parents to send them to private schools?

The answer lies at the very foundation of American democracy: our citizens share a common set of democratic values while preserving their own cultural identity and personal beliefs. Within our shores we encourage pluralism and respect ethnic, political, and religious differences.

The most effective way to transmit these values to our children is by revealing them at work daily at public school. Only here do children witness the wonderful American melting pot: children of many races and creeds, and every socioeconomic level, all learning together. Only when the crucible is flawed, when public schools become segregated along economic, racial, and cultural lines; when a high school diploma no longer means anything; and when educational equity is lacking for poor and minority students, do we realize how vital good public schools are.

IN SEARCH OF THE GOLDEN AGE

Have public schools ever lived up to the ideal of providing every child in this country with a quality education? No, they have not. But never have the consequences of their failure been more keenly felt than today. Historically, African-American students lacked educational equity in poorly funded, segregated schools. Students living in isolated rural areas and disabled children were often excluded from free public school altogether. In the last forty years, schools have redressed the access issue, but the question "Access to what?" remains. If free public schooling is of poor quality, the privilege is worthless.

In generations past, a school dropout or non-English-speaking immigrant could go west and homestead, or build a railroad, or punch cattle. Today, few jobs remain for the unskilled, and many of these are far from major population centers. As our society becomes service-oriented and high technology assumes an important role in more and more jobs, including those on factory assembly lines, every child must have a good education in order to survive economically.

In our cities we now have a second generation of idle workers who cannot feed their families on fast-food wages, much less achieve the American dream of owning their own home. These whom public schools have failed are more likely to engage in drug trafficking, petty theft, abuse within the family, and even violent crime. Once our school dropouts went to the American frontier. Today they go on welfare or to prison. For economic, public safety, and civic reasons we cannot delay the improvement of public education for all children. Failure to act effectively now will certainly bring fundamental changes in our economy and our way of life.

WHAT CAN WE DO?

Listed below are some concrete proposals for improving our public schools.

Concentrate on More Child-Centered Reform

Rather than asking the question how can we raise public school standards, education policymakers should be asking, How can we help *every* child succeed in school? No longer is providing a good education to any child who arrives at school fully prepared to receive it a sufficient or defensible goal for public schools. A host of children do not fit into that category. Yet they, more than any others, need and deserve a good education. Outreach to families during the preschool years and on a continuing basis after children are in school is essential. Approaches to learning that both recognize children's individual differences and close learning gaps without locking children into "slow tracks" should be emphasized. Programs committed to these principles include The Accelerated Schools program developed by Henry Levin at Stanford University, and HOTS (Higher-Order Thinking Skills) begun by Stanley Pogrow at the University of Arizona.

Engage Entire Families in the Public School Experience

This is more easily said than done, according to most educators whose schools draw from low income and minority attendance areas; yet it is not an impossible task, especially when parents are treated with respect as valued partners in their child's education. The effort is well worth the positive outcome. Almost fifty research studies strongly support the link between parent involvement and student achievement.[2] The involvement of low income and minority parents leads to even greater achievement gains than for other families.[3]

Why is this so? Children who do well in school feel that they have some control over their environment. They know that when they work hard, someone will notice and they will be rewarded. A child's sense of control and self-confidence is enhanced when parents are involved in school activities.[4] If parents are treated as unimportant, schools reinforce attitudes that are detrimental to achievement.

It is no coincidence that the areas with the poorest schools have the largest concentrations of families who feel powerless to change their own lives and to make the institutions on which they depend more responsive to their needs. To inner-city and rural parents, many of whom are school dropouts themselves, schools are like fortresses, unwelcoming and forbidding places.

When our organization worked intensively with 150 families of middle school students in West Baltimore, school staff told us they had tried everything to bring these parents to school. But when NCCE asked the parents, they said they were insulted and belittled by school staff. Repeatedly, parents said they were kept waiting an hour or more at school appointments; were required to show an ID at parent-teacher conferences (or were sent home to fetch it); and were told by teachers they were "ignorant," troublemakers, or had an attitude problem. After protesting their treatment at school or advocating for their child, some parents had the idea they were "barred" from the school.

Little wonder, then, that school participation by parents in most cities is abysmally low. Yet it does not have to be that way. The great experiment with school site governance in Chicago demonstrates that blacks, Hispanics, and Asians want to become partners in public schools if given a real chance. Thousands of local parents and citizens in that city have been elected to positions on newly created governing councils in the city's 600 public schools.

Because many poor families place survival issues before school participation, programs designed to engage them must provide links to social services as well as to their child's performance in school. New Beginnings in San Diego and COPS in San Antonio are two programs that place schools at the hub of services for parents and children. With basic food, shelter, and health needs under control, parents are then able to elevate their children's education—and their own—to a place of importance in their daily life.

MAKING SCHOOLS MORE DEMOCRATIC

What an irony that public schooling, the keystone of our democracy, is itself such an undemocratic institution, often barring parents and the community from meaningful participation. In civics class students are taught the importance of self-determination in a free society. Why does that right not extend to allowing teachers to choose their teaching methods and parents to choose their child's school program? A number of like-minded educational reformers have asked this same question. The result is that more self-determination programs are being introduced into the schools in the form of school site management and public school choice programs. These are among the most promising steps being taken currently to involve parents, teachers, and local citizens in public schooling.

Not only is shared decision making the right thing for schools to do and consistent with democratic principles, it should also have a positive effect on student achievement. Pride in ownership and the right to influence one's activities and surroundings are the greatest motivating forces in human behavior. Give people the freedom to choose how and where they will live and what they will do, and they become enterprising and productive citizens. As each individual prospers, so does the entire system.

Our upper and middle classes have prospered because they have been allowed to exercise self-determination, in the schools they send their children to, in the work they do, and in the households they keep. The growing underclass in this country is largely excluded from this American dream. With help, they and their children can be included. If they are not, the survival of our democracy cannot be assured.

NOTES

1. The Center for the Study of Social Policy, *Kids Count Data Book* (Washington, D.C., 1991).

2. Anne Henderson, ed., *The Evidence Continues to Grow: Parent Involvement Improves Student Achievement* (Washington, D.C.: National Committee for Citizens in Education, 1987).

3. David J. Irvine, "Parent Involvement Affects Children's Cognitive Growth," University of the State of New York, State Education Department, Division of Research (Albany, August 1979), and Moncrieff Cochran and Charles R. Henderson, Jr., *Family Matters: Evaluation of the Parent Empowerment Program* (Ithaca, N.Y.: Cornell University Press, 1986).

4. Charles Mowery, "Investigation of the Effects of Parent Participation in Head Start: Non-Technical Report," Department of Health, Education, and Welfare (Washington, D.C., November 1972), and Miriam Sherman Stearns et al., "Parent Involvement

in Compensatory Education Programs: Definitions and Findings," Menlo Park Educational Policy Research Center, Stanford Research Institute (Palo Alto, 1973).

19

Quality Education for Minorities: An Impossible Dream without Public Education

Shirley M. McBay

INTRODUCTION

Our public schools have been historically viewed as places where our children and youth, especially those from low-income families, were taught America's democratic principles and ideals, and where they were provided the basic skills required for the majority of jobs available in the workplace. The factory model approach to public education, established to meet the country's workforce needs, was adequate when only an educated elite managed and directed the rest of the workers. However, as this country seeks to survive in an increasingly competitive global economy, it will require a workforce with higher-level skills throughout and not simply at the top. In the future, as in the past, low-income groups will have to look to the public schools to equip their children and youth with the knowledge and skills required for future success and security in the workplace. The role of public schools as social equalizer and as provider of equal educational opportunities is especially critical to the future well-being of minority children and youth from low-income families in their roles as workers, family members, and citizens.

Shirley M. McBay is President of Quality Education for Minorities (QEM) Network. She holds a Ph.D. in mathematics from the University of Georgia.

The importance of this role is reflected in the vision set forth in the QEM Project Report, *Education That Works: An Action Plan for the Education of Minorities*.[1] That vision is predicated on America's moving forward on the democratic principles of opportunity and access. It sees minorities, from every socioeconomic background, contributing as decision makers and leaders at all levels of society because they will have had access to quality education throughout their lives. Their educational achievement and leadership ability will be due in no small part to the public school system. However, the system envisioned is radically different from the "factory model" now in place. For unlike the system it will replace, this one has as its primary measure of accountability, the achievement of students from those groups that have been historically and disproportionately most underserved by the prior system: African Americans, Alaska Natives, American Indians, Mexican Americans, and Puerto Ricans.

The public school system envisioned in the QEM Report instills in its students such life-long values as:

- an appreciation of the intrinsic joy of learning

- the pleasure of using one's mind to solve problems and come up with ideas

- an appreciation and respect for one's own accomplishments as well as those of others

- the self-confidence to make decisions based on one's own ideas and experiences

- a willingness to work with others toward a common objective

- a respect for points of view that may be different from one's own

- taking responsibility for doing things that need to be done and doing them well, from beginning to end

- understanding that helping others is a responsibility and is its own reward

- understanding that learning is a life-long process and the best way to have the most control over one's life.

In the QEM vision, America turns once more with confidence to its public schools to develop, in partnership with parents and the local community, an understanding and appreciation in its students of democratic values, citizenship responsibilities, and the work ethic. It looks to its public schools to graduate students who are fully prepared to be successful in the workforce or college, and not in need of remedial education.

Is this an impossible dream? The QEM Network, the nonprofit successor organization to the QEM Project, doesn't think so. It believes the vision *is* achievable, but only through the formation of various alliances for the purpose of creating a strong public school system that is held accountable for meeting the needs of *all* American children, particularly those who have been least served in the past. Through a restructured educational system, it would be possible to meet the needs of all students, without neglecting those for whom the system has traditionally worked. The resources now required to support remedial programs could be invested in more intellectually challenging and rewarding programs that would benefit *all* public school children.

The 1990s will be a pivotal decade for achieving this vision of our public schools. National studies of our public educational system are calling for major reforms and restructuring efforts, particularly in school systems that are predominantly minority. At the same time, the country is struggling to maintain its place in a global community, and facing a major shift in demographics as well as a number of social crises (in education, health, homelessness, substance abuse, and crime)—crises of overwhelming proportions, especially in our large cities.

In the near future, the national debate on education will likely intensify over a number of issues and proposals that have been put forth by various groups—the current administration, various business-oriented committees that have focused on workforce needs, and university-associated research groups anxious to test their learning theories on wider audiences. Interestingly, very few of these initiatives have involved parents, teachers, and students. Even fewer have been led by higher education, although unprepared freshmen detract as much from the learning environment and future "output" of universities as do poorly prepared high school graduate employees from business and industry, and the quality of their products.

Issues and proposals fueling the debate relate to access and quality of education provided by our public schools. They include such issues as the practice of educational tracking and ability grouping; parental "choice" of schools and the use of voucher systems; magnet schools earmarked for "excellence" alongside magnet schools for "desegregation" purposes; multicultural infusion and a national curriculum; national professional teaching standards and master teachers; a national student examination system and certificates of mastery determining employment opportunities; race-specific and merit-based scholarships; and "ability to benefit" testing linked to access to postsecondary school.

Each of the issues has major implications for the future of our public school system (quality of instruction, curriculum content, and racial and ethnic composition of its teacher workforce and its student body) and each has direct bearing on the quality and range of educational opportunities available to minorities, from kindergarten through graduate school. These issues and proposals present potential barriers as well as possible opportunities for achieving the vision for our country and for our public school system implicit in both the national goals for education[2] put forth by the president and the governors, and in the goals of *Education That Works.* The implications of these issues for the education of those most poorly served in the past *must* be thoroughly discussed and satisfactorily addressed in *full and equal partnership with minority American parents, students, and educators* if either of these compatible visions is to be achieved.

This essay first examines our changing public school system, focusing on those trends that provide an opportunity for quality education for minorities, as well as on those that potentially throw up new barriers to access to quality education. It then turns to some of the current issues and proposals listed above that have the potential to strengthen or weaken the public school system as a gateway of opportunity for minority youth in this country. Finally, the article returns to the QEM vision, a vision of *quality education for all, an education made possible through a strong and restructured public school system in America.*

TRENDS IN AMERICAN SCHOOLS: OPPORTUNITY OR BARRIER?

In a recent article,[3] educational consultants Marvin J. Cetron and Margaret Evans Gayle list forty-three trends for U.S. schools that they see developing over the coming decades. Many of the changes they envision offer a real opportunity for a restructured public school system to emerge. They argue, first of all, that more *business and school partnerships* and *increased parental participation* are likely developments ahead, along with higher educational standards for which teachers and students will be held accountable. Such trends may well strengthen all schools, thereby helping to provide quality education for *all* students.

But other trends are more ominous for the quality of education available to minorities in the future. The authors cite "accountability" as the buzzword of the 1990s. It is unclear if this accountability will be top-down and mandated through such mechanisms as a "national standardized testing system," or bottom-up, with local schools determining how best to carry out "national" standards. If the former, there are concerns that new and potentially discriminatory standardized testing systems could create additional barriers to the educational advancement and entrance of minorities into the job market. There are corresponding concerns, however, if the meeting of "national" standards is locally determined. Students poorly served by locally controlled schools in the past may be unable to meet new, and presumably higher, national standards without substantial improvement at the local level in the quality of instruction and support they receive there, as well as in the level of expectations many teachers hold for these students.

School finance is another area in which new barriers may be erected to minorities receiving a quality education. For example, Cetron and Gayle argue that "a wide spectrum of school-finance initiatives and experiments will be undertaken in the coming decades, including extreme centralization and financial control at the state level on one end to privatization on the other, where states will finance education through vouchers to parents (based on their choices of schools) rather than by directly financing schools."[4] Because schools with large minority populations have traditionally suffered inequities in financial support, some of these possible "solutions" could actually exacerbate existing barriers to improvement of education for minorities.

The *decreasing percentage of minority public school teachers* is a third trend bearing directly on the education of minorities. Although minorities will become an increasingly larger proportion of the school population, there is no projected reversal reflected in the proportion of minority teachers in the workforce. This discrepancy will be particularly acute in our largest school districts and in inner cities (e.g., in New York City, where the school population is more than 80 percent minority while the teaching workforce is only 20 percent minority). It will also be felt in the Southern states, where minority enrollment ranges from 25 percent to 56 percent, while the proportion of minority teachers ranges from a mere 4 percent to 35 percent.[5] Furthermore, current minority enrollment in teacher education programs is insufficient even to replace the minority teachers who are leaving the profession. To make matters worse, fewer than half of the minority candidates prepared by colleges and universities currently pass the required certification tests in some forty-five states, thereby further reducing the pool of available minority teachers.[6] Clearly, change must take place in the pre-service and in-service education of teachers if this success rate is to improve.

Projected demographic shifts in the workforce are another driving force for change in the educational system. The Hudson Institute's *Workforce 2000: Work and Workers for the 21st Century*[7] described 85 percent of the group representing the net growth in our workforce for the rest of this century as minorities, women, and immigrants. Not only will the workforce look different, so will the work requirements. For the first time in history, a majority of new jobs will require postsecondary education.[8] This places an impossible burden on our tiered public school system whose graduates, except for an educated elite, are unable to meet requirements for college or for the increasing percentage of positions in our workforce utilizing higher-order thinking skills.

Cetron and Gayle[9] argue that increased parental involvement may be the key to effective change in the performance of school systems. Parents are their children's first teachers; therefore, parental involvement in education, in and out of school, is critical. The authors also see a trend, already underway, of parents serving as part-time teachers and teaching assistants, working to increase school budgets, and making certain that their children understand the importance of a good education and have the support needed for higher achievement. Parents of minority and language-minority students are becoming increasingly vocal in their concerns about the ability of the public schools to meet the needs of their children. These families, most of whom are in the lower socioeconomic strata of society, have long held the view that the best hope for their families lies in the quality of education and of job opportunities available for their children.

Therefore, with so many voices calling for reform, restructuring our public schools for the improved education of minorities must surely take its place among the highest priorities on our nation's agenda.

Why Are Restructured Schools So Critical to the Achievement of Minority Students?

Our current hierarchical educational model discourages, rather than promotes, quality education for minority students, especially those from low socioeconomic backgrounds. These students, often as early as kindergarten, are disproportionately relegated to low-track classes in such critical subjects as reading and mathematics, from which they seldom recover. There they are taught by the least experienced teachers with the fewest resources in a climate characterized by low expectations, drill and practice, and rote memorization. Keeping order, labeling of these students as learning-disabled, and calculating average daily attendance for budget allocation purposes take priority over the teaching of higher-order thinking skills, problem solving, group study, and conflict resolution.

The restructured school system envisioned in *Education That Works* would give professional educators the flexibility to develop pedagogical approaches to adapt to diverse circumstances and individual students. It would provide incentives for changes in student achievement and behavior. Accountability in the restructured school would mean improving students' knowledge, skills, and behavior rather than following myriad rules and regulations. Administrators and teachers must have the authority and resources to respond to the unique needs of the students they serve, but at the same time they must be held accountable for results. Lack of accountability allows inexperienced teachers to be assigned to students with the greatest needs and weak teachers to remain in the classroom, unable to respond to the academic and social needs of minority youngsters and too often poisoning the students' expectations.

One example of system-wide restructuring that is being observed is occurring in Dade County, Florida, where teacher professionalization and school-based management are emphasized. Among the broad changes taking place in the Dade County schools, which are 45 percent Hispanic and 25 percent black, is the School-Based Management/Shared Decision-Making Program, in which teachers and administrators jointly develop a system of management for their individual schools, including budget allocation, goal-setting, and evaluation. They have also developed Satellite Learning Centers, in which elementary schools are being set up at central locations convenient to worksites in order to assist working parents and solve after-school day care concerns.

Another example of restructuring can be found in the work done by members of the Coalition of Essential Schools, based at Brown University. Although each of the fifty-six member schools in the coalition follows its own path toward educational equity and excellence, the schools have several things in common: a trend toward teachers functioning not as didactic sources of knowledge but rather as coaches helping students to perform the work of learning; flexible class schedules that respond to the course requirements and not to the constraints of the 45-minute period; closer teacher-student relationships that result from limiting the number of students per teacher to no more than eighty per day; and a focus on competency-based testing, i.e., on demonstrations of achievement rather than multiple choice testing. Essential Schools also promote closer relationships between students and an adult figure, new ways to demonstrate academic achievement, high expectations from teachers as well as students that are generated by a strong sense of belonging, and a common core curriculum in the place of tracking.

Heterogeneous classrooms, along with nontraditional teaching techniques such as cooperative learning and peer tutoring, can reach many of the students we now write off. For example, in an experiment in Baltimore, students use the Cooperative Integrated Reading and Composition Program, in which small learning teams of mixed abilities work together to master material presented first by the teacher. Significant increases were found among these students in reading and language skills over a control group. These innovative teaching techniques provide new windows of opportunity to explore restructuring strategies, not only in school management, finance, governance, and organization, but also in instructional strategies utilized in individual classrooms. From classrooms to entire schools, from local schools to district systems, from districts to states—restructuring must take place simultaneously at all levels of our public educational system.

Much of this restructuring will have to come through new legislation and resources coming to the schools, from the federal, state, and local levels. Hence, the question of restructuring public schools inevitably leads to the issues and policy questions raised earlier that are increasingly being debated in national, state, and local forums.

PUBLIC POLICY AND LEGISLATION: IMPLICATIONS AND ISSUES

At the National Level

National Goals for Education

Much of the current national debate on education is tied to the national education goals adopted by the president and the nation's governors in 1989. The discussion around implementation of these goals is heavily weighted towards *measuring student progress toward the goals.* Very little is heard about ensuring that students from low-income families (who are disproportionately minority) are not overlooked in the rush to make the grade. The focus is on designing assessment models and testing instruments rather than on raising the quality of instruction and improving the learning environment for low-income students in order to enable them to meet national standards and to contribute to the achievement of the national goals. The drive is based upon the erroneous assumption that increasing standards alone will lead to improved quality of instruction. Minority children and youth appear to be forgotten in the rush to raise standards without changing their educational circumstances.

A National Examination System

Consideration currently is being given to establishing a national testing system of student achievement. One such discussion concerns a multicomponent examination (a written performance examination, student projects including group projects, and student portfolios). Thus far, the focus appears to be more on assessment models (and the ability to take the examination many times), than on quality of instruction and strategies for ensuring that youngsters from disadvantaged backgrounds aren't simply sorted once again, but with a different battery of tests. Even administered on a voluntary basis, a national test may join the other major "voluntary" examinations (SAT and ACT) which are voluntary, unless a student wants to go to college. The interests of minority students may be overridden by the need to ensure that test scores rise at any cost.

National Teaching Standards

Legislation was recently approved by Congress to provide $5 million of federal funding for the National Board for Professional Teaching Standards. This board is developing "voluntary" assessments for elementary and secondary teachers. Although there is recognition of the critical need to increase the number of minority teachers in the classroom, attention must also be paid to ensure that National Board assessments do not represent yet another hurdle for minority teachers as many state-administered preprofessional teaching examinations do now, thereby undermining minority teacher recruitment efforts.

"Ability to Benefit" Test

Many issues under consideration by Congress are of concern to minority students. One such issue is that of "ability to benefit" provisions. Currently, students who lack a high school diploma or its equivalent are required to be tested to determine whether they have the "ability to benefit" from the postsecondary program for which they are applying. Since this is intended to apply only to those students seeking financial aid, it has a disproportionate impact on low-income minority students. In fact, some postsecondary schools, out of fear of losing their own ability to obtain federal funds, are requiring all students without a high school diploma or the GED (Graduate Equivalency Diploma) to take the examination, whether or not they are seeking federal financial aid.

Race-Specific Scholarships

The U.S. Department of Education recently issued a memorandum declaring minority scholarship programs to be unconstitutional, and has subsequently wavered in its interpretation of the law on this point. Following a major uproar from within the higher education community, the new Secretary of Education said that institutions should continue their current practices until a thorough study of the issue has been carried out. The availability of scholarships for minority students is as critical to ensuring access to postsecondary education as is receiving a quality public school education.

We can ill-afford to deny any of our young people an opportunity to receive a college or university education simply because of their race or because they cannot financially afford a college education. Nor can we, the most pluralistic, diverse, and democratic nation in the history of humankind, afford to keep large numbers of our citizens on the fringe of society because of their race, ethnicity, or socioeconomic status. Our colleges and universities, as well as our public school system, must reflect the religious, gender, economic, intellectual, and racial diversity of our nation.

Choice

Several issues will be considered by Congress in the area of elementary and secondary education. One issue that Congress is considering is the current administration's proposal for school choice. In the past, Congress has rejected proposals to adopt a voucher plan enabling students to take government funds to a public or private school of their choosing. Now advocates of choice are pointing to increasing support for such initiatives across the country as the driving force behind Congress's reconsideration of its position.

The choice proposal raises considerable concerns, not the least of which is its effect on minority youngsters. It is clear that without adequate knowledge and understanding of options, and without low or no-cost transportation, minority parents are less likely to take advantage of choice, leaving their children in lower quality schools. Furthermore, we have experienced "Freedom of Choice" plans in the past. They have necessitated court-ordered desegregation because they were being used to avoid school integration.

Special Education

Another issue at the national level relates to efforts to expand the eligibility definition of students eligible for services under the Education for Individuals with Disabilities Act in order to include students with a condition known as "attention deficit disorder." This condition is ascribed disproportionately to minority boys. Black and Hispanic male students are already overly represented in special education classes; therefore, an expansion in the definition would represent yet one more way to enroll minority youngsters in special education.

At the State and Local Levels

State Aid Formulas

A number of issues at the state and local levels have national implications for the education of minority students. Courts around the country are examining state aid formulas to determine whether they are equitable in their distribution of funds between school districts, and they have declared some to be unconstitutional. Such decisions have implications for minority youngsters because it is often the case that districts with lower per-pupil expenditures have predominantly minority student populations. Exceptions are usually traceable to increased administrative expenditures rather than instructional costs.

Separate Schools for Black Males

Some local school districts are considering classes or schools especially for black males in an attempt to provide special support geared to the needs of these students. Aside from constitutional issues, there are pedagogical concerns as to whether isolating a group of children might further exacerbate current inequities in education for minority youngsters, and/or undermine the ability of these students to work in a heterogeneous society as adults.

The outcomes of such public policy and legislative discussions will clearly shape the nature of our public school system and the quality of education minorities receive. During the next few years critical legislation will be passed with implications for the education of all students; such legislation must take into account the needs of low-income and minority students.

CONCLUSION

The task before us is clear. Achievement of quality education for minorities—indeed, for all children and youth—requires that we restructure our public schools to ensure an end to the educational neglect of those who continue to be the most underserved. We must do so not only because it is right, though that is reason enough, but because America cannot succeed economically with one-third of its citizens poorly educated. The one force that is sustaining and empowering for all people is the power of education. We must look to our public schools to equip all our young people with the skills and values they need to transform their visions into realities and our lofty goals for them into tasks that can be grasped and achieved. America must be willing to provide the financial and human resources needed to enable our public schools to provide all children, including minority children, with a quality education. Minority children, by right and by virtue of their unlimited potential, surely deserve their own role as builders and as future leaders.

NOTES

1. Quality Education for Minorities Project, *Education That Works: An Action Plan for the Education of Minorities* (Cambridge, Mass.: Massachusetts Institute of Technology, 1990).
2. National Governors' Association, *Educating America: State Strategies for Achieving the National Education Goals* (Washington, D.C., 1990).
3. Marvin J. Cetron and Margaret Evans Gayle, "Educational Renaissance: 43 Trends for U.S. Schools," adapted from Marvin J. Cetron and Margaret Evans Gayle, *Educational Renaissance: Our Schools into the Twenty-First Century* (New York: St. Martin's Press, 1990).
4. Ibid., p. 8.
5. Ibid., p. 3.
6. Ibid., p. 6.

7. William B. Johnston and Arnold H. Parker, *Workforce 2000: Work and Workers for the 21st Century* (Indianapolis, Ind.: Hudson Institute, 1987).

8. Ibid., p. 97.

9. Cetron and Gayle, "Educational Renaissance," p. 2.

20

Why Public Schools?

Michael Casserly

Amidst all the rhetoric from both the Right and the Left; all the calls for reform, restructuring, choice and competition, nearly everyone has lost sight of why we have public schools in the United States and why they constitute both our past and an even more critical portion of our future.

While public schools comprise a good deal of our history, the nation came to them only after some maturation of its initial democratic ideals and after the realization that a private system of schooling was not up to the national task of creating an educated populace that would take the country where it needed to go.

In 1817, Thomas Jefferson prodded the state legislature of Virginia into providing three years of schooling for everyone in the commonwealth at public expense as the foundation of a democratic society. It wasn't until the mid-nineteenth century, however, that Horace Mann called for an increase in the public subsidy to cover six rather than three years of education. And only in 1916 did the philosopher and educator John Dewey call for a broader democratization of public education as a tool for creating a common destiny for us all and an equal chance to attain it. The length of compulsory schooling was gradually increased in the twentieth century from six to ten and then to twelve years, moving in tandem with the matura-

Michael Casserly is Executive Director of the Council of the Great City Schools, a coalition of the nation's largest urban public school systems. He has been with the organization for fifteen years as director of legislation and research.

tion and implementation of this nation's original ideals of democracy and equality.

Public education is being challenged now once again, not just to move with the nation's emerging sense of its own democracy and opportunity, but to address ever greater challenges of both global competition and domestic turmoil. Unfortunately, many now view the country's educational system as not up to the task of getting us where we need to go to meet our immediate challenges. Ironically, the solution being espoused by some is to revert to the kind of elite and privatized system that the nations rejected as insufficient years ago.

What have we lost sight of? The answer rests in the fact that we have collectively forgotten why we have public education in this country, which, for all of its shortcomings and challenges, is necessary to our survival as a nation. Certainly no institution has a more resounding impact on the American society, economy, and culture than the public school. And none is called on to do more: we expect our public schools not only to teach, but also to feed; to nurse; to transport; to shelter; and to provide recreation, values, and self-esteem. To place similar demands upon our banks, ports, museums, farms, parks, businesses, or markets would be ludicrous.

Yet, no other public institution is as frequently criticized, scrutinized, unappreciated, or forgotten as our schools. Imagine if a public official or some other private concerned citizen were to propose cutting by a third the variety of commodities bought and sold on the floor of the Chicago Board of Trade, or phasing out funding for the Port of Baltimore, or turning over to the state the Metropolitan Museum of Art in New York, or compelling residents to redeem a voucher to use San Francisco's Golden Gate Park. The uproar that would greet such proposals would be deafening.

Suppose a private industry that devoted less than 20 percent of its personnel to producing its goods and services actually got headlines for criticizing public schools (which devote 60 percent of their personnel to teaching) for being top-heavy, bureaucratic, and wasteful. Such proposals and comparisons have been made, however, by those who press for greater competition in the schools.

Let me enumerate five reasons why the nation has public schools and why its survival will depend on their health:

1) The future of our country depends upon the strength of our public schools. They are as essential to the national welfare as America's military bases are to the national security.

2) Our country cannot afford to write off any child's future; all children can learn and the nation needs every child to do so. We need an educated workforce to prevent the burden for supporting our country from falling on

fewer and fewer people. It is these children who will run our telecommunications networks, if employed, or drain our economy, if unemployed; who will pay our old-age benefits through their social security taxes or receive welfare benefits paid for by our taxes.

3) The country has a moral imperative articulated by our founders to strive for individual justice and equality. The process of enabling each citizen through education to pursue those individual goals is not only proper, humane, and noble, but is in the highest spirit of our nation's founding principles. Many of these principles have been focused lately on the questions of who has been discriminated against historically and how education can improve opportunity for all. To the extent that the poor and disenfranchised's access to the American dream is blocked, to the extent that the education that opens the door to that dream is neglected, then the dream itself will die.

4) Economic trends point to the need for a better-educated citizenry to compete in more technologically-oriented international markets. The merging high technology boom promises a transformation as sweeping as the Industrial Revolution of the late eighteenth century. The United States will likely continue to yield the manufacturing of heavy industrial goods and simple consumer items to developing countries; those countries in turn will buy sophisticated capital equipment and new kinds of exportable services (such as financial, educational, computer, and telecommunications services) from us. Unless our country is prepared with an educated workforce to develop these fields, we will continue to lose jobs and wealth to other nations.

5) Public schools continue to be the only national mechanism through which our country's common values are articulated and disseminated, even in our polyglot environment.

Just as our banks, ports, factories, farms, and markets are the heart of the American economy, so are our public school students its lifeblood. The ability of our public schools to produce a skilled citizenry will shape the entire national landscape.

For all their national value and purpose, public schools have a more immediate and personal importance to me. I was raised in a conservative, devout Catholic family and graduated from both a Catholic high school and Catholic university, receiving excellent educations from both. My experience in that setting has given me a healthy respect for the capabilities of parochial schools and a certain affection for them as institutions. Yet, I send my only child to the local neighborhood public school and feel rather passionate about doing so. While the area Catholic school is closer to my house and would be within walking distance for my child, there are several strong reasons why I bypassed it in favor of the public school.

First of all, I have a strong sense of accountability about the school, a feeling that the teachers and administrators in it know who their clients are and are answerable to them. I certainly hear a lot about big unresponsive bureaucracies in public education, but I feel much better knowing that with my tax dollars the people I entrust my child to are answerable to a public entity, with public meetings, and on the public record. School people are understandably not anxious for me to come rifling through their files, but I could ask for a breakdown of every dollar that school and its school system spend and get it. That makes me feel better.

If I have a grievance about how my child is treated, how I am treated, how the school spends its money, the qualifications of the teachers, or nearly anything else, I know there is a process by which I can be heard. I may not get my way—and certainly too few parents avail themselves of the opportunity—but I know someone in the public schools has to be accountable to the public for their actions. That makes me feel better both as a client and as a taxpayer.

I am also encouraged by the school's participatory nature. It is constantly seeking parent interest and support, sometimes getting it, sometimes not; but I like the fact that parents are encouraged to play an active role in the activities of the school and to volunteer in the classroom or library.

It is also important to me that my child be exposed to the rainbow of cultures, religions, disabilities, and races that this nation truly is and that she learn to respect and handle the varying perspectives that each brings to the world. While I do not know precisely how many ethnic or racial groups the children at this school come from, it certainly seems a fair reflection of our nation's diversity.

Finally, I feel more tied to the community through my local public school. I have a greater sense of how the school is a rallying point for community activities and how it interlocks with what others in the community are doing.

Do all public schools have these qualities? Certainly not. Are private schools void of these qualities? By no means. But I do think that neither the nation nor its citizens can attain their collective or individual goals in a privatized system. More important, there is no way to reform or spur our nation's educational apparatus to perform better through anything but a public system, nor is there any other way to realize and nourish the nation's democratic ideals and objectives through anything other than a public system, with its mission to the public good.

Public schools still have a long way to go on this latter point. While public schooling was the rock upon which democracy stood, education was not always a democratic process. It sorted, tracked, and discriminated against children for much of its life, a problem evident in many of our other public institutions as well before we, as a nation, came to expect more than just ideals from our Constitution. The difference is that with the public schools, there was and still is an effective and accountable mechanism for addressing those problems, however slow the process.

To succeed a democracy requires two functions from its educational system: equality and excellence. The need for the latter is obvious in the sense that the nation requires ever greater levels of knowledge to compete, solve problems, think critically, and improve the living standard of its people. The need for equality is predicated on the notion that in a democracy all citizens are entitled to the skills and knowledge necessary for participatory citizenship. The necessity of both in a democracy at once is derived from our commitment not to let the differences in our people turn into inequalities, nor to allow educational excellence for some be gained at the expense of others. The acceptance of inequality corrupts our commitment to learning and, more important, our hold on democracy.

In the midst of the shrill, sometimes politically motivated, criticism of the quality of our public schools and the legitimate calls for reform and improvement, we have forgotten that public education has been the backbone of this nation's success. Since World War II, the percentage of seventeen-year-olds graduating from high school each year has risen from 48 percent to 75 percent, fueling an economic upturn, the likes of which the world has never seen. Public education in this nation did not evolve because of a need to provide work for bureaucrats or to form monopolies or to provide cookie cutter products. It evolved because the nation needed it culturally, politically, and morally. No other institution could have produced the citizenry that now fuels the engines of the nation's democracy. No other could rescue an increasing share of its nation's citizens from the cold rain of hopelessness and oppression with the Constitution's wide umbrella of opportunity, freedom, and equality.

Thomas Jefferson saw it, we should, too. Let us not forget it.

21

Why Private School Choice Is Not the Answer

Colin Greer

That we need public schools is an article of faith for some Americans, but others are now completely rejecting that belief. Increasingly, behind a screen of school reform rhetoric, these latter are trying to redefine public education. Education secretary Lamar Alexander has proposed a redefinition that would include the possibility of public schools run by major corporations such as Xerox or Burger King. In his words: "Any school to which a child might go, supported by public funds, answerable to public authorities and regulation, would be a public school whether it's run by the Smithsonian Institution . . . or IBM." Similarly, the Heritage Foundation and the Brookings Institute's John Chubb argue that any school receiving public money should be considered public. President Bush has gone so far as to propose incentives to school districts which provide private school choice options. From this perspective, public schools are seen as so inadequate that we must move to disestablish them. This choice imperative declares that the system of public education has failed and, like a retail chain on the verge of bankruptcy, should sell out to a new vendor—in this instance the old-time local storekeeper. Instead of recognizing the new task of fully educating the children of the poor for opportunity and citizenship in modern society, the move is to dismantle public education. By regarding any institution receiving public money as public, the market becomes the proposed solution to the relatively new problems we face. Those who argue that the private sector is the solution to the failure of public

---

Colin Greer is President of the New World Foundation.

schools misguidedly ignore the reality that goals have changed in 150 years of public school history. The school problems we see now result from unprecedented demands on our public education system—not from its sudden failure to cope with a job it handled well in the past.

The extremity of this proposed redefinition is an accurate measure of the sense of the crisis we face in public schooling. It is not a measure, however, of a public will actually to move toward resolution of it. After all, if the schools had worked in the past as so many believe, it would have been as public institutions that they were successful. Solutions to crisis-level commonweal questions have in the past been resolved by partnership with and intervention of government—from building highways to bailing out limping car manufacturers, from the G.I. Bill to the National Defense Education Act.

The frustration of massive school failure fuels the critics of schools in general and the promoters of redefinition in particular. By school failure they usually mean high dropout rates and poor performance levels across the school-age population, particularly among the poor and people of color. In short, when we want to know how well our public schools are doing, we ask how well children are doing in those schools; specifically, how well they are being taught to read and write. Indeed, since World War II, school performance has become increasingly synonymous with student academic achievement. And at the same time, school curricula have become more and more characterized by reading programs. Yet neither the reading-focused curriculum nor concern for the intellectual achievement of the student was the primary criterion of school evaluation concerns before 1950.

DEFINING THE PUBLIC SCHOOL: AN HISTORICAL SURVEY

Over the years a few key struggles to define public schooling have established the system as we know it: the establishment of public institutions to replace "charity schools" (1860–1890); the move to free and compulsory schooling from grades one through twelve (1890–1920); the tension between local school governance and "good government" centralism (1910–1940); the imperative toward equality of academic opportunity highlighted by reading curricula, IQ testing, and desegregation programs (1949–1970); and now, the debate over whether or not public education is the prerogative of public schools.

The fact is that the American Dream was not always dominated by academic achievement and the school credential, despite the historical presence of public schooling in American life. A Right to Read program, for example, would have meant little to most residents of American cities before the Great Depression and World War II. The right to work was more likely the critical issue—together, perhaps, with the right to withhold work. After 1930, the right to eat became a major theme. By the 1940s the nation's inability to resolve the latter (the right to eat) by the former (the right to work) gave a new salience to public schooling. As the school monopolized conventional expectations for self-improvement and social progress, so did its academic purposes take on quite unprecedented significance as the basis for assessing school efficacy.

In earlier times, an educator asked to assess schools would have considered other issues critical, among them:

- reducing public education taxes and private school costs

- effectively controlling immigrant children

- reducing truancy

- teaching spoken English and American customs to immigrants

- promoting students through the elementary grades until they graduated or were legally allowed to leave school.

When one reads the evaluation of school professionals from the turn of the century, the predominance of internal security and time-cost efficiency is striking. Despite the various reformers who were interested in the significance of the "educational experience," and who wished to build on the individual and ethnic strengths of students to promote cognitive (and, usually, moral) development, internal security remained an overriding issue. By and large, academic success was deemed but one of a number of variables to be considered in assessing school efficiency. Much more critical were the tasks of getting immigrant children off the streets and into the classroom and playgrounds, particularly as industry came to rely increasingly on adult labor as child labor was being phased out (a slow process, incidentally, which was not legislatively completed until 1932). As the school replaced the worksite as prime socializer of working-class children, it explicitly took on the characteristics of the workplace.

In this role, school time was organized with little regard to children's needs and interests. Training for reliable attendance and obedience was far more important. Critical thinking, problem solving, and flexible intelligence are much later goals introduced into the schools by the reforms of the last twenty years. But unfortunately, most of these reforms have been based on the assumption that the system is fundamentally sound and needs only to recapture past achievement.

The grim reality is that for decades, the public schools in this country have been agents of nonchange. They have been unable to respond adequately to the economy's growing demand for a more educated labor force and to the polity's call for informed citizens, even as barriers to full participation have been reduced. Children have consistently been taught to accept responsibility for their failure, so that schools have been producing large numbers of students who acquire more school years than ever before but little academic achievement. Studies reveal that more than nine million children now enrolled in public schools will enter the labor market as functional illiterates; that one in four high schoolers drops out; and that between roughly 25 and 50 percent of those who complete high school are menially employed or unemployed. As for the so-called wonders the public school system worked in the lives of the immigrants, most historical studies of immigrant school performance in major metropolitan areas as well as in smaller towns and cities show a gap of horrific proportions between myth and reality. Truancy and high drop-out rates occurred whenever the labor force beckoned; poor school performance for ethnic groups often remained the same from generation to generation. Thomas Kessner's well-known study of immigrant socioeconomic mobility in *The Golden Door* shows less than 25 percent mobility among Italians and less than 40 percent among Jews who came to America between 1880 and 1915—the period great school believers cite to support their roseate view of the past.

Finally, it's important to point out that the effort to make such correlations between school success and socioeconomic mobility, while useful to disabuse us of school history myths, is quite irrelevant to the purpose of arguing for school efficacy. The fact is that scholastic purposes during the period of floodtide immigration did not include the academic achievement and mobility goals implicit in such correlational analysis. Even if we found a large incidence of immigrant mobility equal to the rates of school completion, this would not mean school success. As Émile Durkheim tried to teach us, social product does not imply institutional intention.

The fundamental historical achievement of schools has been to recast for an urban context the rhetoric of the American Dream. At the turn of the century, that transformation in American life did not require correlations between academic achievement and socioeconomic mobility. No one doubted that there were jobs for newcomers and most of their offspring, but neither was there any question about what kind of jobs they were: low-level and dead-end.

What is true is at its inception public schooling served the American Dream in a role secondary to those of industry and working the land. Just as cognitive development was but one—and by no means a primary—ingredient in what made schools important in these phases, so did the schools reflect, until the Depression, the manual labor and entrepreneurial concerns of early twentieth-century America. But later, IQ and other tests gained primacy. Taking what is a measure of performance and treating it as a measure of potential, the schools' devotion to the standardized IQ measure underscored the extent to which the meritocratic potential of schools has been converted to a latter-day rubber stamp for the privileges, and costs, of birth. Once a student's IQ revealed his or her limited preparedness for school-style cognitive expression that social background had heavily determined, schools went on to track, teach, and guide in conformity with that revelation. While it would be a mistake to construe the shifts to tests and credentials as entirely negative, it is nonetheless true that despite the egalitarian goals which often informed meritocratic developments, the drive to expand the academic measurement and performance focus largely served to promote inequality.

FROM "ASSIMILATION" TO "PERFORMANCE": THE ROLE OF PUBLIC EDUCATION SINCE WORLD WAR II

When immigrants came to American cities and looked for a variety of paths to economic mobility and security, the schools were positioned to take credit for any success that was achieved while concentrating on their assimilation functions. With the growth of a significant service sector, the rise of technology, and the corporate monopoly in business, the school credential became the singular repository of American mobility promises. Socialized to believe in self-improvement, the children of immigrants have become less and less interested in manual labor in an economy which, from the Depression of the 1930s to the recession of the 1990s, has seemed to expect that they would. The school symbolized advance over manual labor, and staying in school was, so the belief went, preparation for promised white-collar security. It was in this context that school became synonymous with social progress as well as individual advancement. Educational issues were, in the 1950s and 1960s, shorthand for wider social and political concerns. Desegregation and decentralization, for example, expressed deep-seated national worries—about race and entitlement, about equity and fairness—in an explicitly educational framework. Like the G.I. Bill of Rights, both desegregation and decentralization underscored the national recourse to public education for dealing with massive manpower problems. In all three, social engineering required an educational agency. The unabsorbable G.I.s, the former Depression unemployed, and blacks, still marginal in American life, were to find economic integration into the mainstream by access to public education—right through college. Education would prepare people for opportunities. Despite the Great Depression, the dominant belief was still that American social problems resulted primarily from poor preparation for the land of opportunity. Rarely was it observed that perhaps a picture of an always bountiful America was questionable, or that the central role of academic success represented a significant revision of some previous expectations for public education.

So, public opinion and educators themselves stressed the past success of schools as the model to be emulated, thereby passing blame for the schools' failure onto the students and their families. The new concern for academic performance seemed to reveal a new failure of schools to work successfully; but in fact, they had never been expected to work that way before.

In the most recent era of public school hiso ry, typified by academic performance testing, schools have sought to keep up with economic developments in the society they serve. Education followed the rise of monopoly capitalism with a credential monopoly narrowly circumscribed by performance tests that have often purported to be tests of potential and aptitude—which they are not. Schools grew in size and in aspiration to expand even further. While the reading and testing emphasis has always been present, they had never characterized school life; now their monopoly on school and student purposes represented a new form in the schools' overall service to social stability through selection and differential preparation, a form of service which schools are now accused of failing to do well.

Unfortunately, the much romanticized notion that education has made it possible for rich and poor alike to learn all that is necessary to enter the mainstream of American society simply isn't true. Where success occurred it occurred, as in private schools, with highly select student bodies. High school attendance was not a successful experience for students in nonselect settings. This remains the problem that both public and private schools share.

Between 1965 and 1975, an extended and varied effort to enable schools to address the new mandate was vigorously undertaken: sometimes allocating blame, sometimes advancing reform agendas. The 1960s' thrusts toward group entitlement and respect for individual and ethnic styles of learning, leading for example to experiments in open classroom techniques and open-access models, found further expression in a demand for more student-sensitive systems of assessment with a diagnostic and pedagogical, not a competitive and exclusionary, imperative.

Reforms like open education, qualitative assessment, problem-solving curricula, and school site councils all have the potential of offering less threatening classroom experiences without necessarily honoring the obligation to stimulate academic success. This has been the case with school reform since this society came to care about academic achievement in its public schools. By and large, structural issues of power and resource equality have not been successfully included in school reform. Desegregation and decentralization projects which did address questions of equalty and power were undermined and short-lived. School process changes, like the "joy in the classroom" movement of the late 1960s, ran the danger of offering more pleasant classrooms for poor children, but not, by and large, in settings (often achieved in private progressive schools) where academic learning was noticeably enhanced.

Alternative schools were a choice option, but one rarely able to impact on the serious problems of mainstream schooling despite their successes with their own students. This was due in part to the relatively short duration of such programs and the private (often foundation) funding base that was not long-lasting either. If choice options are indeed a valuable addition to school reform agenda, why not turn to these once vital experiments which, after all, recognized and understood what I've called the new task of schools?

However, as we move along on the continuum of school reform, it is worth noting that the present reality of even public school choice programs throughout the country is pretty dismal. In Richmond, California, where former superintendent Marks won special commendations from the Bush administration for choice options, fiscal crisis threatens to overwhelm all. In Miami, where choice and local control have made the system nationally known, in many districts people are asking "What choice?" In district after district where public school choice options have been implemented, poor parents are facing additional travel hours for their children (often in badly deteriorating public transportation systems); very often even fewer parents participate in the life of the school due to distance, or else they accept schools located closer to home for their children. With the school reform movement of the 1980s came educators and parents calling for school improvement along with clarion calls for turning back the clock—calls for Back to Basics, for choice and justifications for financial cutbacks (in educational and other social services)—to those times when the very problems we face now were actually institutionalized in their present form. Newly rigid testing standards and revised funding patterns will not deliver that promise either. By definition, the task of exclusion is different from the goal of inclusion; opening private school doors to a few more will do nothing to relieve the prospects of the many who will attend even more inadequate public schools. The parallel reduction of support for public services and corporate and government retreat from the social contract ought to be a clear enough warning. Poor people in previous eras were humiliatingly exploited until public services and regulation improved— fleetingly, it now seems—the conditions of their work lives. It was on the basis of that progress that the agenda for school as the locus of expanded opportunity was built—an agenda some are now proposing to bury deep in the ground alongside the New Deal itself.

PUTTING THE DEAL INTO PRACTICE: THE NEW GOAL OF PUBLIC EDUCATION

To achieve effective universal education we need to cancel the funeral being planned. By the same token, we still need to evolve the public schools we believe we once had, schools that effectively encourage students to achieve aademically regardless of their social condition. But if public schools are to equip students of all origins and backgrounds to function as productively employed citizens who participate fully in our political and economic life, the school has a new task to fulfill. It will not do so by divesting its responsibility to the private sector as if its goal were simply to find efficient ways to recapture past achievement. In order to fulfill this relatively new challenge, public education will have to become more systemically responsive to the socioeconomic realities of those it serves. This means recognizing that social class is a predictor of performance and that schools must work to reverse the social logic implicit therein. Local and private institutions geared to dominant community values and goals and built on a marketplace model are not likely to make headway on this task. This is not the place to detail what can work in this regard, but suffice it to say that from Head Start to "I Have a Dream" programs we have learned how to spend adequate resources to help make school success possible for the least likely pupils.

Finally we do have to set about applying the lessons of such programs; we have to make schools work, in a way that is as radical as the proposals to redefine the private as public. Such a restructuring would begin with recognizing that teachers and schools confront new challenges. It would reestablish the public school context based on the solid datum that educational and income level of parents predicts school performance. To do this we might begin by trying to create jobs in school communities out of school spending (as is underway in some school districts); we would undertake the education of parents by trying to use the citizenship education of voter education and registration activity (aimed at school board elections) as an adult education responsibility of schools. We would try to address the health deficiency and poor medical resources of low-income school communities by replacing their dependence on emergency room service with health care in schools through the inclusion of general practitioner service in public schools as part of residency requirements in big city teaching hospitals. And more, rather than less, money must be spent since even big business agrees now with responsible school people that schools generally get only about half of what they truly need.

These are just a few of the basics that might comprise such a restructuring effort. If public education is going to serve this nation's socioeconomic structure as well as the industrial machine did until the great expansion of service and technological employment, then we will have to give it a comparable order of priority in the allocation of resources and esteem.

The fact is that private schools don't have any record of achievement with the full range of the nation's students. Turning public education into a series of privately run projects is likely to undermine the progress of years of egalitarian struggle, leaving schools at the mercy of consumer prejudice and advertised fashion. If school reform does not restore our investment in public institutions, then the wrong choice will have been made between two contrasting priorities for school change. To be sure, public schools are in need of serious overhaul, but disestablishment is no more an answer here than privatization is in mass transport, garbage collection, or the penal system. Imagine, instead of public schools offering new programs and alternative options, a range of private schools, some like privileged boutiques or first-class sections in trains, others like crowded subway cars.

Private and public schools represent two quite opposite sets of goals for public education: a desire for schools to serve the competitive demands of stratified society versus the desire for schools to play a socially integrative and democratic role, serving the right of all parents to participate in the education of their children regardless of income and other forms of private privilege. The popular critique of public schools is a social and political issue of significance precisely because schools are still agencies of government (i.e., of public purpose) decentralized to every county in the land.

The school as local agency also provides the basis from which communities all over the country connect with and participate in the nation's political processes. Local school boards are the entry into politics for ordinary citizens who move from PTA to school board office—and quite often to larger political office. School board elections are also a vehicle of local political participation: in debates over property taxes, school bonds, curricular concerns, and academic standards, citizens learn to express their point of view politically. In a very real fashion school politics are a barometer of the vitality of the nation's electoral democracy. Apathy and energy at the local school board level is reflected regionally and nationally. To accept current public demoralization about public schools as a finished story comes dangerously close to accepting the current rate of electoral participation (less than 50 percent of eligible voters actually vote, even in presidential elections) as the final word on democratic life in the United States.

Education in a democracy must mean as much as elections; we can't do without either. Turning things over to the market is a bad decision: witness all privatized service from telephones, health care, transportation, and housing—all grossly undersupplied in poor communities. In the same way, school privatization will effectively reinstitutionalize an educational class sytem governed by the market (or rather, by a combination of market strategy and public subsidy, since funds for private education will not be dissimilar to public support for the ailing car and savings and loan industries).

The old charity school model that preceded public schools in the nineteenth century was improved on through the consolidated school model despite all the problems that followed from it. The problems of consolidation—bureaucracy and other issues of scale—are pressing but the kinds of changes needed are well known and can be summarized by the ideal of equality; that is, by reducing the disadvantages of birth and status through public schooling. Redefining the public as private is no solution. Instead there is a great danger that private choices will overwhelm public choices through the prestige they acquire due to resources and selectivity. And the result will be public schools that look more and more like the old charity schools.

22

Keeping the Public in Public Education: Does Choice Serve Democratic Schooling?

Ann Bastian

Thomas Jefferson, the nation's first, and perhaps only, education president, gave a sage instruction to his colleagues as the federal republic was being founded: "Establish the law for educating the common people. This it is the business of the state to effect and on a general plan."

Jefferson's words, inscribed on his memorial in Washington, D.C., contain several of the premises upon which we have built public education in this country. Among them are that education is a central purpose of government; that education belongs in the public sphere; that it should serve the common people beyond a narrow elite; and that it must be effected "on a general plan" or, as we might put it today, implemented as a system.

These premises derive from two broader tenets echoed by Jefferson: that for the individual, education is an essential condition of citizenship and therefore a right; and that for the nation, education is an essential institution in the development of civil society and therefore essential to our capacity for democracy. In other words, public education has a democratic mission that includes both individual entitlement and community empowerment.

These are such basic and familiar principles to Americans that it would

Ann Bastian is an education policy analyst consulting with teacher organizations and parent groups across the country on school restructuring issues. She is also a co-author of *Choosing Equality: The Case for Democratic Schooling.*

seem there is little to dispute. We know that our public education system has far to go to fulfill its democratic mission, on grounds of both quality and equality, but we assume that the mission is intact and that these principles inform our progress. However, it is naive to assume this. We are today at some risk of discarding these principles and abandoning the mission—even worse, we are proceeding without much consciousness or debate over the societal consequences. At the heart of the issue is whether we are sustaining the integrity of a free and universal public education system (including its capacity to improve), or establishing de facto mechanisms for education that serve different principles.

There are at least three interactive forces at work in public education that place its democratic mission in deep jeopardy at the systemic level. One is the stratification of the system, most profoundly on class and race lines. The second is the failure to fund education adequately in the face of declining social priorities and growing tax injustice. The third, and core, topic of this essay is the introduction of marketplace models of schooling, chiefly under the banner of school choice.

I. STRATIFICATION

The persistence of educational double standards has made urban school districts and some poor rural districts barely viable. It has produced drop-out rates of over 50 percent in the inner cities. It has placed more than one-third of children now entering the system at risk of failure, severely diminishing their life chances, including their ability to lobby successfully for social change.

These statistics are not new. Public education has always been stratified in terms of the quality and opportunity available to elites and to the poor. But to our national credit, we did keep the premise and promise of equality alive, thus vindicating the enormous social struggle over its fulfillment. As a result, we have had moments of real progress in widening educational access and in developing effective models for learning among all our children.

The danger is that in the past decade, we have dramatically halted this progression. Following an increasing polarization of wealth, our declining position in the global economy, and a decade of Reaganite social policy, the forces of educational stratification have reasserted themselves. Another generation of the educational underclass has been produced, bounded by poverty, social violence, and racism. Only this time around, opportunities for economic mobility have become narrower and more dependent on educational attainment than ever before. The widening schism between educational "haves" and "have-nots" threatens to negate the promise and progress of our democratic educational mission. On the national policy level, the calls to excellence of the past decade have failed to recognize that this schism and the inequities that underlie it, are at the heart of our education crisis.

While many valuable notions of reform have surfaced in the debate over school restructuring, the actual legislation passed at both state and federal levels has stressed standardization, testing, and magnet programs. President Bush's latest plan for education reform—a national achievement test and a new wave of experimental schools, along with school choice—is no departure. Bush is working on the margins, proposing more regulation through testing and more escape hatches for systems where the pressures of failure are rapidly mounting.

The practical results reinforce the ways schools sort and stratify children. Many exciting models for school improvement have been developed, but the mainstream has been little touched and inner-city school systems are literally collapsing around us. There is no commitment, fiscal or programmatic, to elevating educational results by bringing up the bottom. We are moving from double standards to triple standards of education: sheltered privilege for the affluent, economic functionalism for the middle class, and crude social Darwinism for the poor.

If we find this stratification of our schools unacceptable, then we must pursue educational policies that go far beyond those now on the national agenda: a massive investment in early childhood education, reducing class and school size in overloaded urban systems, retraining the teaching corps to use models that work, extending school-home-community linkages, integrating social and family services into school life, redesigning curricula that are technologically and culturally obsolete—the list could be greatly expanded.

II. FUNDING

The failure to recognize the depth of the equity crisis in our schools is compounded by a failure to address the looming fiscal crisis of education. At least thirty-four states entered fiscal year 1992 with serious budget shortfalls, precipitating cutbacks in aid to education and even deeper cuts in child and family services. An enduring legacy of Reagan's new federalism is that social entitlements rest heavily on the states, as in effect, does most domestic policy. Nearly half the states are also engaged in some form of court challenge over glaring inequities in their school funding formulas. In Texas, for instance, the top one hundred school districts spent an average of $7,233 per pupil in 1990 while the poorest one hundred districts spent an average of only $2,978. The landmark case in Texas, along with parallel cases in Kentucky, New Jersey, and Montana, have shown the potential of school finance issues to propel school reform agendas, but these cases have also begged the underlying question: Who will pay to improve our schools and to narrow the gap between rich and poor districts?

It is fashionable to argue, as President Bush has, that "dollar bills don't educate children." While it is perfectly true that new money without institutional change won't make schools better, although it might keep a few cities afloat, it is equally true that institutional change cannot occur on a meaningful scale without new money, especially the funding to focus on the class size and professional development parts of the agenda.

Unfortunately, the local property tax is an unfair and inadequate instrument that has, in most instances, reached its limits. And since the federal government has virtually divested itself of fiscal responsibility in education, maintaining a viable system has become difficult; changing it will clearly require significant state tax restructuring. Education is thus placed squarely in the larger political arena of tax revolt and tax justice, as has been most recently and sharply experienced in New Jersey and California. It is not a battle that can be avoided much longer in most states.

At risk is the tax base for basic public education services as well as revenues for equity and reform. States are faced with multiple demands to keep resources high at good schools, to dramatically improve failing schools, to bail out insolvent districts, to compensate for shifting tax demographics, to upgrade and replenish the teaching corps, and to inject new programs for school restructuring.

The tax battle must be fought if the democratic mission of public schooling is to go forward. We need to restructure the tax base of public education to reflect general revenues and progressive tax structures and to secure the capital infrastructure to weather business cycles. If we do not address the tax issue, public education will remain trapped in the dilemmas of how many to throw off the boat every time the seas get rough. The discarded will be children who will not be recovered in calmer waters.

III. SCHOOL CHOICE

If the viability of public education as a democratic institution is threatened by resurgent inequity, fiscal austerity, and tax injustice, it also faces a fundamental challenge in the guise of reform itself, the choice movement.

"Choice" is a label covering a broad range of programs seeking to increase the educational options available to students. Some of these programs, such as inter-district transfers, advanced placement in colleges, or magnet schools, have been around for a long time. What is really at issue, however, is choice as a system of open enrollments based on parent and student selection.

Not all choice enrollment systems are the same; different choice designs have very different impacts on education. It is important to sort out the differences before plunging ahead in the choice debate. One defining issue is whether choice is applied only within public schools or allows public funding to support enrollment in private and religious schools. A second issue is whether choice is conceived as restricted (the controlled choice model) or unrestricted (the marketplace model).

In one corner of this matrix are public school, controlled choice programs. They provide a number of promising examples of how school districts can serve diversity, parent and student preference, and school improvement goals. The programs most often cited are East Harlem in New York City; Montclair, New Jersey; and Cambridge, Massachusetts. These controlled choice systems have distinct characteristics: choice is part of an overall school improvement strategy to provide more child-centered education; the choice plan is intra-district and provides reasonable access to all parents and children enrolled; every school in the program is a school of choice and selection carefully respects desegregation mandates; the school missions are diverse, but developed in collaborative and complementary ways; implementation has stressed teacher and parent involvement; and significant additional funding has been provided.

There are also examples of controlled choice programs that lack these elements, with poor or negligible results for educational equity and achievement. Most notorious among choice failures is the Richmond, California, school district. There a controlled choice plan was imposed without parent or teacher consultation, without providing access and transportation, and without adequate funding. The district is now in a state of educational and fiscal bankruptcy.

The point here is that even controlled choice is no miracle cure for what ails public schooling. Where it works it is but one tool in a broad arsenal of school change designs and it only works well if there is a steadfast commitment to improving both equity and funding. In this sense, school choice is a tactic in the larger school improvement battle. I find the label "micro-choice" useful to put this model in context.

In contrast, there is another corner in the choice matrix that promotes choice as the central strategy and structure of school reform, a position I call "macro-choice." In this vision, public funding in education would be allocated by pupils, not schools, in what amounts to a voucher system. Parents and students would be able to enroll in any school that is willing or able to receive them. Presumably, the engine of school improvement would be competition between schools for enrollment dollars. There is a strong push to include private and religious schools through publicly funded vouchers or tuition tax credits.

This macro-choice vision has a very good chance of gaining political ground for two reasons: first, it emanates from national centers of power; it is a centerpiece of the Bush-Alexander education policy and championed by right-wing and neoconservative opinion makers. Second, macro-choice claims to redress the core problems of inequity and austerity that are corroding public education. It is offered both as a way out for the most disadvantaged students trapped in failing schools and as a way to fundamentally reorganize the system without requiring new monies.

But in reality, macro-choice seeks to displace, gradually or radically, the existing framework of public education with that of the marketplace. This vision demands that we understand the difference between a public institution and the market mechanism and look squarely at the dilemmas each poses. Since no system is unproblematic, which set of problems and opportunities do we want for education? This essay measures the potentials in two key areas, equity and governance.

MACRO-CHOICE AND EQUITY

The marketplace that macro-choice models promote for education rests on the competitive dynamic of supply and demand, where individual schools are the units of supply and individual students are the units of demand. The most immediate problem is that there are not enough good schools to go around, especially if we acknowledge the access barriers of distance, time, and culture.

Competition within our current school supply, even including private schools, would increase the level of funding to the richest schools that attract the top students and would accelerate the depletion of resources from inadequate schools. A few students would do better, but poor schools and students would fall further behind. The polarization and stratification of the system would not only increase, but it would be ratified and enforced by the macro-choice design.

This has in fact been the outcome of our most extensive choice experience thus far, the magnet school choice programs in metropolitan desegregation efforts. In the majority of these efforts, magnet schools have been selective or enrollments have been limited. Resources flowed into the magnet programs, but away from the deficient urban neighborhood schools. When the enrollment dust settled, a few highly motivated inner-city children had made it out to suburban schools, but very few suburban students had been attracted to the city. Meanwhile, ghetto schools have continued to languish, becoming more firmly segregated by class and race, more truly separate and unequal.

In this common case, choice has been substituted for a comprehensive and coordinated strategy of school improvement for all schools that could give priority to those who need it most. Freedom of choice is not a substitute for equity, and offering people the chance to choose is not the same as offering them good choices.

Macro-choice advocates respond that we can rely either on greater competition over enrollments to improve inadequate or failing schools or on entrepreneurship to create their replacements. But this again raises the crucial resource question: Which initiative really has a better chance of being institutionally viable—an independent community-based school or a chain initiated by a media mogul? Will the demand-side really prevail over the supply-side in structuring this marketplace?

The study of professional service enterprises, from medical care to legal services, suggests that the so-called free play of supply and demand is largely a myth. Providers not only determine the range and access to services far more than consumers, they also self-regulate their own industries. Moreover, the evidence suggests that service marketplaces are particularly inefficient in providing equity of service; in fact, they are models of "trickle down" economics.

The macro-choice framework raises additional issues of how schools will promote themselves in the marketplace. Given current trends, we will very likely intensify dependence on standardized test scores to measure results and to establish norms of achievement. The dangers of both curriculum and instruction becoming more test-driven are alarming and directly contradict the need to promote higher-order learning skills and multicultural learning styles.

Another range of marketplace problems present themselves: How will schools achieve economies of scale in their facilities? How will they recruit and distribute teachers? How will children's education be protected from dislocations in school enrollments? These are not insoluble problems in the business world, although the 50 percent failure rate of new small businesses should give pause. We must examine, however, whether human services and child development are appropriately directed by the laws of competition.

If we need a chilling comparison, we could look at our present health care marketplace. Are we truly striving to emulate a system that permits the life expectancy of an adult male in Bangladesh to exceed that of a black man in America? There are limits to what can be achieved through the competitive allocation of resources, especially if standards of democratic community are applied to the results.

MACRO-CHOICE AND GOVERNANCE

Democratic standards go beyond equity issues to another set of problems posed by the macro-choice marketplace: governance and accountability. Where schools are individual units of competition and families individual consumers of services, what is the relationship of the school to the community that both sustains those families and funds those enrollment vouchers? Will educational resources flow toward schools that are not only the most exclusive but also the least accountable?

Macro-choice defines the school as a community unto itself, as an aggregate of parents, educators, and managers. It's conceivable that parents would have some direct governing role beyond the ability to take their enrollment dollars elsewhere. But voters, taxpayers, relatives, and neighbors are not an empowered constituency in this framework. Schools would no longer be bound by physical and political communities, posing difficult issues about who will ultimately assess school performance and govern school decision making.

Of course, if we are uncomfortable with the "invisible hand" of the marketplace as a governance mechanism, we can assign such tasks to state regulators, create legislative and judicial mandates, and appoint financial overseers. But we should be clear that the service enterprise will have replaced a very crucial foundation of our current system—the school as a community-based institution.

Many macro-choice advocates believe this is a virtue. In *Politics, Markets, and American Schools*, authors John Chubb and Terry Moe say explicitly: "Bureaucracy is not the most fundamental impediment to more effective schools. That distinction belongs to direct democratic control." They argue that only by separating the school from community politics, with all its contentious compromising of multiple interests, can schools be free to focus creatively on the job of educating children. There is much to argue with in their use of the data on private school performance; certainly it is questionable to measure selective and self-selective private schools against public schools that unconditionally accept all children.

But the basic premise can be challenged on other grounds as well. Chubb and Moe speak for the empowered in public life, even if their radical prescriptions appeal to some who are desperate for change in public education. The disempowered cannot afford to take politics out of the schools. The arena of democratic politics in which public education now operates is the one place where those who are poorly served can contend as an organized constituency for their needs and rights. It is the one place where the entitlement to equity can be battled over, not only on constitutional principles but in everyday school practice. Those who are prevented, by reason of racial, economic, and indeed educational discrimination, from competing fully in the marketplace, may and do participate in the politics of public policy. Vouchers, on the other hand, are not as powerful as votes or social activism; they cannot be collectively exercised to set social priorities or to broaden social entitlements.

The public arena is also the place where communities can define and redefine the spectrum of values and goals that underlie their commitment to education. It is where a "civic culture" is generated that supports and monitors our investment in children as a common social responsibility. It is where the interests of taxpayers and voters weigh in with the interests of parents, extending the constituencies of education beyond those who are enrolled or employed in schools at any given time. And by the same token, the public character of community-based schooling gives schools themselves a valuable role to play in creating community bonds and returning institutional resources to the community.

To whom will the marketplace school belong in a system of atomized and competing enterprises? Markets are the arenas of private interests; even publicly established marketplaces are arenas of privatized, individually competing interests of consumers and suppliers. Unless one is a proponent of nineteenth-century liberal philosophy, we have yet to demonstrate that the sum of private interests or even private values equals the public good. This is why the public education system was instituted in the first place, and significantly, why we encoded the separation of church and state in our Constitution.

This is not to say that everything works smoothly in the public arena or that local communities are always coherent, enlightened, activist, or egalitarian as they engage in democratic governance. Far from it. But when schools are governed in the public arena, through a political rather than an economic process, there is legitimate place to conceive the common interest and the public good, and to have them contend with and against individual rights and private interests. We can keep on the table the issue of how well education serves community (and societal) empowerment which is both an object of struggle and a standard of progress.

To reject the marketplace framework is not to ignore the problems that a public education system entails, aside from the imperfections of democracy. Tremendous obstacles to effective schooling are posed by vested administrative bureaucracies, which consume time and money that is urgently needed at the classroom level. Yet, the marketplace is no stranger to top-heavy management structures or monopolistic behavior. And there is no inherent reason why public schools could not be decentralized through reforms like school-based management and local school governance.

Public schools also suffer from excessive standardization, the stifling of innovation, and the neglect of individual student needs. This problem has many sources, from bureaucracy to poor teacher education programs to overwhelming teaching loads. But the marketplace does not escape the problem of oppressive product conformity; enterprise schools will be particularly vulnerable if standardized testing becomes the central instrument of accountability. The solutions for public education lie in making a collective commitment to discard the factory model and fundamentally restructure our schools. We know many ingredients that work, including human-scale school size, teacher-directed instruction, child-centered learning, active parental involvement, and strong community linkages. We also know that public choice programs, judiciously applied, have much they can contribute and that there are many specific choice designs to explore, from charter schools to controlled choice models.

To reject the marketplace framework, therefore, is not to defend public education as it presently exists, but to defend the public framework of education as the best arena for improving education and a necessary one for promoting its democratic mission. John Dewey once advised that the best solution to the problems of democracy is more democracy. Another way to put it is that public governance will not automatically produce democratic results or achieve the public good, but the marketplace forecloses even the attempt.

CONCLUSION

Thomas Jefferson, no advocate of centralized government, understood that public education stands at the critical intersection of government and civil society. Macro-choice visionaries would like to relocate this institution to stand at the intersection of government and the economy, replacing political mediations with the market mechanism.

We can do that. It would make education more compatible with other trends in our society, and decrease the conflict and resistance we feel when we pursue education's democratic mission in the face of highly stratified economic destinies. The market mechanism would help education better conform with the present political reality that places democratic nation-building behind the maintenance of America's superpower role.

But if we turn to the educational marketplace, it should be clear that we will indeed have made "the choice" to change missions. If we accept macro-choice as a strategic vision, then we must be prepared to accept the consequence—a system that does not presume that education is the business of government, one that does not proceed by a general plan; in short, a system that is in fact not a true system but only a mechanism. We will have made the mission of education more manageable by negating its democratic core and by lowering societal expectations.

Perhaps such warnings are overly alarmist. After all, one of the strengths and weaknesses of public education is that it is so prone to gradualism. Many people who have spent years trying to transform the schools with little result are probably not too worried about the impact of choice. It is unlikely that the entire public school structure will be swept away by a pure marketplace system. But there are other scenarios.

A fine scenario would be that we refine the debate around choice so that we adopt only those plans that offer us a well-honed tool, in the context of comprehensive local school improvement and the strengthening of public education. A poor scenario, perhaps already underway, is that choice becomes the rhetorical cover for inaction on school restructuring, a cosmetic device diverting attention from the deeper problems that require greater commitments. Worse still, choice could become a means for chipping away at the public nature of the system, through deregulation of equity standards, privatization of school services, tax credits and vouchers, and the spread of publicly subsidized enterprise schools—the long-term scenario for macro-choice.

But the worst scenario of all would be that we pursue any version of choice without examining the premises of public education, measuring our progress against democratic values, or testing our values against what we are willing to commit, as a society, to our schools. In this worst-case scenario, it may be possible to visit Washington, D.C., one day and find inscribed on the walls of the Bush Memorial:

"Establish the law for educating the common people so that it won't interfere with educating the elite. For it is the business of government to create an education business and to avoid a general plan."

23

Democratic Schooling and the Revitalization of the Public World

Robert V. Bullough, Jr.

From coast to coast across the United States, one or another choice program is being championed as the key to revitalizing American education. Like the promises that accompanied the deregulation of the savings and loan industry and the airlines, champions of choice augur a more efficient and higher quality education. They add an additional claim: the resulting education will be more democratic than current practices allow. Choice is thought to be the essence of democracy; and the more varied the choices, the more democratic the system.

Before considering this argument, let us step back a few paces and set the historical context within which the present choice debate is taking place.

LESSONS IN DEMOCRACY

The events of this past year have been astonishing. The Soviet Union has ceased to exist, while the Eastern Bloc nations have been shaken to their very foundations. We hear Marx being used as a four-letter word by our new Eastern European friends, and it pleases us. President Bush has pro-

---

Robert V. Bullough, Jr., is a professor of Educational Studies at the University of Utah. He is the author of *The Forgotten Dream of American Public Education*.

claimed an end to the cold war and has told us that we won it! Many of the nations of the world are looking toward America for guidance as they move into uncharted social and economic territories. These are shocking developments. But before smugness sets in and we become too self-congratulatory, we should stop and consider what wisdom we are offering our brothers and sisters to aid them in their rush to embrace democracy.

"What is it that they are hoping to learn from us?" is a good question but, for my purposes, not the right one to ask. A better question is, "What are we able to teach them?" The answer is painfully clear: What we are primarily offering to teach our new-found brothers and sisters is a consumer view of democracy—free markets, capitalism, and freedom of choice among competing products felicitously named "consumer goods." Unlike our brothers and sisters who have only recently heard the sweet song of democracy, we seem no longer to be inspired by it. It is bitterly ironic that just as American political participation has reached an all-time low the world has come to our doors seeking inspiration and direction.

Our offering, ultimately, is an appeal to a hungry world's appetites, to fatten its body while ignoring the ill health of its mind and soul. To be sure, ours is a seductive and a powerful appeal, but one lacking morality and vision. What we offer is a shabby substitute for democracy, an ideology of economic individualism, served by such faithless and fallen high priests of capitalism as Michael Milken and Ivan Boesky. We have turned our backs on the prophets: Thomas Jefferson, James Madison, and Abraham Lincoln.

Perhaps we can forgive ourselves for our loss of memory. For nearly half a century we have defined ourselves as the good guys in an ongoing cold war against the bad guys, the Evil Empire, the Soviet Union. The loss of such a worthy opponent presents us with an opportunity and a challenge: We must either find a new enemy so that we may continue to define ourselves as before, or else face ourselves squarely and consider who and what we are as a nation and what we would like to be.

The popular press is filled with letters to the editor and articles seeking new enemies: Saddam Hussein served us well for a while, and now the Japanese will do. But, happily, there is also an increasing amount of talk of the other kind, which reflects the desire to recapture or rekindle the grand experiment that is democracy, an experiment that was put on hold. These new experimenters wonder about America, and how as a nation we have come to be as we are. And, unlike their enemy-seeking counterparts, they do not take democracy for granted but rather puzzle over its meaning: What is democracy and what does it mean to live in a democratic society? These questions ought to be of the utmost importance to educators.

DEMOCRACY AND EDUCATION

In 1916, John Dewey published *Democracy and Education*. The title of that book captured in a phrase what Jefferson and other early students of democracy understood, although perhaps not fully. Democracy is a theory of education, a theory unlike any other; and within a society striving to call itself democratic, schools have a crucial part to play in building a national life and identity. This insight has been echoed over the years by many of America's finest thinkers, especially at times of crisis. In a letter dated July 26, 1939, Franklin Roosevelt put it this way:

> Everyone knows that democracy cannot long stand unless its foundation is kept constantly reinforced through the processes of education. . . . Education for democracy cannot merely be taken for granted. What goes on in the schools every hour of the day, on the playground and in the classroom, whether reflecting methods of control by the teacher, or opportunities for self-expression by pupils, must be checked against the fact that the children are growing up to live in a democracy. That the schools make worthy citizens is the most important responsibility placed upon them.

As a nation, Americans have taken democracy and education for democracy for granted, as Roosevelt feared, and seem to have forgotten that public education was established in part for the purpose of producing an enlightened and involved citizenship. The results of our neglect have been devastating: like the nation, our public schools are adrift. And, like the nation, our schools are in danger of losing all purpose except what may be found in the economics of consumption. The essence of being an American has become the ability to consume as one chooses, and the purpose of education is to facilitate this choice. Put differently, the purpose of public education is to get a good paying job that will guarantee the ability to consume to our hearts' content. Where this promise fails, parents and students become enemies of the public schools.

Such a purpose cannot possibly sustain our nation's now weakening commitment to public education. This aim leaves nothing special to the public schools; indeed, some private schools may do the job better. But it is perhaps more important to note that while schooling may be essential to obtaining a decent job, it certainly cannot guarantee one. Economics and politics are of far greater importance.

SCHOOLS ADRIFT AND THE PROMISE OF CHOICE

With an educational system adrift, and the promise of jobs given as the standard reason for schooling, both public and private, choice programs have obvious appeal. Choice speaks eloquently to many of our consumer prejudices. Despite virtually no evidence to support the assumption that competitive rather than cooperative modes of social interaction increase production or quality, and considerable evidence to the contrary, we Americans believe in our bones in the value of competition; and choice promises competition of a sort. We believe in a meritocracy and that there ought to be winners and losers in life. In this contest, we believe, good programs, like good people, will prevail. But in reality, when it comes to our own children, we will do virtually anything to assure that they are on the winner's side. Life is a competitive game and we intend to take care of number one, even if it means rigging the outcome against others.

Put more concretely and even more cynically, choice programs offer disillusioned parents an escape from the public school system while absolving them of all responsibility for it. The aim is to escape troubled schools and their problems, rather than to address them. "What's in it for me?" is what matters first and foremost. Furthermore, choice programs make it unnecessary for parents to explore common territory and to compromise differences in the quest for a shared program that is in the best interest of all students. Instead, every interest, however narrow, can be satisfied, with no interests being brought together to challenge one another. Thus, no one, parent or educator, need consider the larger and most important question of what the purpose of American education is. Only specific program purposes matter: all for one, and none for all. When linked to vouchers, choice programs make it possible for parents to keep their children separated from other people's children who represent one or another tainted class. Ultimately and inevitably, common interests are ignored and left unexplored. Provincialism is draped in the dress of diversity, which, ironically, serves as one of the gods before whom the champions of choice prostrate themselves.

The appeal of choice, therefore, is to narrow self-interest of one or another kind: academic, vocational, or religious.

Lacking a school system that presents an inspiring and alternative vision of education, something more than getting a good job, we can only expect that the choice bandwagon will continue to gain speed and with it we can anticipate a further deterioration of the public world we share. This is so because public schooling is perhaps the last remaining common social experience we Americans have that brings us face to face with others whose interests may differ from our own and that requires us to learn to live together for our mutual benefit. With the deterioration of the public world, fewer and fewer Americans will come to recognize that freedom is a social and inter-personal achievement, not a gift, and that it brings with it as many responsi-bilities as rights.

RETHINKING PURPOSES

The challenge before American educators and citizens is nothing less than a rethinking of the purposes of American education both in the light of our history and in anticipation of an uncertain future. Among the striking features of the current debates over restructuring, particularly those that champion choice, is that so few of them consider the purposes of education, especially its social purpose. High test scores and a work force able to beat the Japanese do not a social vision make. The appeal is to our baser instincts and our fears when what is needed is a call to imagine the world not as it is, but as it might be. It is only with an articulated social vision—a description of the kind of life we want to live as a people inside and outside of the school's walls—that judgments can be made about the desirability of the diversity of educational and administrative practices being presented, choice among them. Put succinctly, when debating choice proposals, we ought to first ask, "Choice for what purpose?" The failure to ask this question represents a failure of vision and of leadership, educationally and socially.

In his Gettysburg Address, Abraham Lincoln proclaimed a vision for America, which is worth recalling:

> It is for the living . . . to be dedicated here to the unfinished work which they who fought here have thus far so nobly advanced. It is rather for us to be here dedicated to the great task remaining before us—that from these honored dead we take increased devotion to that cause for which they gave the last full meas-ure of devotion—that we here highly resolve that these dead shall not have died in vain—that this nation, under God, shall have a new birth of freedom—and that government of the people, by the people, for the people, shall not perish from the earth.

Lincoln knew that democracy is never finished. Imagine with him not only a government of, by, and for the people, all the people; but an education of, by, and for the people, all the people, all the children—a democratic education. Only through the exploration of the meaning of democracy as a way of life, a way of being in the world and with others, can a compelling vision and purpose for American public education be found that places the economic motivation to learn to earn in a proper balance with citizenship.

CONSIDERING DEMOCRACY

There are two parts to this exploration. One part seeks an ideal while the other attends to the institutional conditions necessary to achieve it: aims must be coupled with means. It is this point that makes the effort to restructure the schools so important even if at present that effort is misguided on the whole. Our system of public schooling was forged at a time when the factory dominated America's newly emerging urban landscape. The factory was its metaphor and training, not education, its intent. The schools have never paid complete attention to the prophets of democracy. From its inception, American public schooling has been, all too often, autocratic and hierarchical, not democratic in any sense except that all were expected to attend. Recognizing this underscores an important point: Democracy did not fail education; rather, democracy and education have never been joined together and supported structurally.

Democracy presents an illusive ideal, which partially accounts for its limited impact on our schools. It represents more of a direction of development than a state of accomplishment; it is fluid not fixed, dynamic not determinate. As such, each generation must reinterpret the meaning of democracy for its own time and circumstance and thereby make it its own. Democracy lives or dies within the life and mind of each American. It has no separate existence.

The educational ideal of democracy for our time seems to me to begin with two assumptions and three articles of faith. The first assumption is that all humans are educable. Indeed, the optimal development of all human potential is the highest good. The second assumption is that we humans are more alike than different; that we are inextricably bound by the human condition and by virtue of living in a world of finite resources. Thus, we have fundamental common interests that bind us together. Indeed, the sharing of interests is an essential condition for elevating us above the beasts and forms the foundation for the development of community.

The first article of faith is that each person deserves equal access to decent education. The second is that the optimal development of human potential is only possible when humans work in concert with one another, each person attending with care to the effects of his or her actions on others present and absent, including those not yet born. A corollary of this article is that talent finds its fullest expression through being shared, and that all have a responsibility to do so. The third article of faith is that because humans create history, they need not be victims of it. Through the application of reason with good will, and through open and informed discussion, they can identify shared problems and martial the resources sufficient to solve them. Destiny comprises more than simply biology, genealogy, and history.

DEMOCRACY AND THE SCHOOL FACTORY

A factory metaphor for schooling, including its modern derivative equating school with the marketplace, does incredible violence to this conception of democracy and education. It begins from a quite different set of assumptions. The emphasis of the current system on tracking, which will undoubtedly be strengthened by many programs of choice, is based upon the view that not all humans are educable; some are only good for training while others are destined for leadership and deserve special opportunities denied others. Moreover, the emphasis is on human differences, often differences that come primarily, perhaps exclusively, from unevenness of opportunity arising from the happenstance of birth: One child is born into a privileged station, another into poverty.

Factory views also do violence to the articles of faith I have outlined. Again, echoing the terrors of tracking, the factory approach assumes that different kinds of people require fundamentally different kinds of education. The myth of meritocracy reigns supreme. Competition rather than cooperation is most valued. Individual achievement is attributed exclusively to individual striving and talent is seen as a personal possession held for the edification of the owner and the highest bidder. Similarly, excellence is understood as the special realm of a remarkable few who are born to talent, rather than as an expression of diligence and hard work. This view also suggests that both in and out of schools we are all (and should be) in the hands of a few exceptional experts upon whom we must depend for guidance. The vast majority of Americans, teachers included, are in effect merely small children. As such, most problems are well beyond their understanding; the best that can be hoped for is that the experts will govern and direct them wisely and with a measure of kindness. It is best to keep common people and their children out of the way; they will only make trouble and confuse the issue. Even John Kennedy displayed this patronizing view when he said:

> Most of us are conditioned for many years to have a political viewpoint—Republican or Democratic, liberal, conservative, or moderate. The fact of the matter is that most of the problems . . . that we now face are technical problems, are administrative problems. They are very sophisticated judgments, which do not lend themselves to the great sort of passionate movements which have stirred this country so often in the past. [They] deal with questions which are now beyond the comprehension of most men.[1]

Kennedy was wrong. The great problems are problems of purpose, not technique.

What kind of school organization and structure would be consistent with my assumptions and articles of faith? Clearly not the current system. Nor will choice programs necessarily further the cause of democracy. Indeed, as noted, they might very well harm it irreparably. Two alleged pluses of choice programs, that they are likely to lead to increased involvement of parents and to a greater sense of ownership on the part of those who participate, can be achieved in ways other than the choosing by parents of schools, public or private, as I will demonstrate shortly. There are numerous ways of achieving quality; the problem lies in deciding what counts as quality, which requires a frame of reference, one whose focus is democracy as a way of life.

A NEW METAPHOR

Because the factory model for schooling is hostile to it, democracy appears in school only as a subject to be studied like any other subject: a system of government—voting and the steps a bill goes through before it becomes law, something fixed and known—and not as a way of being in the world. This is akin, as Boyd Bode remarked many years ago, to "teaching swimming by correspondence." The challenge is to remake the schools so that students go there not only to study but to carry on a way of life based upon the assumptions and articles of faith that arise from our democratic tradition.

Considering the implications of democracy for the individual's development is extremely important; to be sure, the individual must be taught to "swim." Thinking about creating a structure or organization for schooling that will foster "democratic swimming" shifts the focus momentarily from the individual to the community. The challenge here is to create a community that invites and rewards democratic living but does not compel it. Thus a new metaphor for schooling emerges: School is democratic community, one built on the assumptions and the articles of faith described earlier.

COMMUNITY ELEMENTS

Let us briefly consider some aspects of a democratic school community. It is a diverse community composed of educators, parents, and students bound together by a shared commitment to the optimal development of each member's potential within the context of the community. Individual members share their talents and assist one another in fulfilling their potential, whether it be tutoring younger children to read or assisting teachers to plan a unit of study. All members have extensive and continuous contact with one another (quite in contrast to the results of tracking) and are seen as being responsible for identifying and furthering community interests. Time is set aside explicitly for the study and improvement of group living, and for the identification and solution of community problems. Where conflicts arise, members are committed to their resolution through compromise and respect for the right of others holding differing and even offensive opinions.

The democratic community disciplines its own members, relying extensively on helping the offending parties understand the effects of their actions on others. The wider political, economic, and social world within which the school exists is a subject of study. Attention is given to ways in which individuals can band together to achieve shared aims while always respecting— not simply tolerating—the rights of minorities. The right of the individual to participate in decisions affecting his or her welfare is honored, including participation in the establishment of the rules of governance for the community. The goal is maximal participation with an eye to deepening the individual's sense of membership in the community and his or her intellectual understanding of and commitment to democratic living.

CONCLUSION

American public education has a crucial role to play as we begin to face ourselves as a people and seek to create a new role for ourselves in the world separate from the existence of an enemy. Although the factory metaphor has stifled the potential of the public schools for enhancing our public life, this need not be so. Within the larger context of a changing world, the current movement to restructure public schools presents an opportunity to rethink their purpose within a democracy and to recreate ourselves as a people.

In *Habits of the Heart* (1985), Robert Bellah and his colleagues detected in the Americans they interviewed a longing for a return to community and a hunger for connectedness. Consumption as an ideal, Bellah observes, leaves the spirit malnourished. It is the job of American public schools to feed the spirit as well as the mind of each American young person and to strengthen a fractured public world. Let's get on with the task. Of this we can be certain: privatization of schooling will only lead to further impoverishment of our public world.

NOTE

1. Lewis Lapham, "Democracy in America? Not Only the Economy Is in Decline," *Harper's,* November 1990, p. 54.

Bibliography*

Alley, Robert S., Jr., ed. *The Supreme Court on Church and State.* New York: Oxford University Press, 1988.

Bamber, Chrissie. *Public School Choice: An Equal Chance for All?* Columbia, Md.: National Committee for Citizens in Education, 1990.

Bastian, Ann, et al. *Choosing Equality: The Case for Democratic Schooling.* Philadelphia: Temple University Press, 1986.

Bode, Boyd H. *Democracy as a Way of Life.* New York: Macmillan, 1937.

Buckley, Thomas E. *Church and State in Revolutionary Virginia, 1776–1787.* Charlottesville: University Press of Virginia, 1977.

Bullough, Robert V., Jr. *The Forgotten Dream of American Public Education.* Ames: Iowa State University Press, 1988.

Byrnes, Deborah, and Gary Kiger. "Religious Prejudice and Democracy: Conflict in the Classroom." *Issues in Education* 4 (Fall 1986): 167–76.

Curry, Thomas J. *The First Freedoms: Church and State in America to the Passage of the First Amendment.* New York: Oxford University Press, 1986.

Darling-Hammond, Linda, and Sheila N. Kirby. *Tuition Tax Deductions and Parent School Choice: A Case Study of Minnesota.* Santa Monica, Calif.: RAND, 1985.

Dewey, John. *The Public and Its Problems.* New York: Henry Holt and Company, 1927.

---

*Although this volume has focused primarily on the pitfalls of private school choice, some of the sources in this bibliography and that on pp. 234–35 also deal with the problems inherent in choice programs even when restricted to public schools.

Doerr, Edd, and Albert J. Menendez. *Church Schools and Public Money: The Politics of Parochiaid.* Buffalo, N.Y.: Prometheus Books, 1991.

Elliot, Johnathan, ed. *The Debates in the Several State Conventions on the Adoption of the Federal Constitution.* Philadelphia: J. B. Lippincott and Company, 1941.

Elmore, Richard F. "Educational Choice and Federal Policy." Testimony before the Subcommittee on Elementary, Secondary, and Vocational Education of the House Education and Labor Committee, U.S. Congress, May 21, 1991.

Eve, Ramond A., and Francis B. Harrold. *The Creationist Movement in Modern America.* Boston: Twayne, 1991.

Farrand, Max, ed. *The Records of the Federal Convention of 1787.* New Haven, Conn.: Yale University Press, 1966.

Frey, Donald E. *Tuition Tax Credits for Private Education: An Economic Analysis.* Ames: Iowa State University Press, 1983.

Goodlad, John. *Access to Knowledge.* New York: The College Board Press, 1990.

Greer, Colin. *The Great School Legend: A Revisionist Interpretation of American Public Education.* New York: Penguin Books, 1976.

Gregory, T. B., and G. R. Smith. *High Schools as Communities: The Small School Reconsidered.* Bloomington, Ind.: Phi Delta Kappa Educational Foundation, 1987.

Gunn, Jeremy. *A Standard for Repair: The Establishment of Religion Clause of the United States Constitution.* New York: Garland Press, 1992.

Hunt, Gaillard, ed. *The Writings of James Madison.* New York: G. P. Putnam's Sons, 1900.

Kaestle, Carl F. *Pillars of the Republic: Common Schools and American Society, 1780–1860.* New York: Hill and Want, 1983.

Katznelson, Ira, and Margaret Weir. *Schooling for All: Class, Race, and Decline of the Democratic Ideal.* New York: Basic Books, 1985.

Lapham, Lewis. "Democracy in America? Not Only the Economy Is in Decline." *Harpers,* November 1990, p. 54.

Lee, Gordon C. *Crusade Against Ignorance: Thomas Jefferson on Education.* New York: Teachers College, Columbia University, 1961.

Lemann, Nicholas. "A False Panacea." *The Atlantic Monthly,* January 1991.

Levin, Henry M. "Education as a Public and Private Good." *Journal of Policy Analysis and Management* 6, no. 4 (Summer 1987).

Levy, Leonard. *The Establishment Clause: Religion and the Constitution.* New York: Macmillan, 1986.

Lieberman, Ann, ed. *Schools as Collaborative Cultures: Creating the Future Now.* New York: Falmer Press, 1990.

McDonald, Forrest. *Novus Ordo Seclorum: The Intellectual Origins of the Constitution.* Lawrence: University Press of Kansas, 1985.

Menendez, Albert J., and Edd Doerr. *Religion and Public Education: Common Sense and the Law.* Long Beach, Calif.: Centerline Press, 1991.

Peterson, Merrill D., and Robert C. Vaughn, eds. *The Virginia Statute for Religious Freedom.* New York: Cambridge Unviersity Press, 1988.

Pfeffer, Leo. *Church, State and Freedom.* Rev. ed. Boston: Beacon Press, 1967.

Provenzo, Eugene F., Jr. *Religious Fundamentalism and American Education: The Battle for the Public Schools.* Albany, N.Y.: State University of New York Press, 1990.

Randall, Ruth, and Keith Geiger. *School Choice: Issues and Answers.* Bloomington, Ind.: National Education Service, 1991.

Shanker, Al. "Do Private Schools Outperform Public Schools?" *American Educator,* Fall 1991.

Swomley, John. *Religious Liberty and the Secular State.* Buffalo, N.Y.: Prometheus Books, 1989.

Tashman, Billy. "Hobson's Choice." *Village Voice,* January 21, 1992, pp. 9 and 14.

Thayer, V. T. *The Attack upon the American Secular School.* Boston: Beacon Press, 1951.

Wood, James E., Jr. *Religion, the State, and Education.* Waco, Tex.: Baylor University Institute of Church-State Studies, 1984.

———, ed. *Religion and the State: Essays in Honor of Leo Pfeffer.* Waco, Tex.: Baylor University Press, 1985.

Note: Additional sources may be found in the bibliography at the end of Arnold Fege's article (pp. 234–35).